Software Architecture

Software Architecture

Edited by **Cheryl Jollymore**

WILLFORD PRESS

New York

Published by Willford Press,
118-35 Queens Blvd., Suite 400,
Forest Hills, NY 11375, USA
www.willfordpress.com

Software Architecture
Edited by Cheryl Jollymore

International Standard Book Number: 978-1-68285-078-7 (Hardback)

Printed in the United States of America.

Contents

Preface

This book has been an outcome of determined endeavour from a group of educationists in the field. The primary objective was to involve a broad spectrum of professionals from diverse cultural background involved in the field for developing new researches. The book not only targets students but also scholars pursuing higher research for further enhancement of the theoretical and practical applications of the subject.

The revolutions in software technology in last few decades require a solid foundation of complex structures. Software architecture is an emerging branch of software engineering which presents a blueprint of both, the system and the project developing it. It delves into software frameworks and their properties. This book provides an insight into rapid prototyping, reliability models for creating new software, etc. It is helpful for students, engineers and researchers engaged in this field.

It was an honour to edit such a profound book and also a challenging task to compile and examine all the relevant data for accuracy and originality. I wish to acknowledge the efforts of the contributors for submitting such brilliant and diverse chapters in the field and for endlessly working for the completion of the book. Last, but not the least; I thank my family for being a constant source of support in all my research endeavours.

Editor

Using an empirical study to evaluate the feasibility of a new usability inspection technique for paper based prototypes of web applications

Luis Rivero[*] and Tayana Conte

* Correspondence:
luisrivero.cabrejos@gmail.com
Grupo de Usabilidade e Engenharia
de Software - USES, Instituto de
Computação, Universidade Federal
do Amazonas (UFAM), Manaus, AM,
Brazil

Abstract

Background: Usability is one of the most important factors that determine the quality of Web applications, which can be verified performing usability inspection. This paper presents the Web Design Usability Evaluation (Web DUE) technique, which allows the identification of usability problems in low-fidelity prototypes (or mockups) of Web applications during the design phases of the development. We have also proposed the Mockup Design Usability Evaluation (Mockup DUE) tool which is able to assist inspectors using the Web DUE technique.

Method: In order to verify the feasibility of these technologies, we have performed two empirical studies. During the first study, we compared the effectiveness and efficiency indicators of the Web DUE technique with the ones of its predecessor, the Web Design Perspective (WDP) based usability inspection technique. Also, during the second study, experienced inspectors used the Mockup DUE tool and answered a questionnaire aiming at identifying improvement opportunities in its design.

Results: The analysis of the quantitative data showed that the Web DUE technique allowed the identification of more usability problems in lesser time when compared to the WDP technique. Moreover, the qualitative data from the second empirical study provided information on the tool's perceived ease of use, indicating that inspectors were satisfied and that they would use it to perform a usability inspection with the Web DUE technique.

Conclusions: These results showed that the DUE technologies could be applied in the identification of usability problems early in the design of Web applications. Thus, their use could enable the correction of such problems before the source code of the application is written.

Background

In recent years Web applications have become very important (Oztekin et al., 2009). This type of applications is currently the backbone of business and information exchange, and is being used to present products and services to potential customers (Fernandez et al., 2011). In this context, usability plays a fundamental role since it affects both the acceptability and quality of Web applications (Matera et al., 2006).

The software development industry has invested in the development of a variety of Usability Inspection Methods (UIMs) to address Web usability issues (Matera et al., 2006). UIMs are procedures in which inspectors examine usability-related aspects of a user interface (Rocha and Baranauska, 2003). However, in (Rivero et al., 2013), we identified that there is a lack of UIMs that are able to find usability problems in early stages of the development process.

In this paper we present the proposal and empirical evaluation of the Web Design Usability Evaluation (Web DUE) technique and its tool support, the Mockup Design Usability Evaluation (Mockup DUE) tool. The Web DUE technique allows inspectors to identify usability problems in earlier stages of the development process by evaluating Web low fidelity prototypes or mockups. These mockups are images of how the software would look like after implementation. Furthermore, the Mockup DUE tool assists inspectors using the Web DUE technique by allowing them to: (a) interact with mockups as if they were a real application, and (b) use the Web DUE technique to find usability problems.

This paper is organized as follows. Related work on UIMs for Web applications presents the background knowledge of Usability Inspection Methods for Web applications and related work for this research. In The Web design usability evaluation technique we present the Web DUE technique proposal. Section First empirical study: evaluating the feasibility of the Web DUE technique shows how we carried out and analyzed the results of the feasibility study of the Web DUE technique. We then present the motivation and main functionalities of the Mockup DUE tool in Section The mockup design usability evaluation tool. Next, in Second empirical study: evaluating the mockup DUE tool, we show how we performed an empirical study to address the Mockup DUE tool's perceived ease of use and the satisfaction of its users. Finally Conclusions and future work presents our conclusions and future work.

Related work on UIMs for Web applications

Usability Inspection Methods (UIMs) are evaluation methods in which experienced inspectors or the development team review the usability aspects of the software artifacts. In UIMs, the inspectors base their evaluation in guidelines that check the system's level of achievement of usability attributes. The obtained results can be used to predict whether there will be a usability problem. The main advantage of UIMs is that they can lower the cost of finding usability problems since they do not need any special equipment or laboratory to be performed (Rocha and Baranauska, 2003).

Regarding UIMs for the Web, in our previous work (Rivero et al., 2013) we performed an extension over the systematic mapping from Fernandez et al. (2011) to draw conclusions about the state of art of UIMs for Web applications. During this extension we verified that around 77% of the reviewed papers reported UIMs analyzing finished Web applications or at least functional prototypes. Moreover, the remaining papers described automated techniques in which HTML code was verified, or in which UIMs evaluated if the application model met interaction rules within the Web domain.

There are some UIMs that could be applied in early stages of the development of Web applications (Rivero et al., 2013). Allen et al. (2006) present the Paper-Based Heuristic Evaluation, which was designed for assessing the degree of usability of medical Web applications mockups. During the inspection process, the inspectors evaluate mockups or Web application's print screens using a set of usability heuristics. Furthermore, Molina and Troval (2009) suggest the Model Driven Engineering of Web Information Systems. This method proposes to integrate usability requirements during the specification of Web applications and allows inspectors to check 50 metrics within the navigational models in order to evaluate if they meets usability features. Finally, the Comprehensive Model for Web Sites Quality (Signore, 2005) uses five perspectives in order to evaluate the usability of Web applications: correctness, presentation, content, navigation and interaction. According to Signore (2005), the correctness perspective is directly related to code quality while the other perspectives are related to the users' opinion. During the inspection process, a tool verifies correctness problems and then, the inspectors relate these problems to the other perspectives to identify usability problems in software models.

Despite the academy's effort in developing UIMs for Web applications there is still room for improvement. When analyzing the current state of UIMs for the Web (Rivero and Conte, 2012a), we identified that emerging UIMs for Web applications should be able to: (a) find usability problems in the initial stages of the development process; (b) aid in both the identification and solution of usability problems; and (c) provide assistance by means of a tool to reduce the inspector's effort.

The Web design usability evaluation technique

A. The Web DUE proposal

The Web Design Usability Evaluation (Web DUE) technique is an inspection method based on checklists that was proposed to meet the needs of the software development industry regarding the usability evaluation of Web applications. Consequently, it mainly focuses on identifying usability problems in early stages of the development process. Therefore, the Web DUE technique can be used to evaluate the usability of mockups. This feature is important as finding usability problems in earlier stages of the development process can lower the cost of correcting them (Rivero and Conte, 2012a).

The main innovation of the Web DUE technique is its ability to guide inspectors through the evaluation process by using specific "pieces" that are used to compose Web pages of Web applications. These "pieces" are called Web page zones (Fons et al., 2008) and they contain specific component within Web pages. Table 1 shows the list of the Web page zones used by the Web DUE technique, the suitability of including such zones in a Web page, and a brief description of their contents. In this table,

Table 1 Contents and suitability of Web page zones based on (Fons et al. 2008)

Zone	Suitability	Contents
Navigation	Mandatory	Navigation Links
System's State	Mandatory	Information about the application's state and how we got there.
Information	Depends on the Functionality	Information from the application's data base.
Services	Depends on the Functionality	Access to functionalities related to the information zone.
User Information	Depends on the Functionality	Information about the logged user.
Direct Access	Depends on the Functionality	Links to common Web functionalities (Login, Logout, Home).
Data Entry	Depends on the Functionality	Provides a form to input data to execute certain operations.
Institution	Optional	Information about the institution that is responsible for the Web application.
Custom	Optional	Domain-independent content
Help	*Mandatory*	*Information about how to use the application and how it works.*

"Mandatory" means that the zone is essential; "Optional" means that including/excluding the zone will not affect the provided functionality; and "Depends on the functionality" means that regarding the purpose of the Web page it might be necessary to include the zone. A more thorough description of each Web page zone can be found at (Rivero et al., 2013).

The main advantage of the use of Web page zones is that they can aid inspectors in evaluating only the elements that are present in the evaluated mockup. Another expected benefit of the use of Web page zones is that they can provide inspectors with a guideline to identify the elements within the application.

We based the Web DUE technique in the Web Design Perspective (WDP) based usability evaluation technique (Conte et al., 2009). This technique evolves the Heuristic Evaluation (Nielsen, 1992) in order to evaluate the usability of Web applications. Therefore, it relates the usability of Web applications to three main perspectives: concept, navigation and presentation. Using these perspectives and the heuristics from the Heuristic Evaluation, it creates pairs HxP by combining heuristics and perspectives when there is a relationship between them. For each pair HxP, the WDP provides a set of hints in order to aid inspectors in finding usability problems when evaluating Web applications. Furthermore, the WDP technique has been proved feasible for the usability evaluation of Web applications during several empirical studies (Conte et al., 2009).

We extracted the hints from the WDP technique, and related them to each of the Web page zones creating usability verification items. These verification items check the usable properties of each Web page zone and are grouped in checklists. There is a checklist for each Web page zone. Inspectors use these checklists to verify if the evaluated low-fidelity prototype meets usability principals. Table 2 shows part of the verification items for the Data Entry Web page zone. All the usability verification items from the Web DUE technique can be found at our previous work (Rivero et al., 2013).

B. Web DUE inspection process

The steps of the simplified inspection process of the Web DUE technique are shown in Figure 1. We have used these steps to evaluate the usability of a mockup which was created based on a page of the Journal and Event Management System (JEMS[a]).

The first step for the identification of usability problems is to divide the paper based prototype into Web page zones. Figure 1 shows the identified zones within the mockup: System's State zone, Data Entry zone and Navigation zone. After identifying the Web page zones, inspectors must check if the mockup meets all the items described within each of the checklists per zone. Table 3 shows some of the usability verification items that were not met by the prototyped Web page and their associated Web page zones.

Table 2 Data entry zone: description and part of the usability verification items

Description of the data entry zone	Usability verification items
This zone is responsible for providing the user with a form to input data in order to execute certain operations. Then, a submit-like button links the input data with the associated functionality.	1) It is easy to see (find, locate) the zone to input data in the system.
	2) The interface indicates which data must be mandatory filled.
	3) The interface indicates the correct format for a determined data entrance.

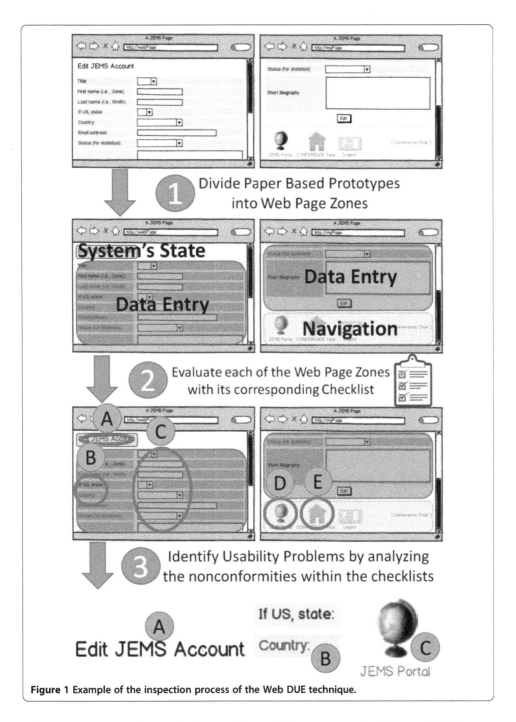

Figure 1 Example of the inspection process of the Web DUE technique.

Inspectors must point out in the mockups which components within each Web page zone did not meet the usability verification items. If we look at Figure 1 and Table 3 simultaneously, we can relate the nonconformity of the usability verification items in Table 3 with the augmented elements A, B and C in Figure 1. We will address each of the encountered usability problems as follows.

Regarding the System's State zone, the usability verification item 01 indicated that, despite showing the actual state of the system, the prototype does not show it logically (see Figure 1 element A). In other words, the prototype does not show how the user reached that state.

Table 3 Verification items that were not met by the prototyped Web page of the JEMS system

N°	Web page zone	Usability verification items
01	System's State	The System's State is naturally and logically presented to the user.
02	Data Entry	The data to be input (whatever the means of input) by the user are requested in a natural and logical order.
03	Navigation	The terms (words or symbols) make sense considering the domain of the application and follow conventions of the real world.

Regarding the Data Entry zone, we identified the nonconformity 02 which indicates that the mockup does not request data in a logical way. Asking for the country's state before informing the country is not coherent (see Figure 1 element B).

During the evaluation of the Navigation zone we encountered nonconformity 03 which indicates that the symbols used within the navigation zone are difficult to understand. A user would find it confusing that the "globe" symbol would leave to the JEMS portal (see Figure 1 element C).

We have shown the simplified inspection process of the Web DUE technique by evaluating a low-fidelity prototype of a Web page. As mentioned before, in order to evaluate the entire Web application, all Web pages within the Web application must be evaluated. Furthermore, the amount of mockups (number of sketched Web pages) must be enough to simulate a user task or user case in the Web application. Also, these mockups must provide enough detail (layout and elements) for the inspector to understand the overall design of the application and its interaction steps.

First empirical study: evaluating the feasibility of the Web DUE technique

According to Shull et al. (2001), the first study that must be carried out to evaluate a new technology is a feasibility study. Therefore, we have designed and executed a feasibility study to verify if the Web DUE technique is feasible regarding the number of detected defects and the time spent. In this study we compared the Web DUE technique with the WDP technique (Conte et al., 2009). Despite the fact that the WDP is not a technique for the evaluation of paper based prototypes, it is the Web DUE's predecessor, since the Web DUE is based on the WDP. Therefore, we believe it is reasonable to compare if the Web DUE presents better results than the WDP when evaluating mockups.

During this study we have controlled the following independent variables: the subjects' experience, the evaluated Web application mockups, and the applied techniques. Furthermore, we have measured the following dependent variables: number of defects, number of false positives, time, effectiveness and efficiency per technique. These variables will be explained as they are cited throughout the text. Moreover, we gathered the subjects' opinion to better understand the results from this empirical study.

A. Description of the empirical study

Goal

In Table 4, we present the goal of this feasibility study using the GQM paradigm (Basili and Rombach 1998). We have characterized the feasibility of the Web DUE technique

Table 4 Goal of the feasibility study of the Web DUE technique presented using the GQM paradigm

Analyze	The web design usability evaluation technique.
For the purpose of	Characterize.
With respect to	Its feasibility in terms of the effectiveness and efficiency indicators compared to the WDP technique.
From the point of view	Of Software Engineering Researchers.
In the context of	A usability evaluation of the mockups of a Web based system by usability inspectors.

by analyzing its effectiveness and efficiency indicators. For these indicators, we have used the same definition used in (Conte et al., 2009) and (Fernandez et al., 2010):

- Effectiveness is the ratio between the number of detected problems and the total of existing problems.
- Efficiency is the ratio between the number of detected problems and the time spent in finding them.

Subjects

We carried out the feasibility study in April 2012 with students of the Computer Science course from Federal University of Amazonas. There were a total of eight undergraduate and postgraduate students who agreed to participate. All subjects signed a consent form and filled out a characterization form. The characterization form addressed the subjects' expertise concerning: (a) expertise in usability knowledge, (b) expertise in usability evaluation, and (c) expertise in application design. All subjects answered objective questions regarding their degree of knowledge and professional experience. The characterization data were analyzed and each subject was classified as having Low, Medium or High experience according to the provided information within his/her characterization form. For instance, in the characterization of the inspectors' experience in Human Computer Interaction (HCI), we considered: (a) Low, if the subject had no practical experience in HCI and/or had not studied HCI; (b) Medium, if the subject had studied HCI, but had poor practical experience in usability evaluations; and (c) High, if the subject had studied HCI in books and class, and had participated in projects involving usability evaluation. In order to reduce the bias of having more experienced inspectors using one or another technique, we equally distributed the subjects into two teams. One team used the Web DUE technique and the other one the WDP technique. Table 5 shows both teams and the expertise of their members.

There were other participants in this empirical study: (a) the moderator of the inspection, who was responsible for planning and collecting the data during the empirical study; (b) the technique lecturers, who provided the training on each technique; and (c) the discrimination team, which was responsible for deciding which of the pointed out defects were real usability problems.

Materials

Each team used either the Web DUE technique or the WDP technique to evaluate the usability of a set of paper based prototypes. For each technique they received a set of

Table 5 Quantitative results of the feasibility study of the Web DUE technique

	Group							
	Web DUE				WDP			
Subject	1	2	3	4	5	6	7	8
HCI experience	M	L	L	H	L	L	H	M
Inspections	L	L	L	L	L	L	L	H
Design	L	M	L	H	L	M	M	L
Time spent (min)	100	67	200	160	147	132	124	279
Total discrepancies	38	23	27	22	12	33	9	30
False positives	19	2	5	4	1	5	0	8
Total defects	19	21	22	18	11	28	9	22
Effectiveness (%)	24.05	26.58	27.85	22.78	13.92	35.44	11.39	27.85
Efficiency (Defects per hour)	11.40	18.81	6.60	6.75	4.49	12.73	4.35	4.73
Average effectiveness (%)	25.32				22.15			
Average efficiency (Defects per hour)	10.89				6.58			

checklists to report the encountered usability problems. The mockups were prepared based on a coupon website. Coupon websites offer social coupons which are quickly emerging as a marketing tool for businesses, and an attractive shopping tool for consumers. We decided to perform the inspection over this type of Website since its popularity is raising (Kumar, 2012). To aid inspectors in the navigation among the prototyped Web pages, we provided a navigation map indicating which page should be shown after pressing buttons. Figure 2 shows one of the prepared mockups (see Mockup 05) and its navigation map (see Navigation Map for Mockup 05). It is noteworthy that the mockups and navigation map are in Portuguese since the Web application had Brazilians as target users.

Procedure

In order to use the Web DUE technique or the WDP technique, it is necessary to receive previous training in usability inspections and how to identify a usability problem during the problems detection phase from the assigned technique. Therefore, to provide background in usability inspections, all subjects had lectures on: (a) usability, (b) examples of typical usability problems, and (c) how to apply an inspection method like the Heuristic Evaluation. Furthermore, before the inspection, each team was trained in the technique it was assigned. Consequently, each team had contact with just one of the techniques in order to avoid biased results. The main reason for this measure is that knowing both techniques could affect the overall performance and opinions of the inspectors.

Each subject had three days to complete the inspection and prepare a defect report which contained discrepancies (issues reported by the inspector that could be real defects or false-positives) and the time spent to perform the inspection, which was measured by the inspector himself. After finishing the inspection, each subject sent back his/her report and a follow-up questionnaire with comments regarding the Web DUE or the WDP technique.

Data collection

All inspections reports were delivered on time and none of them were discarded. The moderator checked all discrepancies within the defect reports for incorrect or missing information and also gathered the discrepancies. Finally he generated a new discrepancies

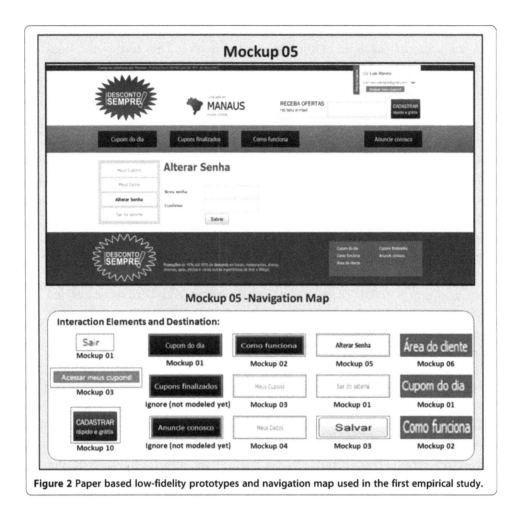

Figure 2 Paper based low-fidelity prototypes and navigation map used in the first empirical study.

report which contained all discrepancies found without showing the duplicated ones. Readers must note that both the collection activity and the discrepancies report were also verified by another researcher to avoid bias.

After the collection activity there was a discrimination meeting. This meeting was attended by the moderator and two other researchers who were not involved with the study. These researchers possessed good usability knowledge and prior experience in usability evaluation. For each reported discrepancy, the other researchers verified if it was a usability error by evaluating the paper based prototypes. It is noteworthy that the moderator, who was involved in the study, did not classify any of the discrepancies in order to reduce biased opinions. Considering all discrepancies, there were a total of 79 real defects. This number was used in the calculation of the effectiveness indicator as shown in the next subsection.

B. Analysis of the results of the feasibility study

We have analyzed quantitative and qualitative data. We obtained the quantitative data from the discrepancies' list resulting from the discrimination meeting, and the qualitative data from the answers to the questionnaires.

Quantitative analysis

As mentioned in the previous subsection, the total number of known usability defects is 79. Table 5 presents both the results per inspector and the overall results per technique. Using these data, we applied the Mann–Whitney U test to perform the statistical analysis of the experiment results. This test is the non-parametric equivalent of the t-Student test and we used it because we had two groups to compare (inspection techniques), different participants in each condition, and no assumption about the data distribution. Furthermore, in this analysis, we used α = 0.10 due to the small sample used within this study (Dyba et al., 2006).

It is noteworthy that a thorough description of our hypotheses and their statistical evaluation is available at our previous work (Rivero and Conte, 2012b). Interested readers can refer to that paper for further information.

The boxplot graph comparing the effectiveness indicator is shown in Figure 3. When analyzing the graph, we can see that the median from the Web DUE group is slightly higher than the median from the WDP group. However, the comparison using the Mann–Whitney statistic method showed that there was no significant difference between the groups (p = 0.885). These results suggest that the Web DUE technique and the WDP technique provided similar effectiveness when used to inspect paper based Web pages of a Coupon Website.

The boxplot graph comparing the efficiency indicator is shown in Figure 4. When analyzing the graph, we can see that the median from the Web DUE group is higher than the median from the WDP group. Therefore, the group that used the Web DUE technique was able to find more defects in lesser time than the group that used the WDP technique. Nevertheless, the comparison using the Mann–Whitney statistic method showed that there was no significant difference between the groups (p = 0.149). These results suggest that: (a) the Web DUE technique and the WDP technique provided different efficiency when used to inspect paper based Web pages of a Coupon Website; and (b) this difference is not significant from a statistical point of view.

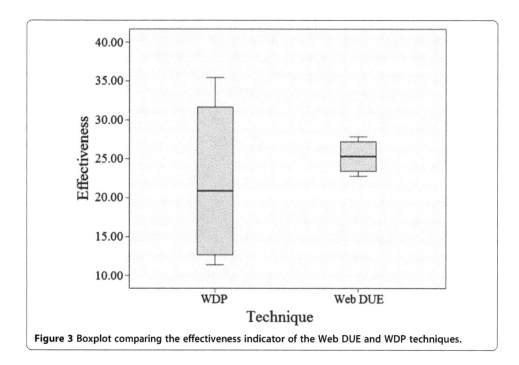

Figure 3 Boxplot comparing the effectiveness indicator of the Web DUE and WDP techniques.

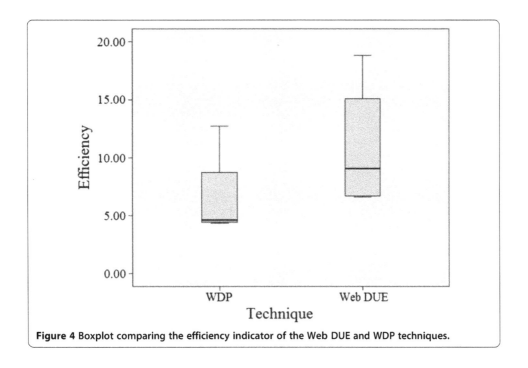

Figure 4 Boxplot comparing the efficiency indicator of the Web DUE and WDP techniques.

Qualitative analysis

The data analysis began with the examination of the answers within the follow-up questionnaires of the subjects who used the Web DUE technique. Figure 5 shows the main questions within the questionnaires which aimed to obtain information about the subjects' overall opinion of the main components of the Web DUE technique. We also collected data regarding the adequacy and perceived ease of use of the technique.

Regarding the subjects' opinion towards the use of Web Page zones, all inspectors agreed that it was easy to understand and identify all Web page zones within paper based Web applications. This is illustrated in the following quote.

- "Yes, they were really clarifying; I had no trouble understanding them." - Inspector 1.

Inspector 4 added that maybe it would be easier to carry out the inspection, if the Web DUE allowed an easy way to verify repeated Web page zones within a Web page. This could have caused an increase in the time spent during the inspection.

- "... In case of a data entry zone, a Web page could contain more than one data entry zone with different purposes. The technique could allow the verification of all these repeated zones in a particular way." - Inspector 4.

Regarding the Web DUE's verification items, Inspectors 1, 3 and 4 agreed that they were helpful when combined with the Web page zones (See quote from Inspector 4). However, Inspector 2 pointed out that some verification items could be used to evaluate the same Web page zone (See quote from Inspector 2). This could mean that some Web pages can be used to evaluate the same components, which confuses the inspectors; or that some verification items are too broad to allow the identification of specific

1. From the point of view of usability inspection, what is your opinion about the ease of use of the Web DUE technique?
2. From the point of view of usability inspection, what is your opinion about the adequacy of the Web DUE technique for the inspection of paper based low fidelity prototypes?
3. Were the proposed Web page zones (navigation, system's state, data entry, etc.) described in such a way that their meanings could be easily understood? If not, what could be improved?
4. Did the use of the usability verification items for each Web page zone result in any kind of difficulty or facility in the discrepancies detection?
5. Regarding the examples/explanations provided for each usability verification item, was there any you could not understand? If so, what could be changed to make them more understandable?
6. Regarding the usability verification items and their examples/explanations, was there any you disagreed with? If so, which was it and why?
7. In a new usability evaluation, would you consider using this technique to evaluate the usability of paper based low fidelity prototypes?
8. Regarding the mapping of the paper based Web pages, comment about the difficulties/facilities in understanding and simulating the interaction between the user and the system. Do you have any suggestion to simplify the inspection process of paper based Web pages?
9. Comment about the Web DUE's application and the identified problems.

Figure 5 Follow-up questionnaire of the feasibility study of the Web DUE technique.

features of the evaluated Web page zone. Furthermore, Inspector 3 stated that some items did not help him decide whether there was a usability problem or not (See quote from Inspector 3). This means that some verification items could not provide a clear description of which nonconformities must be found, or that the verification items are too subjective for the inspector to decide.

- "..., the usability verification items contributed to find more discrepancies when analyzing a determined part of the page." - Inspector 4.
- "Data entry zones, for example, possess verification items that could be adequate for the evaluation of the help zone. This ambiguity made it difficult to find terms that defined the problems encountered during the inspection." - Inspector 2.
- "... However, some verification items judge features, which are not totally wrong or right." - Inspector 3.

Regarding the subjects' opinion towards the examples and explanations provided along with the verification items, all inspectors agreed they were easy to understand and that they also made it easier to understand the usability verification items. However, when asked about the technique's adequacy, one inspector (Inspector 3) found the technique inadequate. Nevertheless, this inspector was not referring to the technique, but to the mapping process of the Web pages. All inspectors agreed that the technique could aid in finding usability problems in Web page prototypes. However, the fact that inspectors had to manually simulate the interaction between the user and the system turned the inspection process very tiring. The following quotes illustrate the inspector's opinion towards the difficulty in simulating interaction.

- "Applying the technique in mockups is really confusing when navigating through the pages. Mainly in bigger systems, with a higher number of pages. Furthermore, there is no interaction with the system." - Inspector 3.
- "It was too difficult to simulate using Web pages. Linking Web pages is complex even with the use of the navigation map." - Inspector 3.

Regarding the technique's perceived ease of use we found out that Inspector 4 found the technique very difficult. He argued that the Web DUE technique was too detailed and very repetitive (See quote from Inspector 4). The other inspectors did not stress that the technique was difficult, but that it was difficult to simulate the interaction as pointed out before.

- "The technique did not seem easy at all. It was too detailed and repetitive during most of the evaluation. On the other hand, it includes a very complete view of the contents of the pages." - Inspector 4.

Inspectors also stated advantages and suggestions of the evaluation of paper based prototypes. According to Inspector 4, mockups allow to directly point out the usability problems. Regarding suggestions for the evaluation of low fidelity prototypes, Inspector 3 indicated that colored mockups could make them more realistic and Inspector 2 said that the organization of the mockups is important for simulating the interaction between the system and the user.

- "I found the technique appropriate because in the mockups we can scribble and then, we can relate what we drew in the checklists options." - Inspector 4.
- "For a more artistic/visual view of the site, it could be interesting to provide colored mockups." - Inspector 3.
- "The use of a graph explaining the interaction among pages, or the organization of the pages according to the activities that are being executed can help in understanding the interaction." - Inspector 2.

The overall results show that the technique can be applied in the evaluation of paper based low-fidelity prototypes of Web applications. However, as the qualitative data indicate, there is still room for improvement. In the following subsection, we present the threats to validity of the feasibility study of the Web DUE technique.

Threats to validity

In this study we considered four main threats to the internal validity, which is concerned with if, in fact, the treatment causes the results (Wohlin et al., 2000). Regarding the first issue, training effect, there could be a risk if the quality of the training of the WDP technique had been inferior to the training of the Web DUE technique. However, we controlled this risk by using the same examples of encountered usability problems in both trainings. Furthermore, in order to mitigate the threat of the subject's knowledge affecting the results, we divided them into balanced groups according to their experience. Moreover, the inspector with the highest experience in inspections and usability was assigned to the WDP technique to avoid bias. To mitigate the bias of the subjects' classification we used three criteria that were assessed through an objective questionnaire. Finally, despite asking the subjects to be very precise in their time measurement, we cannot guarantee that these measures were carefully obtained.

Regarding the external validity in this study, which is concerned with the generalization of the results (Wohlin et al., 2000), we will discuss four issues. As for the first issue, the use of students as inspectors, we can argue that since we were looking for inspectors with the same degree of usability knowledge and we balanced both teams, students could be used as subjects since none of them had previous experience with any of the techniques. Furthermore, even though we used an academic environment to carry out the feasibility study, we based the mockups and their interaction in a real Web application, which can help resemble a real industry environment. Regarding the use of a coupon Website, we cannot guarantee that it is not a threat since there are many Web application categories (Kappel et al., 2006). Finally, using the WDP technique for comparison purposes is a validity threat. Nevertheless, since the Web DUE technique is based on the WDP technique, it is reasonable to compare if the Web DUE presents better results than the WDP when evaluating mockups.

According to Wohlin et al. (2000), the conclusion validity is concerned with the relationship between the treatment and the results. In this study, the biggest problem is the statistical power. Since the number of subjects is low, the data extracted from this study can only be considered indicators and not conclusive.

Finally, the criteria used to measure the feasibility of the technique can be considered a threat to the construct validity (relationship between the theory and the observation) if not properly chosen (Wohlin et al., 2000). However, as effectiveness and efficiency are two common criteria used for investigating the productivity of new techniques (Fernandez et al., 2010), this threat cannot be considered a risk to the validity of our results.

The mockup design usability evaluation tool
A. Motivation and features of the mockup DUE tool

The results of the empirical study in Section IV indicated that the fact that inspectors had to manually simulate the interaction between the user and the Web mockups turned the inspection process very tiring. Furthermore, the inspectors cited the main advantages of using mockups for usability inspection:

- Colored mockups can show how the Web application will look.
- The inspectors can directly point out the encountered usability problems.
- The inspectors can add notes or suggestions.

The Mockup DUE tool was conceived in order to: (a) automatically simulate the interaction among mockups, and (b) maintain the main features that made the use of mockups appropriate for usability inspection. To do so, we divided the inspection process into two main activities: (i) planning of the interaction, and (ii) detection. Using these activities the Mockup DUE tool supports the overall inspection process of the Web DUE technique.

During the planning stage, the moderators, who are preparing the mockups for inspection, can load their mockups in the tool and connect them by adding links (see Figure 1 stage 1). Furthermore, they can visualize and simulate the interaction steps by clicking in the mockups. This feature allows the creation of clickable mockups, which are close to real finished applications.

During the detection phase, inspectors use the previously mapped mockups and perform an inspection using the Web DUE technique. In this stage, the inspector mentally divides the mockups into Web page zones (see Figure 1 stage 2). For each of the identified zones, the inspector checks the usability verification items which are grouped and shown by the Mockup DUE tool (see Figure 1 stage 3). Moreover, the inspector can also interact with the mockups to verify the interaction. If he/she identifies a usability problem, he/she can add that problem and point it out in the mockup. Furthermore, the inspector can add notes with suggestions or considerations at any time.

In the next subsection we will show, through an example, how to use the Mockup DUE tool. It is noteworthy that all the screenshots from the Mockup DUE tool are in Portuguese since the first version of the Mockup DUE tool was originally developed in Brazil.

B. Using the mockup DUE tool to carry out an inspection

In order to carry out an inspection using the Mockup DUE tool the inspectors must be familiar with the overall inspection process of the Web DUE technique, either by using it without the tool or by being trained in it. In this subsection, we will discuss the main features of the Mockup DUE tool by analyzing some print screens of its graphical user interface. Figure 6 shows print screens in which we used the tool to map the interaction between Web mockups. In Part 1 we loaded two mockups to the Mockup DUE tool, and marked them as: (a) Elements A: a mockup that provides user information, and (b) Element B: a mockup of a page in which the user can edit his/her user information. When the user clicks in one of the mockups he added, the Mockup DUE tool shows it in real size in the visualization area (see Figure 6 Element C).

In Figure 6 part 2 we also show how to link mockups to simulate interaction. When the user clicks in the "add link" button (see Figure 6 Element D), the system asks the user which mockup will be shown once the link is clicked (see Figure 6 Element E). After imputing this information, the user can locate and resize the link (see Figure 6 Element F).

To check if the links lead to the correct mockups, users can visualize the mapping of the mockups (see Figure 7) and interact with them. Therefore, users can click in the previously added links (Figure 7 part 1) and then the tool will take the user to the related destination (Figure 7 part 2). This step is important as the moderator of the inspection can evaluate if the simulated interaction will be presented to the inspectors as intended by the designers of the Web application.

In Figure 8 we show the how to find usability problems using the Mockup DUE tool. Initially the inspector loads a project which consists of a set of previously mapped Web mockups. Then, the tool shows the first mockup to be evaluated, and next to it, the Web pages zones and the usability verification items of the Web DUE technique. The inspector must select a Web page zone (see Figure 8 Element A) to load its respective usability verification items list (see one of the items from the list in

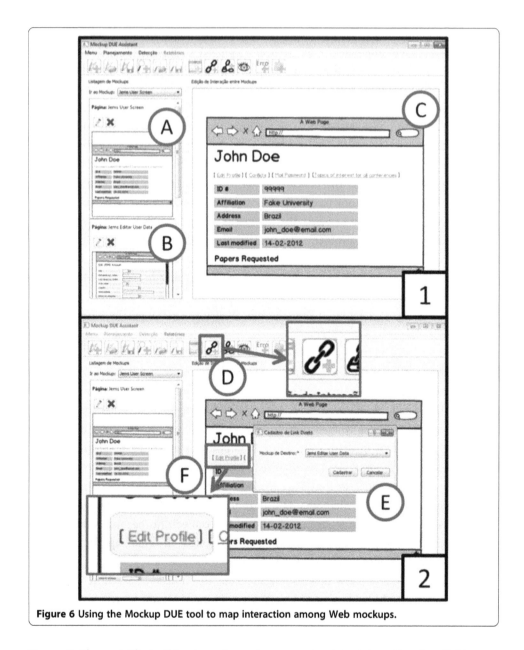

Figure 6 Using the Mockup DUE tool to map interaction among Web mockups.

Figure 8 Element B). In this stage, inspectors can simulate interaction by clicking on the links (see Figure 8 Element C).

When using the Mockup DUE tool, inspectors must verify if the verification items from the Web DUE technique are met by the Web mockups. When a mockup violates a usability verification item, the inspector clicks in the "point error" button (see Figure 8 Element D). After that, the tool draws a red empty circle in the mockup. This circle will be used by the inspector to indicate which part of the mockup has the usability error. The inspector can resize and locate the circle according to his/her needs (see Figure 8 Element E). Furthermore, if the inspector needs to make comments or suggestions, he can use the "add note" button (see Figure 8 Element F) to place a note.

After finishing the inspection of the mockups, the Mockup DUE tool can be used to generate a report for further analysis. Such report contains all the violated usability

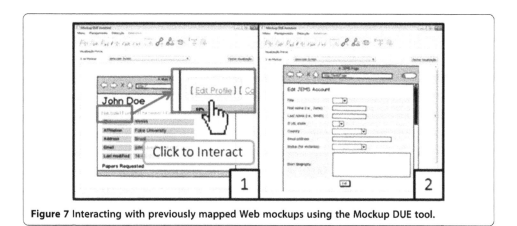

Figure 7 Interacting with previously mapped Web mockups using the Mockup DUE tool.

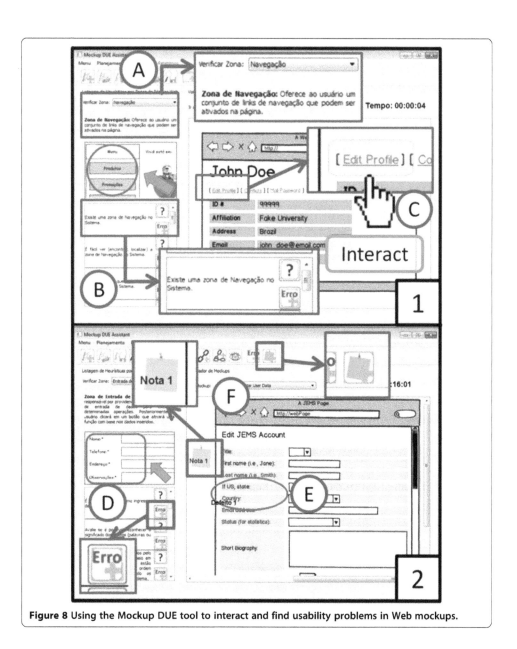

Figure 8 Using the Mockup DUE tool to interact and find usability problems in Web mockups.

verifications items and their location in the mockup. In the following section we will discuss the empirical study of the Mockup DUE tool and its results.

Second empirical study: evaluating the mockup DUE tool

We have designed and executed an empirical study to evaluate the users' satisfaction when using the Mockup DUE tool. In this study, we have performed a cooperative evaluation of the Mockup DUE tool. In a cooperative evaluation, design teams and users collaborate in order to evaluate a product and identify usability issues and their solutions (Rocha and Baranauska, 2003).

During this study we have controlled the following independent variables: the subjects' experience, the evaluated Web application mockups, and the applied tool. Furthermore, although it was not completely quantified, we have gathered the subjects' opinion as dependent variable. These variables will be explained as they are cited throughout the text.

A. Description of the empirical study

Goal

The goal of this empirical study is shown in Table 6 using the GQM paradigm (Basili and Rombach 1998). We aim to evaluate the Mockup DUE tool by analyzing the user satisfaction indicator and the perceived ease of use it provides to its users. Therefore, we have analyzed the inspectors' opinion during and after their experience with the tool.

Subjects

We carried out the feasibility study in June 2012 with usability experts from Federal University of Amazonas. There were a total of four postgraduate students who agreed to participate. All subjects signed a consent form and filled out the same characterization form used in the first empirical study (see Section IV). The characterization data were analyzed and each subject was classified as having Low, Medium or High experience, according to the provided information within his/her characterization form. The results from the overall characterization (See Table 7) show that, in general, the inspectors possessed from medium to high experience levels in HCI and usability inspections. Furthermore, the inspectors had no previous contact with the Mockup DUE tool in order to avoid learning biased opinions.

Materials

Each subject tested the main features of the Mockup DUE tool using two sets of Web mockups. The first set, which was used to test the mapping and simulation activities from the Mockup DUE tool, was based on the Google[b] Web site. The

Table 6 Goal of the empirical study of the Mockup DUE tool presented using the GQM paradigm

Analyze	The web design usability evaluation tool.
For the purpose of	Characterize.
With respect to	Its feasibility in terms of user opinion about their degree of satisfaction and the degree of usability of the tool.
From the point of view	Of Human Computer Interaction Researchers.
In the context of	A usability evaluation of the mockups of a Web based system by medium and high experienced usability inspectors.

Table 7 Characterization of the subjects who participated of the cooperative evaluation in the second empirical study

	Subject			
Experience in:	1	2	3	4
Human computer interaction	High	High	High	High
Usability inspections	Medium	High	Medium	High
Design	High	Low	Medium	Low

second set was based on the JEMS system. We previously mapped the interaction among the mockups from the second set as the subjects would use it to test the activity of usability problems detection. It is noteworthy that we selected these mockups because of the degree of the familiarity that subjects had with them. The first set was based on Google as it was necessary for the subjects to know the application because they would have to link its mockups, while the second set was based on the JEMS system as the subjects would not need any previous experience in the interaction provided by the application. Some inspectors, however, had used the JEMS system to submit their work for evaluation and therefore, had a little experience with the application.

We also used the Morae^c usability testing software to obtain richer qualitative data from the cooperative evaluation. This software allows the researcher to record and visualize the user reaction towards the tested software, and identify the interaction steps in which a problem can occur.

Procedure

All subjects received a set of tasks to be performed using the Mockup DUE tool: (a) to map the interaction of Web mockups; (b) to simulate the interaction between the user and the Web application; and (c) to detect usability problems. The subjects were told that the purpose of the evaluation was to identify usability problems regarding the Mockup DUE tool. Furthermore, they were encouraged to speak what they were thinking and suggest improvements so that the tool could be more easily used. During the cooperative evaluation, the moderator also asked questions regarding the system's ease of use. Moreover, if the subject encountered any difficulty in using the tool, the moderator would take notes and try to identify the cause. Additionally, we recorded the cooperative evaluation using the Morae software, for further analysis. Figure 9 shows a subject carrying out the cooperative evaluation of the Mockup DUE tool.

Each subject had as much time as he/she considered necessary to perform the tasks. Readers must note that the subjects did not perform a complete inspection over the evaluated mockups. As the goal of the study was to evaluate if inspectors could actually use the tool to perform an inspection, there was no need for performing a complete inspection. Finally, at the end of the cooperative evaluation, the subjects filled out a follow-up questionnaire with comments regarding the Mockup DUE tool.

Data collection

We gathered three types of information: (a) the notes taken by the moderator during the execution of the cooperative evaluation; (b) the follow-up questionnaires with

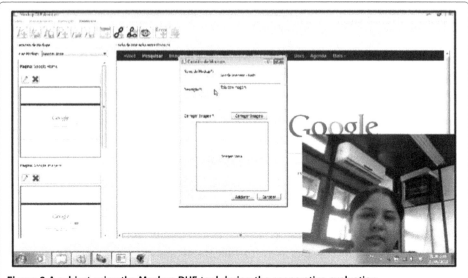

Figure 9 A subject using the Mockup DUE tool during the cooperative evaluation.

comments from the subjects and their overall satisfaction rating; and (c) the videos from the recording of the cooperative evaluations. In the next subsection we present the results of this empirical study and its qualitative analysis.

B. Qualitative analysis of the results of the empirical study

The data analysis began with the examination of the answers within the follow-up questionnaires. In these questionnaires we asked the subjects to rank their overall degree of satisfaction in a Visual Analogue Scale - VAS. A VAS is a measurement instrument that tries to determine a characteristic or attitude that is believed to range across a continuum of values and cannot easily be directly measured (Schaik and Ling, 2003). As shown in Figure 10, all subjects marked their overall satisfaction rate in the VAS scale after interacting and carrying out the inspection tasks with the Mockup DUE tool. In our VAS, 0 represents very displeased and 10 represents very satisfied. Furthermore, Figure 11 shows the follow-up questionnaire from this empirical study. We will now relate the results from the study to the subject's answers and our observations during the cooperative evaluation.

The results for Q1 (Is the tool easy to use?) and Q6 (Which were the aspects that made the tool easy or difficult to use?) showed that the inspectors' opinions were divided. Inspectors 1 and 2, found the tool difficult to use as they argued that they

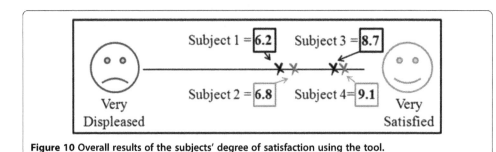

Figure 10 Overall results of the subjects' degree of satisfaction using the tool.

1. From the point of view of usability inspection, what is your opinion about the ease of use of the Mockup DUE tool?
2. From the point of view of usability inspection, what is your opinion about the adequacy of the Mockup DUE tool for the inspection of mockups?
3. If you had to perform a usability inspection using the Mockup DUE tool. Would you say it is possible to use it without any training? If not, what makes it difficult to use it without training?
4. Were the provided functionalities within the Mockup DUE tool intuitive and easy to perform? If not, what could be improve to facilitate the use of the tool?
5. Was the layout and disposition of the items within the Mockup DUE tool facilitating the use of the functionalities and easy to understand?
6. What do you think were the aspects that turned the Mockup DUE tool easy or difficult to understand?
7. In a new usability evaluation, would you consider using this tool to evaluate the usability of mockups?

Figure 11 Questions regarding the ease of use of the Mockup DUE tool.

needed more information in order to start using it. Inspectors 3 and 4 stated that over-all the tool was easy to use, but that it was necessary to make some changes to improve its ease of use. Below we present some quotes from the subjects in order to support these statements:

- "The tool needs to improve its usability. I felt lost when I started to map the mockups and to start the inspection." - Inspector 1.
- "The tool should improve some of the interface elements. There are some ambiguities regarding the activities of the user and the activities of the inspection." - Inspector 2.
- "The tool is easy to use because the icons are intuitive... However, when I added a usability error, I couldn't read the description..." - Inspector 3.
- "It's very neat, nice. But there are some details that made it confusing... When working with the links I had no information which mockup I had left..." - Inspector 4.

The answers for Q2 (Is the tool adequate for Web mockups inspections?) indicated that all inspectors agreed that the tool was very adequate (see quote from Inspector 3). Nevertheless, inspector 4 argued that it was not clear whether it was possible to point out a usability problem that was not in the usability verification lists.

- "I liked it very much and certainly it's way better than just using Web mockups..." - Inspector 3.
- "It is adequate. However, there are some details that confuse the user, for example: I thought I could only point out the usability problems from the lists." - Inspector 4.

The results for Q3 (Is training necessary before using the tool?) showed that some inspectors needed more information before starting using the tool (see quotes from Inspectors 1 and 2). However, Inspectors 3 and 4 argued that the activities were easy to perform without previous training, but that some usability problems needed to be corrected (see quote from Inspector 4).

- "No, some hints should be offered when starting the activities." - Inspector 1.
- "Without the observer's influence it could be very difficult to use the tool without training. Some icons, functionalities and modules possess names that are inadequate. ... Some functionalities could be grouped differently to enhance user experience." - Inspector 2.
- "Yes, despite being a bit confusing and difficult to learn, it is possible to use without training. Maybe there could be a general description of the functionalities..." - Inspector 4.

Regarding question Q4 (Are the offered functionalities intuitive and easy to perform?) and Q5 (Is the layout of the application easy to understand?), we identified that the layout had a direct effect over how easy it was to execute the functionalities. Inspectors stated that overall they were able to carry out all the activities. However, the location, size and description of the of the user interface elements made it difficult to execute the activities. Quotes from Inspectors 1 and 4 illustrate this fact.

- "Some user interface elements should be improved... In the detection phase the items should be better organized, as well as the verification items and 'add error' buttons." - Inspector 1.
- "I understood everything I had contact with. However, I had to read the hints to understand the functionalities of the buttons... I believe some of the elements from the interface are not well located." - Inspector 4.

Finally, the answers to question Q7 (Would it be possible to consider using the tool for Web mockups inspections?) showed that all inspectors would use the tool to carry out a usability inspection of Web mockups. However, most of them argued that in order to provide a better interaction, the previously mentioned usability problems should be corrected (See quotes from Inspectors 2 and 3).

- "Yes, but improve the words and terms, and some items and their location." - Inspector 2.
- "Of course I would use it again if the previously described errors were corrected." - Inspector 3.

Overall, the average degree of the subjects' satisfaction when using the tool was 7.7 (based on the VAS scale in Figure 10), which means that the inspectors were pleased when using the tool. We identified there was a relationship between the perceived ease of use and the degree of satisfaction of the inspectors. Inspectors 3 and 4 rated the Mockup DUE tool with an acceptable satisfaction rate. We identified that these inspectors found the tool easy to use right from the beginning and that they did not need any training. However, Inspectors 1 and 2, argued that the tool did not provide enough information for new users, therefore affecting the evaluation of their satisfaction rate.

In order to identify which user interface elements had caused a detrimental effect over the inspectors' opinion towards the tool, we analyzed the recordings and the notes taken during the cooperative evaluation. In Table 8 we provide some of the pointed out elements and what should be corrected to improve the usability of the Mockup DUE tool.

Threats to validity

We considered five threats to validity: (a) students are probably not good substitutes for professional inspectors, (b) academic environments do not represent day to day experience in the industry, (c) if the Google and JEMS Websites were representative applications of all Web applications, (d) the number of subjects involved in the study, and (e) if the criteria used to measure the feasibility of the tool were properly chosen.

As for the first issue, the use of students as inspectors, we can argue that since the subjects possessed high levels of usability knowledge and usability inspection experience, they could be used as experienced inspectors. Furthermore, even though we used an academic environment to carry out the feasibility study, we based the mockups and the interaction between the system and the user, in a real Web application which can help resemble a real industry environment (threat b). Regarding the use of the Google and JEMS Websites, we cannot guarantee that it is not a threat since there are many Web application categories (Kappel et al., 2006).

In this study, the biggest problem is the number of subjects who participated of the cooperative evaluation. Since there were only four subjects, the data extracted from this study can only be considered indicators and not conclusive. Finally, as satisfaction and perceived ease of use are two common criteria used for investigating the productivity of new software, threat (e) cannot be considered a risk to the validity of the results (Tanaka and Rocha, 2011).

Conclusions and future work

This paper has described and evaluated the Web DUE technique and the Mockup DUE tool for low-fidelity prototypes of Web applications. Furthermore, the empirical evaluation of these technologies showed indicators of their feasibility. For instance, the Web DUE technique managed better effectiveness and efficiency than its predecessor (the WDP technique) when evaluating the mockups of a coupon website. Moreover, the experienced inspectors who used the Mockup DUE tool stated that they would use it to carry out usability inspections within the context of Web mockups.

Table 8 Problematic elements in the Mockup DUE tool and a possible solution to minimize their effects

Element	Problem	Solution
Mapping Stage – Mockup List: Edit Button.	The name of the button suggests that the user will edit the mockup, while he will only edit the interaction.	Change the name of the button to: "Edit Mapping".
Mapping Stage – Whole Interface.	There is no indication where the user is.	Add system's state information.
Detection Stage – Notes.	The user can only see the note he added after waiting for the hint to appear.	Show the note's text if the user clicks the note icon.
Whole Interface.	There is no information about the execution process of the activities in the tool.	Provide a help menu or hints that describe which activities must be performed and how.

Regarding the evolution of the Web DUE technique future work involves: (a) verifying which usability verification items can be combined within the Web page zones to reduce effort during the inspection; (b) analyzing and suggesting an alternative inspection process in order to reduce repetitive instructions; and (c) analyzing which usability verification items or examples/explanations are not clear or ambiguous in order to reduce the inspector's effort and confusion.

Future work concerning the evolution of the Mockup DUE tool involves: (a) analyzing and suggesting a new organization for the supported activities; (b) modifying the user interface according to the suggestions from its feasibility study; and (c) preparing a help menu to aid inspectors that are not familiar with the tool in performing the mapping and inspection of Web mockups.

We also intend to perform new empirical studies to validate the obtained results and to better understand both the technique and tool. In these studies we intend to use further resources to achieve richer data. For instance, we will use existing satisfaction questionnaires found in the literature for further qualitative data, and likert scales so that it is possible to perform quantitative analyses regarding the proposed technologies. Furthermore, we will compare the Web DUE technique with a technique specifically created for the evaluation of low fidelity prototypes.

We also believe it is important to test the performance of the Web DUE technique and the Mockup DUE tool in Web development processes which take benefit from early Web artifacts with a high degree of expressiveness. Consequently, we intend to perform new empirical studies within the context of agile development and model-driven development to gather information about the impact of using the proposed technologies in such contexts. Finally, we intend to analyze the agreement rate among the evaluators and to what extent are their experience levels impacting these results.

Endnotes

The endnotes that appear in this paper refer to: (a) https://submissoes.sbc.org.br/, (b) http://www.google.com.br/ and (c) http://www.techsmith.com/morae.html.

Acknowledgements

We thank the financial support granted by CAPES to the first author of this paper. Furthermore, we thank the Natasha Costa and Priscila Fernandes for their assistance during the discrimination meeting.

References

Allen M, Currie L, Patel S, Cimino J (2006) Heuristic evaluation of paper-based Web pages: a simplified inspection usability methodology. J Biomed Inform 39(4):412–423

Basili V, Rombach H (1998) The tame project: towards improvement-oriented software environments. IEEE Transactions on Software Engineering 14(6):758–773

Conte T, Massollar J, Mendes E, Travassos G (2009) Web usability inspection technique based on design perspectives. IET Software 3(2):106–123

Dyba T, Kampenes V, Sjoberg D (2006) A systematic review of statistical power in software engineering experiments. Information and Software Technology 48(8):745–755

Fernandez A, Abrahao S, Insfran E (2010) Towards to the validation of a usability evaluation method for model-driven Web development. Proceedings of the IV International Symposium on Empirical Software Engineering and Measurement, USA, pp 54–57

Fernandez A, Insfran E, Abrahao S (2011) Usability evaluation methods for the Web: a systematic mapping study. Information and Software Technology 53(8):789–817

Fons J, Pelechano V, Pastor O, Valderas P, Torres V (2008) Applying the OOWS model-driven approach for developing Web applications: The internet movie database case study. In: Web Engineering: Modeling and Implementing Web Applications. Springer, USA

Kappel G, Proll B, Reich S, Retschitzegger W (2006) An Introduction to Web Engineering. In: Web Engineering: The Discipline of Systematic Development of Web Applications. Wiley, USA

Kumar V (2012) Social coupons as a marketing strategy: a multifaceted perspective. Journal of the Academy of Marketing Science 40(1):120–136

Matera M, Rizzo F, Carughi G (2006) Web Usability: Principles and Evaluation Methods. In: Web Engineering. Springer, USA

Molina F, Toval A (2009) Integrating usability requirements that can be evaluated in design time into Model Driven Engineering of Web Information Systems. Advances in Engineering Software 40(12):1306–1317

Nielsen J (1992) Finding usability problems through heuristic evaluation. Proceedings of the Computer Human Interaction 92, UK, pp 373–380

Oztekin A, Nikov A, Zaim S (2009) UWIS: an assessment methodology for usability of Web-based information systems. Journal of Systems and Software 8(12):2038–2050

Rivero L, Conte T (2012a) Using the Results from a Systematic Mapping Extension to Define a Usability Inspection Method for Web Applications. Proceedings of the 24th International Conference on Software Engineering and Knowledge Engineering, USA, pp 582–587

Rivero L, Conte T (2012b) Using an Empirical Study to Evaluate the Feasibility of a New Usability Inspection Technique for Paper Based Prototypes of Web Applications. Proceedings of the 26th Brazilian Symposium on Software Engineering, Brazil, pp 81–90

Rivero L, Barreto R, Conte T (2013) Characterizing usability inspection methods through the analysis of a systematic mapping study extension. Latin-american Center for Informatics Studies Electronic Journal 16(1)

Rocha H, Baranauska M (2003) Design and Evaluation of Human Computer Interfaces. Nied, Brazil (In Portuguese)

Schaik P, Ling J (2003) Using on-line surveys to measure three key constructs of the quality of human-computer interaction in Web sites: psychometric properties and implications. International Journal of Human-Computer Studies 5(5):545–567

Shull F, Carver J, Travassos G (2001) An empirical methodology for introducing software processes. ACM SIGSOFT Software Engineering Notes 26(5):288–296

Signore O (2005) A comprehensive model for Web sites quality. Proceedings of the 7th IEEE International Symposium on Web Site Evolution, Hungary, pp 30–36

Tanaka E, Rocha E (2011) Evaluation of Web Accessibility Tools. Proceedings of the X Brazilian Symposium on Human Factors in Computing Systems and the V Latin American Conference on Human-Computer Interaction, Brazil, In, pp 272–279

Wohlin C, Runeson P, Host M, Ohlsson M, Regnell B, Wessl A (2000) Experimentation in software engineering: an introduction. Kluwer Academic Publishers, USA

2

Towards guidelines for building a business case and gathering evidence of software reference architectures in industry

Silverio Martínez-Fernández[1]*, Claudia P Ayala[1], Xavier Franch[1], Helena Martins Marques[2] and David Ameller[1]

*Correspondence: smartinez@essi.upc.edu
[1] GESSI Research Group, Universitat Politècnica de Catalunya, Jordi Girona, 1-3, 08034 Barcelona, Spain
Full list of author information is available at the end of the article

Abstract

Background: Software reference architectures are becoming widely adopted by organizations that need to support the design and maintenance of software applications of a shared domain. For organizations that plan to adopt this architecture-centric approach, it becomes fundamental to know the return on investment and to understand how software reference architectures are designed, maintained, and used. Unfortunately, there is little evidence-based support to help organizations with these challenges.

Methods: We have conducted action research in an industry-academia collaboration between the GESSI research group and *everis*, a multinational IT consulting firm based in Spain.

Results: The results from such collaboration are being packaged in order to create guidelines that could be used in similar contexts as the one of *everis*. The main result of this paper is the construction of empirically-grounded guidelines that support organizations to decide on the adoption of software reference architectures and to gather evidence to improve RA-related practices.

Conclusions: The created guidelines could be used by other organizations outside of our industry-academia collaboration. With this goal in mind, we describe the guidelines in detail for their use.

Keywords: Software architecture; Reference architecture; Empirical software engineering; Business case; Cost-benefit analysis; Reference architecture context; Industry-academia collaboration

1   Background

Nowadays, the size and complexity of information systems, together with critical time-to-market needs, demand new software engineering approaches to design Software Architectures (SA) (Nakagawa et al. 2011). One of these approaches is the use of software Reference Architectures (RA) that allows to systematically reuse knowledge and components when developing a concrete SA (Cloutier et al. 2010; Galster and Avgeriou 2011). Hence, RAs provide guidance for the development and evolution of a class of software systems in a cost-effective manner (Martínez-Fernández et al. 2013b).

As defined by Bass et al. (2003), a Reference Model (RM) is "a division of functionality together with data flow between the pieces" and an RA is "a reference model mapped onto software elements and the data flows between them". It is important to denote that this RA definition already emphasizes two fundamental assets of an RA: the RM that defines its fundamental properties, and the software elements that makes the RM operational by its implementation (Bass et al. 2003; Galster and Avgeriou 2011).

A more detailed definition of RAs is given by Nakagawa et al. (2011). They define an RA as an architecture that encompasses the knowledge about how to design SAs of systems of a given application or technological domain. Therefore, an RA must address: business rules; architectural styles that address quality attributes; best practices of software development such as architectural decisions, domain constraints, legislation, and standards; and the software elements that support development of systems for that domain. All of this must be supported by a unified, unambiguous, and widely understood domain terminology (Nakagawa et al. 2011).

In this paper, we consider that an RA may have the elements that these two RA definitions state. We show the relationships among RM, RM-based RA and RA-based concrete SA in Figure 1. Throughout the paper, we use the term RM to refer to industry-specific RM, although RMs can also be defined by other agents such as research centers or nonprofit organizations. Also, we use the term RA to refer to RM-based RA and SA to refer to RA-based concrete SA. Angelov et al. have identified the generic nature of RAs as the main feature that distinguishes them from concrete SAs (Angelov et al. 2012). Every application has its own and unique SA, which is derived from an RA. This is possible because RAs are abstract enough to allow their usage in differing contexts (Angelov et al. 2012).

The motives behind RAs are: to facilitate reuse, and thereby harvest potential savings through reduced cycle times, cost, risk and increased quality (Cloutier et al. 2010); to help with the evolution of a set of systems that stem from the same RA (Galster and Avgeriou 2011); and to ensure standardization and interoperability (Angelov et al. 2012). Due to this, RAs are becoming a key asset of organizations (Cloutier et al. 2010).

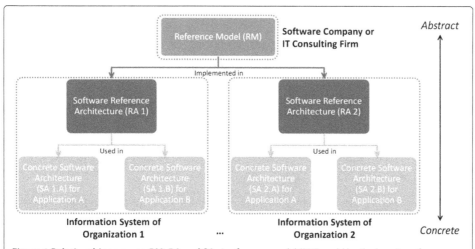

Figure 1 Relationships among RM, RA and SA. A reference model (RM) could be the baseline of many software Reference Architectures (RA). Likewise, RAs serve as a reference for the concrete Software Architecture (SA) of the applications of an information system. These three artifacts go from a high level of abstraction to a low level of abstraction.

1.1 Research problem

Although the adoption of an RA might have plenty of benefits for an organization, it also implies several challenges, such as the need for an initial investment (Martínez-Fernández et al. 2013b) and getting real evidence for driving its design and use (Angelov et al. 2013). Currently, organizations have little support for dealing with these two challenges.

First, there is a shortage of economic models to precisely evaluate the benefit of RAs in order to make informed decisions about their adoption in an organization (Martínez-Fernández et al. 2013b). Organizations with a wide portfolio of applications, which may consider adopting an existing or new RA to create and maintain such applications, lack an approach to know whether it is worth for them to invest on the adoption of an RA. This situation could be addressed by making a business case with the help of an economic model that perform cost-benefit analysis about the adoption of an RA (Reifer 2002).

Second, there is also a shortage of experience reports disseminating the context of RAs in industry. For instance, a recent literature review about evidence in software architecture, in which only two papers were about RAs, shows that there is limited knowledge about RAs (Qureshi et al. 2013). As a result, practitioners usually find the current literature about RA scarce and abstract (Angelov et al. 2012), limiting the industrial uptake of research results in the field. In this context, we argue that in order to enable practitioners to fully exploit the benefits of RA adoption and usage, the research community must clarify the context of RA in practice. We propose conducting empirical studies to accumulate real evidence for understanding the context of RAs from essential types of stakeholders. Such evidence aims to help practitioners to better understand RA-related practices and, then, to identify the current challenges to improve these practices in their organization. Throughout the paper, we use the term "RA-related practices" to refer to common practices in RA projects, such as defining the goals of an RA, RA design, RA review, RA use and so on.

1.2 Research goals and contribution

In this context, the goal of this research is to support organizations (i.e., software companies, information technology consulting firms) to deal with the following Research Questions (RQ):

- RQ 1: Is it worth for an organization to invest on the adoption of an RA?
- RQ 2: How can an organization get corporate evidence that is useful for RA-related practices?

In addition, we aim for a third research question:

- RQ 3: How the results from RQ1 and RQ2 could be articulated to provide prescriptive support utilities (i.e., guidelines and artifacts) to support organizations in such endeavors?

These support utilities aim to allow organizations to set up and carry out empirical studies aimed to extract evidence to support RQ1 and RQ2.

1.3 Paper structure

The paper is structured as follows. In Section 2, we explain the research methodology used. In Section 3, we report the details of how RQ 1 was approached and its results. In

Section 4, we report the details of how RQ 2 was approached and its results. In Section 5, we report how the results from RQ 1 and RQ 2 have been packaged to answer the RQ 3, and we present the guidelines for building a business case and gathering evidence of RAs and their context of use. Finally, in Section 6, we end up with conclusions and future work.

The work presented in this paper is a follow-up of the work presented in (Martínez-Fernández et al. 2013a). It substantially extends such work by:

- Providing further details of the research methodology applied (see Section 2).
- Adding results obtained in RQ 1 (see Section 3): providing new results about the application of an economic model to build a business case of an RA (see new Section 3.2).
- Making more narrow the scope of RQ 2 (see Section 4), updating the set of criteria to understand and evaluate RAs (see Section 4.1), and providing new results about why RAs are used in organizations (see new Section 4.2.1).
- Providing details of the formative and summative stages of the guidelines obtained from the RQ 1 and RQ 2 results (see Section 5). To analyze if the proposed guidelines could be used by other organizations, we also add the context of RA projects as reported by other researchers and practitioners (see new Section 5.1.1).

2   Methods

This section explains the research methodology used, and the context of this research. The research is being done under an industry-academia collaboration (Martínez-Fernández and Marques 2014) between the GESSI research group and *everis*, a multinational IT consulting firm based in Spain.

The architecture group of *everis* faced the two problems stated in Section 1.1. The main motivation of *everis* for conducting this research is twofold:

- strategic/organizational: providing quantitative evidence to its clients about the potential economic benefits of applying an RA;
- technical: identifying strengths and weaknesses of RA-related practices in RA projects in order to disseminate them and, if necessary, to improve them.

2.1   Action research

This research consists of an ongoing action research initiative among the GESSI research group and *everis*. Action research is "learning by doing" - a group of people identify a problem, do something to resolve it, see how successful their efforts are, and if not satisfied, try again (Brydon-Miller et al. 2003). The action research cycle consists of: 1) diagnosis of a problem, 2) examination of options to solve the problem, 3) selection of options and execution, 4) analysis of the results, and, 5) repetition for improvement.

However, the idea behind this research is not only to help *everis* to cope with RQ 1 and RQ 2. With the goal of RQ 3 in mind, we also aim to package the solution in such a way that it can be easily used by other organizations dealing with similar problems as *everis*. The guidelines that will be proposed in this paper are shaped throughout our involvement with *everis* to cope with the RQ 1 and the RQ 2.

2.2   Context of RAs in everis

We analyze the context of RA projects from our experience with *everis*. We focus on the case in which *everis* has designed an RA with the purpose of deriving concrete SAs for each application of a client organization. This usually happens when *everis* is regularly contracted to create or maintain information systems in client organizations. Each information system of the client organization is built upon the RA and includes many software applications (see Figure 2). RAs enable reuse of architectural knowledge and software components (normally associated to particular technologies) for the design of concrete SAs in client organizations. Therefore, RAs provide a baseline that facilitates standardization and interoperability as well as the attainment of business goals during applications' development and maintenance.

Besides, a special characteristic of *everis* is its previous experience in multiple RA projects. This experience allows *everis* to build a more abstract industry RM. This RM includes best practices from previous successful experiences, which serve as a reference for new RAs that inherit a certain level of quality.

The context of *everis* is very similar to other IT consulting firms. As a recent Gartner report shows, IT consulting firms "leverages industry-specific or industry reference models to accelerate client delivery and ensure quality and consistency across client engagements" (Brand 2014). However, "clients must ensure that generic industry or reference models [...] are sufficiently customized and tailored to enable their unique business

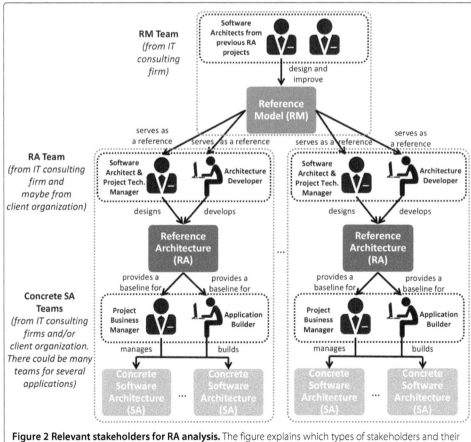

Figure 2 Relevant stakeholders for RA analysis. The figure explains which types of stakeholders and their roles in each type of project (RM, RA and SA projects).

capabilities and environments" (Brand 2014), so that the RM does not stifle competitive advantage of the RA.

Next subsections respectively show the types of projects that can be found on the *everis* context and the stakeholders that participate in each project.

Types of projects   There are three types of projects with different targets (Figure 2).

1.   RM projects.
2.   RA projects.
3.   SA projects.

Stakeholders for RA analysis   Stakeholders need to be clearly defined for RA assessment purposes (Angelov et al. 2008). The people involved in an RA assessment are the evaluation team, which conducts the empirical studies of the guidelines, and stakeholders from architectural projects. In the three types of projects defined above performed by IT consulting firms, we consider the following five stakeholders essential for RA assessment: project business manager, project technological manager, software architect, architecture developer, and application builder. Each of these stakeholders has a vested interest in different architectural aspects, which are important to analyze and reason about the appropriateness and the quality of the three types of projects (Gallagher 2000). However, there could be more people involved in an architectural evaluation, as Clements et al. indicate in (Clements et al. 2001). As a consequence, although this context is generic for IT consulting firms, projects' stakeholders may vary between firms. Below, we describe to which type of project essential stakeholders belong and their interests.

RM project   It is composed of software architects from the IT consulting firm that worked in previous successful RA projects. They are specialized in architectural knowledge management. Their goal is to gather the best practices from previous RA projects' experiences in order to design and/or improve the corporate RM.

RA projects   RA projects involve people from the IT consulting firm and likely from the client organization. Their members (project technological managers, software architects and architecture developers) are specialized in architectural design and have a medium knowledge of the organization business domain.

Project technological managers from the IT consulting firm are responsible for meeting schedule and interface with the project business managers from the client organization.

Software architects (also called as RA managers) usually come from the IT consulting firm, although it may happen that the client organization has software architects in which organization's managers rely on. In the latter case, software architects from both sides cooperatively work to figure out a solution to accomplish the desired quality attributes and architecturally-significant requirements.

Architecture developers come from the IT consulting firm and are responsible for coding, maintaining, integrating, testing and documenting RA software components.

SA projects   Enterprise application projects can involve people from the client organization and/or subcontracted IT consulting firms (which may even be different than the RM owner) whose members are usually very familiar with the specific organization domain. The participation of the client organization in RA and SA projects is one possible strategy for ensuring the continuity of their information systems without having much dependency on subcontracted IT consulting firms.

Project business managers (i.e., customer) come from client organizations. They have the power to speak authoritatively for the project, and to manage resources. Their aim is to provide their organization with useful applications that meet the market expectations on time.

Application builders take the RA reusable components and instantiate them to build an application.

3 Building the business case of RAs in everis

This section details our action research initiative with regard to RQ 1, which is intended to quantify the benefits and costs of RAs through a business case. "A business case is a tool that helps you make business decisions by predicting how they will affect your organization. Initially, the decision will be a go/no-go for pursuing a new business opportunity or approach" (Northrop and Clements 2014). A useful economic function for business cases is the Return On Investment (ROI). The ROI is a "measure of how much profit an investment earns computed by dividing net income by the assets used to generate it" (Reifer 2002). Although the ROI is the most popular function in business cases, there are many others (Ali et al. 2009). For instance, Net Present Value (NPV) estimation with discounted cash flow is mostly used to address the time value of money, and the Internal Rate of Return (IRR) compares the profitability of investments. Sarmad Ali et al. summarize the economic functions used for software product lines (Ali et al. 2009).

Figure 3 shows the action research cycles conducted in order to answer RQ 1.

In the first cycle of the RQ 1, we diagnosed the problem of the lack of approaches to justify the investment on RAs to *everis'* clients in monetary terms. As a consequence, we

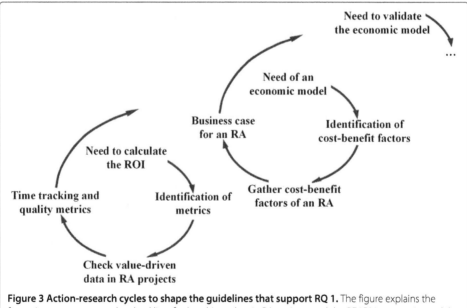

Figure 3 Action-research cycles to shape the guidelines that support RQ 1. The figure explains the formative stage to create the checklist of value-driven data in RA projects and the REARM economic model.

designed online questionnaires to ask stakeholders the metrics available in RA projects and conducted them in several RA projects. As a result, we observed that effort metrics could be derived from time tracking practices and that cost-benefit factors could be computed by using reuse-based metrics from the source code of the RA projects. The results from the online questionnaires to study the metrics available in RA projects are reported in Section 3.1.

In the beginning of the second cycle of action research, we diagnosed the need of having an economic model that would use the available data. Then, we identified economic functions meaningful to *everis* to justify RA investments. We also identified cost-benefits factors from the literature that can be calculated from the available metrics. Later, we computed these cost-benefit factors for a real RA project. At the end of this second cycle, we could build the business case for that RA project. In Section 3.2, we report an application of REARM, which is the economic model that we created.

Currently, we are at the beginning of a third cycle in which we diagnosed the problem of validating the economic model in another RA project.

3.1 First cycle: survey to check existing value-driven data in RA projects

In this survey, a sample of 5 *everis*' RA projects and 5 SA projects were selected on the basis of their suitability and feasibility to contact at least with one person that participated in the projects.

The main perceived economic benefits on the use of RAs are the cost savings in the development and maintenance of systems due to the reuse of software elements, and the adoption of best practices of software development that increase the productivity of developers (Martínez-Fernández et al. 2013c). To quantify these cost savings, we used online questionnaires to ask project technical managers and application builders about existing information from past projects. An excerpt of the questions of this survey is shown in Table 1, whereas Additional file 1 includes all the questions. When the client organization has no experience in RAs, these data need to be estimated, which could be potentially error-prone.

3.1.1 Results: costs and benefits metrics for RAs

In this section we describe the information that was available in order to calculate the costs and benefits of adopting an RA. We divide existing information in two categories: effort and software metrics. First, the invested effort from the tracked activities allows the calculation of the costs of the project. Second, software metrics help to analyze the benefits that can be found in the source code.

Effort metrics to calculate projects' costs In RA projects, 4 out of 5 client organizations tracked development efforts, while maintenance effort was tracked in all 5. In SA projects, 4 out of 5 client organizations tracked development and maintenance effort.

The development effort is the total amount of hours invested in the development of the RA and the SAs of applications. It could be extracted from the spent time for each development's activity of the projects. The maintenance effort is the total amount of hours invested in the maintenance of the RA and the SAs of applications. Maintenance activities include changes, incidences, support and queries.

Table 1 An excerpt of the template survey for software architects to check existing value-driven data in RA projects

Type of question	Question
Questions about data available for the RA.	Is it possible to access to a code quality management tool (e.g., Sonar) used in the RA project? If not, is it possible to install Sonar to take metrics from the source code of the RA?
	Would it be possible to estimate the degree of reuse in each of the modules of the RA with respect to the RM? (optional)
	Did the RA stakeholders track the time spent on each task in the development of the RA? If so, with which granularity?
	Is there data about personnel and time invested in maintaining the RA? If so, with which granularity?
	Would it be possible to give an estimate of the additional training time that an application builder needs to use the RA?
	Would it be possible to specify a standard hourly rate of performing tasks on the RA?
Questions about data available for the applications based on the RA.	How many applications are (or will be) based on the RA? Make a list of the applications with a contact person.
	Do you have an overview of the development of applications based on the RA? If so, go on. If not, we will contact the person who you indicated in the previous answer.
	For which of the above applications is it possible to know which RA modules have been reused and the degree of reuse?
	Is additional effort needed to reuse RA modules?
	Can you estimate how long it would take to develop RA modules instead of reusing them?
	Is it possible to access to a code quality management tool (e.g., Sonar) used for the RA-based applications? If not, is it possible to install Sonar to take metrics from the source code of the applications?
	Please, indicate the generic characteristics (e.g., reuse percentage of RA modules, size of applications) of three ideal types of RA-based applications with low, medium and high complexity.
	Did the RA stakeholders track the time spent on each task in the development of the RA-based applications? If so, with which granularity?
	Is there data about personnel and time invested in maintaining the RA-based applications? If so, with which granularity?
	Would it be possible to specify a standard hourly rate of performing tasks on the RA-based applications?
	Have you done any comparison between the costs and the benefits between RA-based applications and ad-hoc applications?
	Currently, are there indicators or metrics to evaluate the improvement of the quality attributes in the applications because of the RA usage?
Questions for adding comments and propose metrics to calculate the ROI of the RA.	In addition to the information discussed above, do you think that there is other available information to evaluate how the RA affects the applications development?
	Do you think that other metric, not mentioned above, could be useful to calculate the ROI of building applications based on the RA?
	Our economic model to calculate the ROI of an RA is based on the reuse and maintenance of code. Do you think there are other quality attributes or important factors for evaluating an RA?
	Before sending the survey, would you like to add any comments that may help to understand the context of your answers?

Software metrics to calculate benefits in reuse and maintainability Source code in RA and SA projects was obviously available in all projects. However, due to confidentiality issues with client organizations, it is not always allowed to access source code.

The analysis of the code from RA and SA projects allow quantifying the size of these projects in terms of LOC or function points (e.g., number of methods). Having calculated the project costs as indicated above, we can calculate the average cost of a LOC or a function point. Since the cost of applications' development and maintenance is lower because of the reuse of RA modules, we can calculate the benefits of RA by estimating the benefits of reusing them. Poulin defines a model for measuring the benefits of software reuse (Poulin 1997). Maintenance savings due to a modular design could be calculated with design structured matrices (MacCormack et al. 2012). For a detailed explanation about how such metrics can be used in a cost-benefit analysis, the reader is referred to (Martínez-Fernández et al. 2013b).

3.1.2 Lessons learned

Improvements in the quality attributes of an RA (e.g., reuse, maintainability, security) are extremely difficult to evaluate in an analytic and quantitative fashion contrary to the efficacy of the business (e.g., sales) (Carriere et al. 2010). This is because software development is a naturally low-validity environment and reliable expert intuition can only be acquired in a high-validity environment (Erdogmus and Favaro 2012). In order to evaluate RAs based on an economics-driven approach, software development needs to move to a high-validity environment. The good news is that it could be done with the help of good practices like time tracking, continuous feedback, test-driven development and continuous integration. In order to get the metrics defined above, tools such as JIRA (Atlassian 2014) and Redmine (Redmine 2014) allow managing the tasks and their invested time, general software metrics (like LOC) and percentages of tests and rules compliance can be calculated by Sonar (SonarSource 2014) and (Jenkins 2014). We think that adopting good and repeatable practices to collect data is the basis for moving software development to a high-validity environment and consequently being able of performing an accurate cost-benefit analysis.

3.2 Second cycle: a case study to apply an economic model to calculate the ROI of adopting an RA

In this case study, a sample of 1 everis' client organization RA project in a public administration and 1 SA project was selected. These projects were selected because the public administration that adopted the RA was interested in the study results. Besides, by the time we conducted the study, everis' started the aforementioned SA project, being highly feasible to collect quantitative data. Although we were aware of other SA projects with participants that do not belong to everis, it was not possible to contact with them.

Results from the previous survey (see Section 3.1) revealed that the data available in order to calculate costs and benefits were effort and software metrics. We collected these metrics, which are presented in (Martínez-Fernández et al. 2013b), from two types of tools. In order to collect data, JIRA (Atlassian 2014) was used to collect the invested effort from training, development and maintenance activities. Keeping track of activities is common in practice for project management and auditing. In addition to that, Sonar (SonarSource 2014) was used to gather software metrics to analyze the benefits that can be found in the source code. Sonar offers tool support for obtaining general software metrics such as LOC, dependencies between modules, technical debt, and percentages of tests and rules compliance.

3.2.1 Results

After retrospectively collecting the data of the past RA and SA projects, we analyzed which cost-benefit factors of adopting an RA could be calculated and envisaged the REARM economic model (Martínez-Fernández et al. 2013b) in order to calculate the ROI of the RA investment. By the time we conducted the study, the public organization had already: (1) adopted an RA designed by *everis*, (2) created an application using the RA, and (3) fixed errors discovered in the RA software elements that were reused by the application.

We calculated a three-year ROI of 42% with a payback period of 16,5 months and 7 applications in the public organization (see Figure 4).

Moreover, applications are introduced into the market earlier from the seventh month on. This is due to the effort avoidance of reusing the RA in the development of new applications.

The results of this study are further reported in (Martínez-Fernández et al. 2013b).

3.2.2 Lessons learned

As Clement et al. point out in their book (Clements and Northrop 2002), experts agree that the number of applications you need to build for a reuse-based architecture-centric approach to pay off is between 2 and 3. We also agree with that statement. In our study it turned out to be 7 because the application from which we collected data was small and only 20% of the RA was reused. However, in applications in which this percentage is higher, the benefit from the RA is greater. If we perform sensitivity analysis to REARM, with a higher reuse of the RA in applications (for instance higher than 70%, which is likely in medium to large applications), the RA pays off with 2 applications.

4   Gathering evidence of RAs in everis

This section details our action research initiative with regard to the RQ 2. Figure 5 shows the action research cycles conducted in order to answer RQ 2.

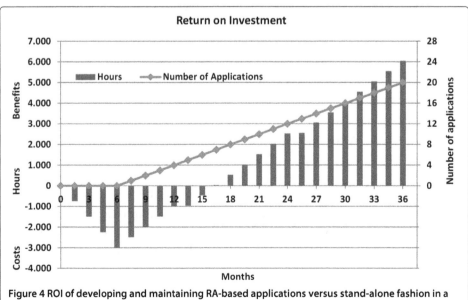

Figure 4 ROI of developing and maintaining RA-based applications versus stand-alone fashion in a public administration. The public administration of this study will realize a three-year ROI of 42% with a payback period of 16,5 months and 7 applications.

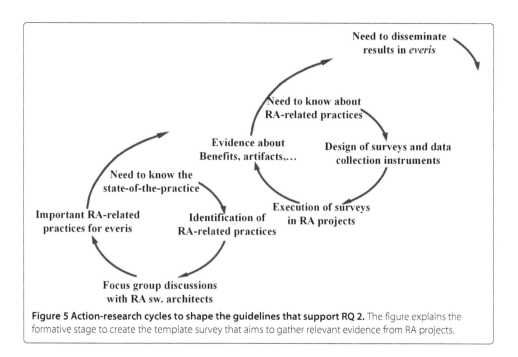

Figure 5 Action-research cycles to shape the guidelines that support RQ 2. The figure explains the formative stage to create the template survey that aims to gather relevant evidence from RA projects.

In the first cycle of the RQ 2, we diagnosed the need of knowing about the state of past and present RA projects in *everis* in order to reuse architectural knowledge and improve RA-related practices in prospective RA projects. As a consequence, we planned to identify a set of criteria about RAs that are relevant for practitioners. Finally, we identified five aspects that indicate what evidence to gather in order to support RA-related practices, which are presented in Section 4.1.

In the second cycle of this action research, we planned to gather evidence about these aspects. We designed surveys to gather mostly qualitative evidence about such aspects. Then, we executed these surveys in a case study with several RA projects in *everis*. As a consequence, we obtained results about why *everis'* clients adopted RAs, and the benefits and drawbacks of RAs. These results are reported in Section 4.2.

Currently, we are at the beginning of a third cycle of the RQ 2 in which we diagnosed the problem of disseminating these results in *everis*.

4.1   First cycle: identifying practical review criteria for RAs

In order to gather evidence of RAs, it becomes necessary to previously identify the aspects that are relevant for practitioners about RAs. In this section we identify an initial set of criteria, which might be further refined after gathering evidence from RAs. To do so, we analyzed the key criteria mentioned by *everis'* software architects during the meetings and focus group discussions of our action research initiative, and we also studied the literature. We prioritized the *everis'* vision to make a more practitioner-oriented set of criteria.

Although a commonly accepted set of criteria to evaluate RAs does not exist (Angelov et al. 2008; Gallagher 2000; Graaf et al. 2005), it has been claimed that RAs have to be evaluated for the same aspects as SAs (Angelov et al. 2008). For this reason, we started by analyzing some available works on SA evaluation (Bass et al. 2008; Clements et al. 2001; Falessi et al. 2010). However, existing evaluation methods for SAs are not directly applicable to RAs or other architecture-centric approaches such as product lines architectures because they do not cover their generic nature (Angelov et al. 2008). The development of a family of software systems has some characteristics that distinguish it from the development of software systems (Montagud et al. 2011). Therefore, existing evidences for product line architectures can be also used to evaluate RAs, namely: generic characteristics such as "variability, reusability, commonality, and compositionality" (Montagud et al. 2011); the propagation of architectural decisions while reusing common assets (Montagud et al. 2011); and lower development costs with respect to developing systems individually (Ali et al. 2009; Linden et al. 2004; Montagud et al. 2011).

Due to these reasons, the authors of the paper and two more software architects from *everis* elaborated further this analysis considering the specific characteristics of RAs as described in (Angelov et al. 2008, 2012; Galster and Avgeriou 2011; Graaf et al. 2005; Nakagawa et al. 2011), commonalities with other architecture-centric approaches such as product line architectures (Ali et al. 2009; Deelstra et al. 2005; Linden et al. 2004; Montagud et al. 2011), and experience from *everis*. The resulting aspects for understanding and evaluating RAs are detailed below and summarized in Table 2.

Aspect 1 refers to the need of determining the context and classifying an RA. As Angelov et al. point out (Angelov et al. 2012), there are five types of RAs depending on their characteristics. Among the most important characteristics are (Angelov et al. 2012):

- the organization(s) that will use the RA (e.g., a *single organization* or *multiple organizations* that share a domain),
- who defines the RA (e.g., *software companies* as IT consulting firms, *software groups* from the organization that use the RA, and so on),
- the origin and motivation of the RA (e.g., *preliminary* when the RA solves a new problem or *classical* when it is based on previous experiences),
- the goal of the RA and the domain of the RA-based applications (e.g., *standardization* of SAs or *facilitation* of the design of SAs),
- and the RA elements it may include (e.g., *components and connectors, policies and guidelines*, and so on).

The classification of an RA is vital to better understand its limits, to ensure its congruency, and to facilitate its evaluation.

Table 2 Summary of relevant aspects for software reference architecture understanding and evaluation as seen by practitioners

Aspect	Description of the RA Aspect
1	Overview and classification of an RA
2	Requirements and quality attributes analysis
3	Architectural knowledge and decisions
4	Supportive technologies
5	Business qualities and architecture competence

Aspect 2 consists of the quality attributes targeted by an RA. The achievement of quality attributes is in fact an SA most compelling reason for existence (Bass et al. 2003). However, SAs and RAs do not strictly determine all of an application's qualities. One example is usability: "whether the user sees red or blue backgrounds, a radio button or a dialog box" (Clements et al. 2001) is not determined by an SA or an RA. A list of quality attributes that lie squarely in the realm of SAs is defined by the architecture trade-off analysis method (Clements et al. 2001): performance, reliability, availability, security, modifiability, portability, functionality, variability, subsetability and conceptual integrity. For instance, variability shows how well an RA could be expanded or modified to produce new SAs of applications. Besides, an RA could address more architectural qualities than an SA (e.g., variability, reusability, commonality, compositionality, and applicability) (Angelov et al. 2008; Montagud et al. 2011). Quality attributes analysis should be wider for RAs in this sense.

Aspect 3 comprises architectural decisions. Many prominent researchers (Angelov et al. 2008; Falessi et al. 2010) highlight the importance of architectural decisions for the SA design process and the architectural evaluation. For RAs, architectural decisions are even more important than in a single software system since, owing to systematic reuse, an inadequate design decision could be propagated to several software systems (Montagud et al. 2011).

Aspect 4 consists of the supportive technologies such as methods, techniques and tools (Falessi et al. 2010; Nakagawa et al. 2011) that aim to improve the RA design process and support the use of the RA during the development of applications. Moreover, this aspect is very important for practitioners, since they are interested in knowing the latest versions of technologies and tools used in the RA projects, and providing application builders with tools that improve their productivity.

Aspect 5 refers to business qualities of an RA. SAs also address business qualities (Angelov et al. 2008) (e.g., cost, time-to-market) that are business goals, i.e. the objectives of an organization that affect their competence (Bass et al. 2008). These business qualities are even more important in the context of families of applications, such as RAs: "the main arguments for introducing software product family engineering are to increase productivity, improve predictability, decrease the time to market, and increase quality (dependability)" (Linden et al. 2004).

We recommend gathering evidence about these five aspects, which are summarized in Table 2, in order to improve RA-related practices. Next, Section 4.2 explains how we are gathering evidence about these aspects. Currently, there are no guidelines to support the gathering of these aspects altogether. This has motivated our work.

4.2   Second cycle: surveys to gather evidence to improve RA-related practices

In these surveys, the target populations were RA projects and SA projects executed by *everis*. A sample of 9 representative *everis'* projects in client organizations were selected. All these projects were from Europe (7 from Spain).

In order to collect data, semi-structured interviews were used for project technological managers, software architects, and client's project business managers. The reason of using interviews is that these roles have higher knowledge than the other roles about the architectural aspects of the Table 2, or another perspective in the case of client's project business managers, so we wanted to collect as much information as possible from them. Prior to the interviews, questionnaires were delivered to collect personal information about the interviewee and to inform him/her about the interview. On the other hand, online questionnaires were used for architecture developers and application builders, since most of their questions are about supportive technologies and their responses can be previously listed, simplifying the data collection process.

To perform data analysis, the research team held several discussion meetings during and after data collection, and established specific protocols and templates for data analysis. In the case of the interviews, we used an Excel-based template to organize each participant's answer to each question using tables. For doing this, we used the interview transcripts and individual notes taken by different researchers during the interviews. Then, we analyzed the data from two perspectives that lead us to a better understanding and interpretation of the results. First, we analyzed the answers at the project level, in order to understand the specific context of each project and the perspective of its stakeholders. Second, we analyzed the answers at whole by assessing all participants' answers related to each question, in order to categorize their answers using template tables that described (in each column): the name of the category, a detailed description of the cases covered by the category, the participant, and the explicit sentences that support the category. Such categories were then further discussed and analyzed by the entire team in order to better analyze the evidence and improve our understanding until reaching an agreement. As a result, some categories were split, modified, discarded or added to ensure that all answers were well-represented.

The complete version of the surveys protocol, which contains interview guides and questionnaires, is available at the Additional file 2. An excerpt of the questions for software architects of this survey, which only includes the questions used for the results described in the next two subsections, is shown in Table 3.

4.2.1   *Results: motivations to use RAs for designing SAs of applications*

In this subsection, we present results about the Aspect 1, which was defined in Section 4.1. Such results answer why RAs were adapted for creating SAs of *everis* client organizations' applications. Next, we report the motives that trigger the origin behind each RA project. These results can help organizations to analyze if they need an RA. Table 4 shows the characteristics and objectives of each RA project.

The motivations why *everis*' client organizations adopted an RA are shown below. We report between brackets the identifier of the client organization that indicated such motivation (see Table 4).

- 5 out of 9 projects (B, C, D, F, H) reported the update of technologies to develop applications since they were obsolete or application maintenance was costly.
- 4 out of 9 projects (A, B, G, H) mentioned the need to homogenize the development of similar applications and identify their common elements to foster reuse.
- 4 out of 9 projects (C, D, F, G) aimed to simplify application development (e.g., use of widely-known technologies) and improve productivity of application builders in order to hire profiles less specialized and reduce development time.

- 2 out of 9 projects (C, I) needed to improve business processes of the organization because of organizational changes or applications misalignment with business needs.
- 2 out of 9 projects (C, E) were started because the client organization had difficulties in developing applications without the help of a software vendor.
- 2 out of 9 projects (A, B) mentioned the need to support and enable application development in any platform (e.g., web, smartphone, POS terminal, ATM).
- 2 out of 9 projects (B, D) stated the need to migrate functionality from legacy systems to new systems (also known as "downsizing") to reduce maintenance costs.
- 1 out of 9 projects (A) reported the lack of products on the market adapted to its needs and business processes.

4.2.2 Results: strengths and weaknesses of RAs

In this section we present preliminary results about the Aspect 5 defined in Section 4.1. Such results answer how the adoption of RAs provide observable benefits to the different involved actors in RA projects in *everis*. Below, the resulting benefits and aspects to consider are reported, and it is indicated between brackets the identifier of the client organization that mentioned such benefits (see Table 4).

Benefits in *everis*' RA projects We grouped benefits in four categories. Below each category, explicit sentences from software architects are also indicated.

Table 3 An excerpt of the template survey for software architects to gather evidence about Aspects 1 and Aspect 5 of RA projects

Type of question	Question
Questions about the classification of the RA.	What do you understand by RA?
	What was the objective of the project?
	Which was the client organization's problem that motivated the project?
	What was the relationship with the client organization during the design and maintenance of the RA?
Questions about the business qualities of the RA for the client organization.	What benefits does the client organization experience from adopting your RA? And developers from using it?
	Which problems does the client organization experience from adopting your RA? And developers from using it?
	How the training for the client organization was conducted in order to them use your RA?
	Did the use of your RA cause any organizational change in the client organization?
	How does the use of your RA reduce the time-to-market of RA-based applications in the client organization?
	What types of non-functional requirements are reinforced because of using your RA in applications?
	To sum up, what conclusions do you draw from the facilities provided by your RA for the client organization?
Questions about the business qualities of the RA for the IT consulting firm (optional).	How is your RA based on an RM and any other existing architectural knowledge and software components in your company?
	What do you think should be replaced, included or updated in prospective versions of the RM?
	To sum up, what conclusions do you draw from the facilities provided by the RM for the IT consulting firm?

- 7 out of 9 projects (A, B, C, E, F, G, I) stated "reduction of the development time and faster delivery of applications".

  - An RA allows starting developing applications since the first day by following architectural decisions already taken.
  - An RA decreases the development time of applications since the RA's modules that implement needed functionality are reused in the application.

- 7 out of 9 projects (A, B, C, D, E, H, I) mentioned "increased productivity of application builders".

  - An RA facilitates material and tools for the development, testing and documentation of applications, and for training application builders.
  - An RA generates or automatizes the creation of code in the applications.
  - An RA indicates the guidelines to be followed by the application builders.
  - An RA reduces the complexity of applications' developments because part of the functionality is already resolved in the RA.

Table 4 Overview and characteristics of selected *everis'* RA projects

Id.	Domain	RA objective	Examples of applications	RA project type
A	Industry	Web-based applications to allow vendors updating information about clients in a department store.	Application that allows vendors to manage client information.	Design
B	Banking	Multi-platform applications that are fast, satisfy practices of the market and support transaction processing.	Application for online banking. There are approximately 300 applications.	Design, Evolution
C	Banking	Multi-platform applications of a bank. To improve the productivity of applications builders and to facilitate the development of applications.	Application to integrate some existing applications with the same look and feel. Application to improve the business process of depositing money. There are approximately 10 applications.	Design, Evolution
D	Insurance	Applications that satisfy internal request for proposals.	Applications to hire insurance policy (home insurance, life insurance...).	Design, Evolution
E	Public sector	Java web applications, with flexible front-end, integration and batch processes.	Application to support billing and technical services.	Design, Evolution
F	Public sector	Web-based applications for the different departments of a public administration.	Application to deliver forms and pdfs. There are around 50 applications of different departments of a public administration.	Design, Evolution
G	Public sector	Applications with enhanced reuse and reduced development costs.	Application for enterprise resource planning and customer relationship management.	Design
H	Insurance	Applications integrated with services of an insurance company.	Application to manage health care and payments.	Design
I	Public sector	Applications that include the business processes of a utility organization.	Application for urban management reports.	Design

- – An RA facilitates the configuration of its modules and the integration with legacy systems or external systems.

- 6 out of 9 projects (A, B, C, D, E, G) stated "cost savings in the maintenance of the applications".

  - – An RA increases the control over applications through their homogeneity.
  - – An RA maintains only once reused services by all applications.
  - – An RA allows adding or changing functionalities by means of a modular design.
  - – An RA establishes long term support standards and "de facto" technologies.

- 4 out of 9 projects (C, F, G, I) mentioned "increased quality of the enterprise applications".

  - – An RA helps to accomplish business needs by improving key quality attributes.
  - – An RA helps to improve the business processes of an organization.
  - – An RA reuses architectural knowledge of previous successful experiences.

Aspects to consider that eventually could become risks in *everis*' RA projects

- 5 out of 9 projects (B, C, E, F, H) considered "additional learning curve". An RA implies an additional training for their own tools and modules, even if its technologies are standard or "de facto" already known by the application builder.
- 4 out of 9 projects (B, C, D, E) stated "dependency on the RA". Applications depend on the reused modules of the RA. If it is necessary to make changes in a reused module of the RA or to add a new functionality, application builders have to wait for the architecture developers to include it in the RA for all the applications.
- 2 out of 9 projects (A, D) considered "limited flexibility of the applications". The use of an RA implies following its guidelines during the application development and adopting its architectural design. If business needs require a different type of application, the RA would limit the flexibility of that application.

The results of this study are further reported in (Martínez-Fernández et al. 2013c).

4.2.3 Lessons learned

During the pilot of the survey, we learnt the following lessons about its design:

- The same term could have slightly different meaning in the academia and in the industry (for instance, the term "enterprise architecture" is sometimes used in the industry to mean "RA for a single organization").
- The software development methodology used during the development of applications is seldom prescribed by the RA, so we removed it as relevant aspect for RAs (it was an aspect in previous versions).
- Contacting stakeholders from client organizations was harder than contacting interviewees from *everis*. This is mainly because it was *everis* who requested the study, so they had a clear interest on it.

5 Results and discussion

In this section, we present how the results from RQ1 and RQ2 have been articulated into guidelines to support organizations building a business case and gathering evidence of RAs. The guidelines have been incrementally constructed based on our action research approach with *everis*. For its shaping and validation, the construction of the guidelines is respectively divided in two stages: the formative and the summative stages.

5.1 Formative stage: shaping the guidelines

In the formative stage, the goal is to incrementally shape the guidelines from the feedback of the action research. In order to analyze whether other organizations deal with similar problems as *everis*, we highlight the similarities of RAs designed by *everis* with other RA contexts that have been reported in the literature and by practitioners. After this analysis, we will only package into the guidelines the material that could be used under other organizations context.

5.1.1 Similar contexts of RAs in practice

The results from our action research in *everis* are particular to the context described in Section 2.2. IT consulting firms, such as Accenture (Brand 2014) and Capgemini (Herold and Mair 2013) also fit into such context (i.e., they use industry-specific RM, and they carry out the three types of projects described there). However, to properly create the guidelines for other RA contexts, it is vital to first characterize RA projects conducted by other companies.

Architecture-centric approaches to develop families of software applications are not new. Deelstra et al. give a classification of these approaches with respect to the level of reuse (Deelstra et al. 2005): 1) standardized infrastructure; 2) platform: 3) software product line, and 4) configurable product family. In this classification, RAs can be positioned as standardized infrastructures or platforms (Graaf et al. 2005), whereas software product lines and configurable product families are based on Product Lines Architectures (PLA). Several authors has stated that RAs are more generic than PLAs (Martínez-Fernández et al. 2013b). Next, we classify RAs in the industry under the two former categories.

On the one hand, standardized infrastructures have been used by public administrations in Germany (Herold and Mair 2013), in the Netherlands (Galster et al. 2013), and in Spain (García-Alonso et al. 2010). These RAs provide software assets as inspiration for the design of applications, but little domain engineering effort is performed (i.e., little domain specific functionality is included in the RA). They are popular in public administration because there is a need to cover multiple organizations from different business domains (i.e., ministries or departments of the government) and little common functionality exist. Also, the high distribution of development teams implies that these RAs play only an informative or instructive role rather than regulative.

On the other hand, platforms additionally "require a certain amount of domain engineering to create and maintain the assets that implement the common functionality" (Deelstra et al. 2005). There are several business domains that have used this type of RAs.

In the space domain, the NASA has detected that "many Earth science data system components and architectural patterns are reconstructed for each mission" (Mattmann and Downs 2010). In order to reuse these assets in new systems, they created the NASA's ESDS RA (NASA 2012).

In the banking domain, RAs are usually used to integrate legacy systems and migrated service-oriented systems that contain the business logic. The common scenario is that these RAs provide common services that then may be reused in the different front-ends or channels (e.g., desktop applications, web client applications, mobile applications, ATMs and so on). An example is Credit Suisse (Murer and Hagen 2013).

The most mature domain for RAs may be the embedded systems domain. For instance, Océ, one of the world's leading copier manufacturers, uses an RA to derive an SA for engines incorporated in a specific series of Océ printers (Graaf et al. 2005). Besides, in the automotive industry, car manufacturers such as Volvo (Eklund et al. 2005) and BMW (Reichart and Haneberg 2004) started to use RAs to develop the software of electronic/engine control unit based on basic software components that were unique to them. As a further step, AUTOSAR has become popular later because it standardizes basic software components for many car manufacturers, suppliers and other related companies (AUTOSAR 2014). This enables the reuse of software developed by original equipment manufacturers in multiple car manufacturers. This has led to software ecosystems that are characterized by a network of developers rather than a single organization providing the final product to the customer (Eklund and Bosch 2014).

To sum up, we can conclude that core idea of using an RA for the development and maintenance of a family of software products is common in all these contexts. However, RM are only commonly used in IT consulting firms. As a consequence, the study of RM during the application of the guidelines will be optional so that it can be used in these other contexts.

It is also important to note that all RAs described in this section are based on practical experience in the industry. The guidelines will target this type of RA, also known as *classical* (Angelov et al. 2012). Conversely, the guidelines would be hardly applicable in *preliminary* RAs, i.e., those that are "defined when the technology, software solutions, or algorithms demanded for its application do not yet exist in practice by the time of its design" (Angelov et al. 2012).

5.1.2 *Packaging the guidelines*

everis' results are being suitably packaged with the aim of being applied in prospective RA projects and also in similar organizations. Figure 6 summarizes the guidelines for building a business case and gathering evidence of RAs in industry.

First of all, organizations that may want to use these guidelines need to fit into the context depicted in Section 5.1.1. This means that they need to design an RA based on practical experience, and to use such RA for the development and maintenance of a family of applications in industry. This is because the input for using the guidelines is evidence from real RA projects.

The guidelines support organizations:

1. To decide whether to invest on an RA by providing them with:

    - A checklist to analyze existing value-driven data in RA projects.
    - An economic model that uses such value-driven data to calculate the ROI of adopting an RA.

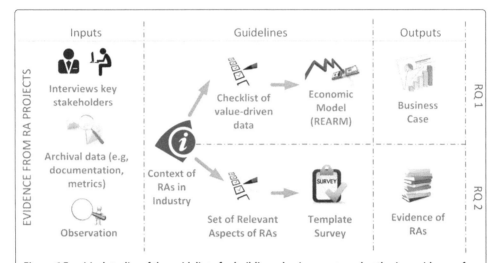

Figure 6 Empirical studies of the guidelines for building a business case and gathering evidence of RAs in industry. The guidelines are composed of the context of RAs in industry, and four empirical studies. The four empirical studies are used as follows. To answer RQ 1, there are two studies: a survey to check existing value-driven data in organizations and a case study to calculate the ROI of adopting an RA. To answer RQ 2, there are two studies: a focus group to determine the set of criteria about RAs important for an organizations and a template survey to gather evidence about the previously identified relevant aspects of RAs.

2.   To improve RA-related practices based on corporate evidence by providing them with:

   • A practitioner-oriented set of criteria to understand and evaluate an RA.
   • Templates of interview guides and online questionnaires to gather relevant evidence.

On the one hand, to analyze whether it is worth to invest on an RA, a checklist of value-driven data that an organization might have is facilitated to check if the provided economic model provided can be executed. On the other hand, to improve RA-related practices with evidence, a set of relevant aspects for RAs is facilitated to check which ones are important for an organization and then use the provided template surveys to gather evidence.

To gather evidence with the help of the aforementioned artifacts, empirical studies can be set up and carried out. Several data collection techniques exist (Lethbridge et al. 2005). We propose surveys that use interviews and questionnaires, case studies that require documentation analysis and metrics gathering, and focus groups. Below, we explain the dimension, context, objective and method applied in each empirical study of the guidelines. To see the threats to validity in *everis*, the reader is referred to (Martínez-Fernández 2013).

I) A survey to check existing value-driven data in RA projects

Dimensions   RQ 1.

Context   Typically, organizations do not have resources to compare the real cost of creating applications with and without an RA and historical data may be scarce. Thus, alternatives should be considered.

Objective   The objective of this survey is to identify the quantitative information that can commonly be retrieved in RA projects in order to quantitatively calculate the costs and benefits of adopting an RA in an organization. This is an initial step to create repeatable techniques for performing a cost-benefit analysis.

Method   Exploratory surveys with personalized questionnaires applied to relevant stakeholders (e.g., manager, architect, developer) to find out the quantitative data that has been collected in RA projects and SA projects. An example of conducting this empirical study and its approach for data collection is described in Section 3.1.

II) A case study to apply REARM to calculate the ROI of adopting an RA

Dimensions   RQ 1.

Context   Before deciding to launch an RA, organizations need to analyze whether to undertake or not the investment. Offering organizations an economic model that is based on former RA projects data can help them to make more informed decisions.

Objective   The objective is to analyze whether it is worth investing on an RA with the help of an economic model, in order to improve the communication among architects and management, and to improve their decisions.

Method   A case study that applies an economic model to calculate the ROI of adopting an RA. Depending on the maturity of the organization, two approaches can be applied. If the organization does not have experience with an RA, the economic model should be fed with estimated data. Nevertheless, when the organization already has experience with RAs (i.e., the case of IT consulting firms), real data can be gathered by means of an exploratory quantitative post-mortem analysis. Then, the economic model quantifies the potential advantages and limitations of using an RA. Some related works explain how to calculate the ROI of a product (Forrester 2014), software reuse (Frakes and Terry 1996; Poulin 1997), and software product lines (Ali et al. 2009). We suggest the use of REARM, which is an economic model specific for RAs presented in (Martínez-Fernández et al. (Martínez-Fernández et al. 2013b)). An example of conducting this empirical study and its approach for data collection is described in Section 3.2.

III) A focus group to study the relevant criteria of RAs for an organization

Dimensions   RQ 2.

Context   Typically, organizations drive the design and use of RAs in an unsystematic manner (Eklund et al. 2005). To drive RA-related practices based on evidence, it becomes fundamental to identify the relevant aspects of RAs as seen by practitioners.

Objective   The objective of this study is to identify the aspects that are important for each organization in order to support RA-related practices.

Method   A focus group with relevant stakeholders (e.g., manager, architect, developer) to find out which aspects of RAs are important to them. A focus group is considered a proven and tested technique to obtain the perception of a group of selected people on a defined area of interest (Lethbridge et al. 2005). An example of conducting this empirical study and its approach for data collection is described in Section 4.1.

IV) Surveys to gather evidence to improve RA-related practices

Dimensions   RQ 2.

Context   To reuse architectural knowledge and improve RA-related practices in prospective RA projects, organizations need to understand RA's characteristics, as well as its potential benefits and limitations. Gathering evidence from previous RA projects is a feasible way to start gaining such an understanding.

Objective   The purpose of the survey is to understand the impact of using RAs for designing the SAs of the applications of an information system of a client organization. This is a descriptive survey that measures what occurred while using RAs rather than why. The following questions are important for organizations in order to understand relevant Aspects 1 to 5 of RAs (defined in Table 2):

1.   Why is an RA adapted for creating SAs of the organizations' applications? What type of RA is being designed and used in the organization?
2.   What is the state of practice in requirement engineering for RA projects in the organization?
3.   What is the state of practice in architectural design for RA projects in the organization?
4.   Which tools and technologies are currently being used in RAs projects by the organization?
5.   How does the adoption of RAs provide observable benefits to the different actors involved in RA projects in the organization?

Method   Exploratory surveys with personalized questionnaires applied to relevant stakeholders (e.g., architects, developers) to gather their perceptions and needs. An example of conducting this empirical study and its approach for data collection is described in Section 4.2.

Finally, the output for using guidelines for RQ 1 is a business case that evaluates whether it is worth or not to invest on an RA. On the other hand, the output of gathering evidence about Aspects 1 to 5 of Table 2 is a corporate knowledge base about these aspects. It is important to note that, although it is not strictly necessary, it is recommended to gather Aspects 1 to 5 for building the business case. In other words, guidelines are complementary and support each other (e.g., results from a preceding study can be used to corroborate or further develop other results). For instance, in our industry-academia collaboration, the qualitative results about the benefits and drawbacks of RAs supported the unquantifiable benefits, and uncertainties and risk of the business case.

5.2 Summative stage: validating the guidelines

The summative stage will take place once the guidelines will have been adequately shaped and improved. The primary role of this stage will be to validate the version of the guidelines after applying it in *everis* with more practitioners. This evaluation consists of the use of the guidelines in other organizations to design and conduct empirical studies. Organizations analyzing whether to make the strategic move to RA adoption and organizations that face the design and use of RAs based on evidence will benefit from these guidelines.

6 Conclusions

Conducting empirical studies is becoming one of the main sources of communication between practitioners and the academia. We are conducting an action research initiative in *everis*. This has allowed gathering industrial evidence:

- To build a business case of adopting an RA in a public administration of Spain, which is an *everis*' client (Martínez-Fernández et al. 2013b). The feedback from this study improved the checklist of value-driven data and the REARM economic model. We learned the importance of good practices like time tracking, continuous feedback, test-driven development and continuous integration in order to quantitatively evaluate RAs. We performed a cost-benefit analysis of an RA adoption in a public administration and it showed that the RA pays off after creating 7 small applications. With medium to large applications, this number could be reduced to 2 applications.

- To create an evidence-based information about RAs in *everis*. It includes evidence about: (a) the motivations of *everis*' client organizations to adopt RAs; (b) benefits and drawbacks of using RAs (Martínez-Fernández et al. 2013c); and (c) artifacts of RAs (Martínez-Fernández et al. 2014). The feedback from these studies improved the set of relevant criteria of RAs, and our template survey to gather evidence about RAs. Among the main benefits, stakeholders indicated that the adoption of an RA bring cost savings in the development and maintenance of applications and improved productivity during the design of concrete SAs.

These results have been evaluated by the *everis*' managers involved in the research. Besides, for their widespread use in *everis*, they have been published in form of proposed solutions, internal reports, executive summaries, and pilots run in real projects (Martínez-Fernández and Marques 2014).

The main contribution of this work is the formulation of guidelines for conducting empirical studies to support building a business case and gathering evidence of RAs. These guidelines consist of stating the context of RAs in industry and their stakeholders, and an assortment of four complementary empirical studies that allow understanding and evaluating RAs. The created guidelines could be used by other organizations outside of our industry-academia collaboration. With this goal in mind, we describe the guidelines in detail for their use. However, practitioners should be aware that conducting empirical studies is time consuming and they should dedicate proper effort.

Future work spreads into two directions. In terms of shaping the guidelines (the formative stage), we need to validate REARM in another *everis*' RA project and to analyze the rest of qualitative data from the survey to gather evidence about RAs. With respect to validation (the summative stage), we plan to apply the guidelines in other organizations if possible.

Additional files

> **Additional file 1: List of questions of the survey to check existing value-driven data in RA projects (in Spanish).**
>
> **Additional file 2: Protocol of surveys to gather evidence and to create a corporate knowledge base about RAs.**

Competing interests
The authors declare that they have no competing interests.

Authors' contributions
Every author was important for the completion of this article, however, their previous activities are also important to reach the research results, then, these activities are listed in this section. SMF, CA and XF envisaged the guidelines and the protocol of the studies. HM was responsible of looking for RA projects at *everis*, contacting the participants of the studies to schedule meetings with SMF and DA and provide more information when necessary. The guidelines have been shaped in periodic meeting at *everis* among SMF, CA, XF and HM. SMF and DA performed the face-to-face interviews to the survey participants. All authors read and approved the final manuscript.

Acknowledgements
This work has been supported by "Cátedra *everis*" and the Spanish project TIN2010-19130-C02-01. We would also like to thank all participants of the surveys for their kind cooperation.

Author details
[1]GESSI Research Group, Universitat Politècnica de Catalunya, Jordi Girona, 1-3, 08034 Barcelona, Spain. [2]Everis, Diagonal, 605, 08028 Barcelona, Spain.

References
Ali MS, Babar MA, Schmid K (2009) A comparative survey of economic models for software product lines. In: Software Engineering and Advanced Applications, 2009. SEAA'09. 35th Euromicro Conference on. IEEE, pp 275–278. http://ieeexplore.ieee.org/xpl/login.jsp?tp=&arnumber=5349963&url=http%3A%2F%2Fieeexplore.ieee.org%2Fxpls%2Fabs_all.jsp%3Farnumber%3D5349963.

Angelov S, Trienekens JJ, Grefen P (2008) Towards a method for the evaluation of reference architectures: Experiences from a case. In: Software Architecture. Springer, Berlin Heidelberg, pp 225–240. http://link.springer.com/chapter/10.1007%2F978-3-540-88030-1_17.

Angelov S, Grefen P, Greefhorst D (2012) A framework for analysis and design of software reference architectures. Inform Software Tech 54(4):417–431

Angelov S, Trienekens J, Kusters R (2013) Software reference architectures-exploring their usage and design in practice. In: Software Architecture. Springer, Berlin Heidelberg, pp 17–24. http://link.springer.com/chapter/10.1007%2F978-3-642-39031-9_2.

Atlassian (2014) Jira: Issue and project tracking software. https://www.atlassian.com/es/software/jira. Accessed 12 Feb 2014

AUTOSAR (2014) Automotive open system architecture (autosar). http://www.autosar.org/. Accessed 12 Feb 2014

Bass L, Clements P, Kazman R (2003) Software architecture in practice. Addison-Wesley Professional. http://resources.sei.cmu.edu/library/asset-view.cfm?assetid=30659.

Bass L, Clements P, Kazman R, Klein M (2008) Evaluating the software architecture competence of organizations. In: Software Architecture, 2008. WICSA 2008. Seventh Working IEEE/IFIP Conference on, IEEE, pp 249–252. http://ieeexplore.ieee.org/xpl/login.jsp?tp=&arnumber=4459163&url=http%3A%2F%2Fieeexplore.ieee.org%2Fiel5%2F4459128%2F4459129%2F04459163.

Brand S (2014) Accenture has business-outcome-driven ea capabilities, but doesn't automatically begin with this approach. https://www.gartner.com/doc/2651816/accenture-businessoutcomedriven-ea-capabilities-doesnt. Accessed 25 Feb 2014

Brydon-Miller M, Greenwood D, Maguire P (2003) Why action research? Action Res 1(1):9–28. doi:10.1177/14767503030011002, http://arj.sagepub.com/content/1/1/9.short.

Carriere J, Kazman R, Ozkaya I (2010) A cost-benefit framework for making architectural decisions in a business context. In: Software Engineering, 2010, ACM/IEEE 32nd International Conference on, IEEE, vol 2, pp 149–157. http://ieeexplore.ieee.org/xpl/login.jsp?tp=&arnumber=6062148&url=http%3A%2F%2Fieeexplore.ieee.org%2Fxpls%2Fabs_all.jsp%3Farnumber%3D6062148.

Clements P, Northrop L (2002) Software product lines: practices and patterns. Addison-Wesley Professional. http://www.addison-wesley.de/9780201703320.html.

Clements P, Kazman R, Klein M (2001) Evaluating software architectures: methods and case studies. Addison-Wesley Professional. http://resources.sei.cmu.edu/library/asset-view.cfm?assetid=30698.

Cloutier R, Muller G, Verma D, Nilchiani R, Hole E, Bone M (2010) The concept of reference architectures. Syst Eng 13(1):14–27

Deelstra S, Sinnema M, Bosch J (2005) Product derivation in software product families: a case study. J Syst Soft 74(2):173–194. doi:10.1016/j.jss.2003.11.012, http://www.sciencedirect.com/science/article/pii/S0164121203003121.

Eklund U, Bosch J (2014) Architecture for embedded open software ecosystems. J Syst Softw. doi:10.1016/j.jss.2014.01.009, http://dx.doi.org/10.1016/j.jss.2014.01.009, http://www.sciencedirect.com/science/article/pii/S0164121214000211.

Eklund U, Askerdal Ö, Granholm J, Alminger A, Axelsson J (2005) Experience of introducing reference architectures in the development of automotive electronic systems. In: ACM SIGSOFT Software Engineering Notes, vol 30. ACM, New York, pp 1–6

Erdogmus H, Favaro J (2012) The value proposition for agility–a dual perspective. http://www.infoq.com/presentations/Agility-Value. Accessed 3 Mar 2014

Falessi D, Babar MA, Cantone G, Kruchten P (2010) Applying empirical software engineering to software architecture: challenges and lessons learned. Empir Software Eng 15(3):250–276

Forrester (2014) Forrester's total economic impact (tei). http://www.forrester.com/marketing/product/consulting/tei.html. Accessed 12 Feb 2014

Frakes W, Terry C (1996) Software reuse: metrics and models. ACM Comput Surv (CSUR) 28(2):415–435

Gallagher BP (2000) Using the architecture tradeoff analysis method to evaluate a reference architecture: A case study. Tech. rep., Software Engineering Institute, CMU/SEI-2000-TN-007

Galster M, Avgeriou P (2011) Empirically-grounded reference architectures: a proposal In: Proceedings of the joint ACM SIGSOFT conference–QoSA and ACM SIGSOFT symposium–ISARCS on Quality of software architectures–QoSA and architecting critical systems–ISARCS. ACM, New York, pp 153–158

Galster M, Avgeriou P, Tofan D (2013) Constraints for the design of variability-intensive service-oriented reference architectures–an industrial case study. Inf Softw Technol 2(55):428–441. http://dx.doi.org/10.1016/j.infsof.2012.09.011

García-Alonso J, Olmeda JB, Murillo JM (2010) Java para aplicaciones corporativas de la administración. In: Teniente E, Abrahão S (eds) JISBD. IBERGARCETA Pub. S.L. 2010, pp 263–266. http://www.informatik.uni-trier.de/~ley/db/conf/jisbd/jisbd2010.html#Garcia-AlonsoOM10

Graaf B, Van Dijk H, van Deursen A (2005) Evaluating an embedded software reference architecture. industrial experience report In: Software Maintenance and Reengineering, 2005. CSMR 2005. Ninth European Conference on, IEEE, pp 354–363. http://ieeexplore.ieee.org/xpl/articleDetails.jsp?arnumber=1402153.

Herold S, Mair M (2013) Checking conformance with reference architectures: a case study In: Enterprise Distributed Object Computing Conference (EDOC)2013 17th IEEE International. http://ieeexplore.ieee.org/xpl/articleDetails.jsp?arnumber=6658265.

Jenkins (2014) An extendable open source continuous integration server. http://jenkins-ci.org/. Accessed 12 Feb 2014

Lethbridge T, Sim S, Singer J (2005) Studying software engineers: data collection techniques for software field studies. Empir Software Eng:311–341. http://link.springer.com/article/10.1007/s10664-005-1290-x.

Northrop LM, Clements PC (2014) A framework for software product line practice, version 5.0. http://www.sei.cmu.edu/productlines/frame_report/index.html. Accessed 1 Mar 2014

Linden FVD, Bosch J, Kamsties E (2004) Software product family evaluation In: Software Product Lines. Springer, Berlin Heidelberg, pp 110–129. http://link.springer.com/chapter/10.1007%2F978-3-540-24667-1_27.

MacCormack A, Baldwin C, Rusnak J (2012) Exploring the duality between product and organizational architectures: a test of the mirroring hypothesis. Res Pol 41(8):1309–1324

Martínez-Fernández S (2013) Towards supporting the adoption of software reference architectures: an empirically-grounded framework In: Proceedings 11th International Doctoral Symposium on Empirical Software Engineering (IDoESE) at the Empirical Software Engineering International Week; Baltimore, Maryland, USA. available at http://umbc.edu/eseiw2013/idoese/pdf/eseiw2013_IDoESE_180.pdf. Accessed 12 Feb 2014

Martínez-Fernández S, Marques H (2014) Practical experiences in designing and conducting empirical studies in industry-academia collaboration In: Conducting Empirical Studies in Industry (CESI), 2014 2nd International Workshop on. ACM, New York, pp 15–20. http://doi.acm.org/10.1145/2593690.2593696.

Martínez-Fernández S, Ayala C, Franch X, Ameller D (2013a) A framework for software reference architecture analysis and review In: Memorias del X Workshop Latinoamericano de Ingeniería en Software Experimental ESELAW2013; Montevideo, Uruguay. available at: http://cibse2013.ort.edu.uy/pdf/ESELAW-ISBN-978-9974-8379-3-5.pdf. Accessed 12 Feb 2014

Martínez-Fernández S, Ayala C, Franch X, Marques H (2013b) Rearm: a reuse-based economic model for software reference architectures. In: Favaro J, Morisio M (eds) Safe and Secure Software Reuse, Lecture Notes in Computer Science, vol 7925, pp 97–112. doi:10.1007/978-3-642-38977-1_7

Martínez-Fernández S, Ayala C, Franch X, Martins Marques H (2013c) Benefits and drawbacks of reference architectures. In: Drira K (ed) Software Architecture, Lecture Notes in Computer Science, vol 7957, pp 307–310. doi:10.1007/978-3-642-39031-9_26

Martínez-Fernández S, Ayala C, Franch X, Marques H (2014) Artifacts of software reference architectures: a case study In: Proceedings of the 18th International Conference on Evaluation and Assessment in Software Engineering. doi:10.1145/2601248.2601282

Mattmann C, Downs R (2010) Reuse of software assets for the NASA Earth science decadal survey missions. Geoscience and Remote Sensing Symposium (IGARSS)2010 IEEE International, vol 1. http://ieeexplore.ieee.org/xpls/abs_all.jsp?arnumber=5653018.

Montagud S, Abrahão S, Insfran E (2011) A systematic review of quality attributes and measures for software product lines. Software Qual J 20:425–486. doi:10.1007/s11219-011-9146-7, http://link.springer.com/10.1007/s11219-011-9146-7.

Murer S, Hagen C (2013) 15 Years of Service Oriented Architecture at Credit Suisse:1–30. http://ieeexplore.ieee.org/xpls/abs_all.jsp?arnumber=6654116. Accessed 25 Feb 2014

Nakagawa EY, Antonino PO, Becker M (2011) Reference architecture and product line architecture: a subtle but critical difference In: Software Architecture. Springer, Berlin Heidelberg, pp 207–211. http://link.springer.com/chapter/10.1007%2F978-3-642-23798-0_22.

NASA (2012) Esds reference architecture working group: Esds reference architecture for the decadal survey era. https://earthdata.nasa.gov/sites/default/files/field/document/ESDS%20Reference%20Architecture%20v1.1.pdf. Accessed 12 Feb 2014

Poulin JS (1997) Measuring software reuse: principles, practices, and economic models. Addison-Wesley Longman Publishing Co., Inc., Boston

Qureshi N, Usman M, Ikram N (2013) Evidence in software architecture, a systematic literature review In: Proceedings of
      the 17th International Conference on Evaluation and Assessment in Software Engineering. ACM, New York, pp 97–106
Redmine (2014) A flexible project management web application. http://www.redmine.org/. Accessed 12 Feb 2014
Reichart G, Haneberg M (2004) Key drivers for a future system architecture in vehicles In: Convergence International
      Congress & Exposition On Transportation Electronics. SAE International. http://papers.sae.org/2004-21-0025/.
Reifer DJ (2002) Making the software business case: improvement by the numbers. Pearson Education. http://books.
      google.es/books?id=W61QAAAAMAAJ.
SonarSource (2014) Continuous inspection of code quality. http://www.sonarsource.com/. Accessed 12 Feb 2014

3

F3T: a tool to support the F3 approach on the development and reuse of frameworks

Matheus C Viana[1,2]*, Rosângela AD Penteado[2], Antônio F do Prado[2] and Rafael S Durelli[3]

*Correspondence:
matheus_viana@dc.ufscar.br
[1] Federal Institute of Sao Paulo,
Campus Sao Carlos, Rod.
Washington Luis, km 235, Block AT6,
13565-905 Sao Carlos, Brazil
[2] Department of Computing,
Federal University of Sao Carlos,
Rod. Washington Luis, km 235,
13565-905 Sao Carlos, Brazil
Full list of author information is
available at the end of the article

Abstract

Background: Frameworks are used to enhance the quality of applications and the productivity of the development process, since applications may be designed and implemented by reusing framework classes. However, frameworks are hard to develop, learn and reuse, due to their adaptive nature. From Feature to Frameworks (F3) is an approach that supports framework development in two steps: Domain Modeling, to model domain features of the framework; and Framework Construction, to develop framework source-code based on the modeled domain and on patterns provided by this approach.

Methods: In this article, it is presented the From Features to Framework Tool (F3T), which supports the use of the F3 approach on framework development.

Results: This tool provides an editor for domain modeling and generates framework source-code according to the patterns of the F3 approach. In addition, F3T also generates a Domain-Specific Modeling Language that allows the modeling of applications and the generation of their source-code. F3T has been evaluated in two experiments and the results are presented in this article.

Conclusions: F3T facilitates framework development and reuse by omitting implementation complexities and performing code generation.

Keywords: Reuse; Framework; Domain; Feature; Generator

1 Introduction

Frameworks are reusable software composed of abstract classes that implement the basic functionality of a domain. When an application is developed through framework reuse, the functionality provided by the framework classes is complemented with the application requirements. As this application has not been not developed from scratch, the time spent in its development was reduced and its quality was improved (Abi-Antoun 2007; Johnson 1997; Stanojevic et al. 2011).

Frameworks are often used to implement common application requirements, such as persistence Hibernate 2013 and user interface (Spring Framework 2013). Besides, frameworks are also used as core assets in the development of closely related applications in a Software Product Line (SPL) (Kim et al. 2004; Weiss and Lai 1999). The common features of the SPL domain are implemented in the framework and applications implement these features by reusing framework classes.

Despite those advantages, frameworks are hard to develop since their classes must be abstract enough to be reused by applications that are unknown beforehand. Therefore, it is necessary to define two things (Parsons et al. 1999; Weiss and Lai 1999): 1) the domain of applications the framework is able to instantiate; and 2) how the framework accesses application-specific classes. Frameworks are also hard to reuse because they have a steep learning curve (Srinivasan 1999). They may be very complex, composed by a large number of classes and modules that even developers who are conversant with it may make mistakes.

In a previous paper, an approach for building Domain-Specific Modeling Languages (DSML) was proposed to support framework reuse (Viana et al. 2012). A DSML can be built by identifying framework features and the information required to instantiate them. Then, the application source-code can be generated from models created with this DSML. Experiments have shown that DSMLs protect developers from framework complexities and reduce the time spent on framework instantiation.

In another paper, the From Features to Framework (F3) approach was presented. It aims to reduce framework development complexities (Viana et al. 2013). In this approach, framework domain is defined in an F3 model, as described in Section 2.1. A set of patterns guides the developer when designing and implementing a white box framework according to its domain. Besides showing how developers shall proceed, the F3 patterns systematizes framework development process, allowing it to be automatized by a tool.

In this article, the From Features to Framework Tool (F3T) is presented as a plug-in for the Eclipse IDE that supports the F3 approach on framework development and reuse. By using this tool, developers can define a domain in an F3 model. Then, framework source-code and DSML are generated from this model. This DSML can be used to model applications and to generate their source-code, which reuses the framework previously generated.

Two experiments have also been carried out in order to evaluate F3T. In the first one, it was analyzed whether F3T facilitates framework development or not and, in the second presents a comparison between F3T and Pure::variants (Pure::Variants 2013).

The remainder of this article is organized as follows: background concepts are discussed in Section 2; the F3 approach is described in Section 2.1; F3T is presented in Section 3; two experiments to evaluate F3T are presented in Section 4; the related works are discussed in Section 5; and the conclusions and future work are presented in Section 6.

2 Background

The basic concepts applied to F3T and its approach are presented in this section. Reuse is a practice that aims: to reduce the time spent in the development process, since software was not developed from scratch; and to increase the software quality, since reusable practices, models or code were previously tested (Shiva and Shala 2007). Patterns, frameworks, generators and domain engineering are common ways to apply reuse to software development (Frakes and Kang 2005).

Patterns are successful solutions that may be reapplied to different contexts (Johnson 1997). They provide reuse of experience, which helps developers to solve recurrent problems (Fowler 2003). A pattern documentation mainly contains its name, the context it may be applied, the problem it intends to solve, the solution it proposes, illustrative class models and examples of use. There are patterns for several purposes, such as design, analysis, architectural, implementation, process and organizational patterns (Pressman 2009).

Frameworks act like skeletons that can be instantiated to implement applications (Johnson 1997). Their classes embody an abstract design that provides solutions for application domains (Srinivasan 1999). Applications are connected to a framework by reusing its classes. According to the way a framework is reused, it is classified as: white box, when its classes need to be extended; black box, when it works like a set of components; and gray box, when it is reused on the two previous ways (Abi-Antoun 2007).

Despite the advantages frameworks offer, they are more complex to develop than applications (Kirk et al. 2007), since frameworks demand an adaptable design. Their classes will be reused by applications that are unknown during framework development, thereby frameworks need mechanisms to identify and to access application-specific classes. Thus, design patterns and advanced resources of programming languages, such as abstract classes, interfaces, polymorphism, generics and reflection, are often used in framework development. In addition to design and implementation complexities, it is also necessary to determine the domain of applications the framework will be able to instantiate, the features that compose this domain and the rules that constrain these features (Stanojevic et al. 2011). Some solutions to this issue propose adaptations of the traditional software development process (Amatriain and Arumi P 2011) or the refactoring of applications that share common features in order to implement a framework (Xu and Butler 2006).

The reuse of frameworks provides higher quality and efficiency to software development process. However, frameworks require the developer to have detailed knowledge about their internal structure and their hot spots so that they can be properly used (Abi-Antoun 2007; Srinivasan 1999). Some solutions have been applied in order to facilitate the difficulties in reusing frameworks, such as manuals, cookbooks and pattern languages. These solutions may guide the application developer through framework instantiation. However, the task of identifying and configuring the hot spots according to the application requirements is still executed by the developer and relies on his/her skills and knowledge (Antkiewicz et al. 2009).

Generators are tools that transform an artifact into another (Lolong and Kistijantoro 2011; Sarasa-Cabezuelo et al. 2012. There are many types of generators. As frameworks, generators are also related to domains, although some are configurable and may change their domain (Liem and Nugroho 2008). In this case, templates are used to define the artifacts that can be generated.

A domain of software consists of a set of applications that share common features. A feature is a distinguishing characteristic that aggregates value to applications (Bayer et al. 1999; Gomaa 2004; Jezequel 2012; Kang et al. 1990; Lee et al. 2002). Domain features are defined in feature models. Features may be mandatory or optional, have variations and require or exclude other features. The feature that represents the purpose of the domain is added to the root and a top-down approach is applied to add the other features.

Domains may also be modeled with metamodel languages, which are used to create Domain-Specific Modeling Languages (DSML). Metamodels, as defined in the MetaObject Facility (MOF) (OMG's MetaObject Facility 2013), are similar to class models, which makes them more appropriate to developers accustomed to UML. While in feature models, only features and their constraints are defined, metaclasses in the metamodels may contain attributes and operations. On the other hand, feature models can define dependencies between features, while metamodels depend on declarative languages to do so (Gronback 2009).

2.1 F3 Approach

From Features to Framework (F3) is a Domain Engineering approach that aims to develop domain specific frameworks. It has two steps: 1) Domain Modeling, to define and model a domain of applications; and 2) Framework Construction, to design and implement a framework for the domain defined in the previous step.

In Domain Modeling step, the domain is defined as an extended version of feature model, called F3 model. This extended version is used in the F3 approach since feature models are too abstract to contain enough information for framework development and also because metamodels depend on other languages to define dependencies and constraints. F3 models incorporate characteristics from both feature models and metamodels. As in conventional feature models, features in the F3 models may also be arranged in a tree-view. The root feature is the main one and it is placed on top of the tree. However, F3 models do not necessarily form a tree, since a feature may have a relationship targeting a sibling or even itself, as in metamodels. The elements and relationships in F3 models are:

- **Feature**: graphically represented by a rounded square, it must have a name and it may contain any number of attributes and operations;
- **Decomposition**: relationship that indicates that a feature is composed of another feature. This relationship specifies a minimum and a maximum multiplicity. The minimum multiplicity indicates whether the target feature is optional (0) or mandatory (1). The maximum multiplicity indicates how many instances of the target feature may be associated to each instance of the source feature. Valid values of the maximum multiplicity are: 1 (simple), for a single feature instance; * (multiple), for a list of instances of a single feature subclass; and ** (variant), for a list of instances of different subclasses of a feature.
- **Generalization**: relationship that indicates a feature is a variation generalized by another feature.
- **Dependency**: relationship that defines a condition for a feature to be instantiated. There are two types of dependency: requires, when feature A requires feature B, an application that contains feature A also has to include feature B; and excludes, when feature A excludes feature B, no application may include both features.

Framework Construction step has a white box framework as output. The F3 approach defines patterns that assist developers to design and implement frameworks from F3 models as well as to know the code units that shall be created to implement domain functionality and its variability. F3 patterns address problems that range from the creation of classes that represent features to the definition of framework interface. Some of the F3 patterns are presented in Table 1.

Besides indicating the code units that shall be created to implement framework functionality, F3 patterns also determine how the framework may be reused by the applications. For instance, some patterns suggest implementing abstract operations that allow the framework to access application-specific information. In addition, F3 patterns make the process of framework development systematic, allowing it to be automatized. Thus,

Table 1 Some of the F3 patterns

Pattern	Purpose
Domain Feature	Indicates structures that should be created for a feature.
Mandatory Decomposition	Indicates code units that should be created when there is a mandatory decomposition linking two features.
Optional Decomposition	Indicates code units that should be created when there is an optional decomposition linking two features.
Simple Decomposition	Indicates code units that should be created when there is a simple decomposition linking two features.
Multiple Decomposition	Indicates code units that should be created when there is a multiple decomposition linking two features.
Variant Decomposition	Indicates code units that should be created when there is a variant decomposition linking two features.
Variant Feature	Defines a class hierarchy for features with variants.
Modular Hierarchy	Defines a class hierarchy for features with common attributes and operations.
Requiring Dependency	Indicates code units that should be created when a feature requires another one.
Excluding Dependency	Indicates code units that should be created when a feature excludes another one.

F3T was created to automatize the use of the F3 approach, enhancing the processes of framework development.

3   From features to frameworks tool

Although all advantages provided by the F3 approach make framework development easier, it still requires developers to model domains and apply the F3 patterns properly to implement the frameworks. For instance, a developer could forget to apply an F3 pattern during Framework Construction step. Thus, computational support should be provided during code implementation, in order to improve productivity and reduce the occurrence of human errors.

F3T assists developers to apply the F3 approach in the development of white box frameworks and in the reuse of these frameworks through their DSML (Viana et al. 2012, 2013). In order to use the tool it is necessary to follow the steps of this approach. The tool provides an editor to F3 models and generates framework source-code based on the F3 patterns. The role of the framework DSML is to facilitate framework instantiation.

F3T is a plug-in for Eclipse IDE, so developers may make use of F3T resources, such as domain modeling, framework construction, application modeling through framework DSML, application construction and other resources provided by Eclipse IDE. F3T is composed of three modules, as seen in Figure 1: 1) Domain Module; 2) Framework Module; and 3) Application Module. Each module represents a resource that developers may use to create the artifacts required by the F3 approach to develop and reuse frameworks.

3.1   Domain module

Domain Module (DM) is an editor for developers to create an F3 model with the domain features, as illustrated in Figure 1. This module has been developed with the support of the Eclipse Modeling Framework (EMF) and the Graphical Modeling Framework (GMF) (Gronback 2009). EMF was used to create the metamodel that defines the elements, relationships and rules of F3 models, as described in the Section 2.1. This metamodel is shown

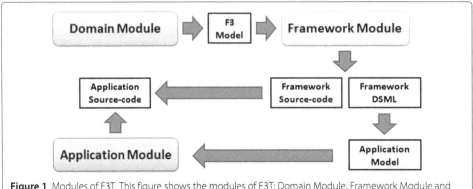

Figure 1 Modules of F3T. This figure shows the modules of F3T: Domain Module, Framework Module and Application Module. Each module is composed by a set of Eclipse IDE plug-ins.

in Figure 2. From this metamodel, EMF generated the source-code of the Model and the Controller layers of the F3 model editor.

GMF has been used to define the graphical notation of F3 models. This graphical notation may also be seen as the View layer of the F3 model editor, as it defines how features and relationships are graphically represented. Then, GMF generates the source-code of the graphical notation. The F3 model editor is shown in Figure 3 and it is composed of three parts: 1) editor panel, which is used to create and visualize F3 models; 2) menu bar, which provides the F3 elements and relationships to be included in the models; and 3)properties panel, which displays all properties of a selected element or relationship in the model.

For instance, the F3 model for the domain of rental and trade transactions is shown in Figure 3. This domain deals with rental and trade transactions of resources to destination parties. The root feature is a generic `ResourceTransaction`, specialized by the features `ResourceTrade` and `ResourceRental`. The `DestinationParty` feature represents the party that requires the transaction. For instance, a destination party may be treated as a customer in an application. `DestinationParty` is optional by default. However, once `ResourceRental` is used, `DestinationParty` is mandatory. That is why there is a `requires` relationship between these features. The `Resource` feature represents the resources that may be traded or rented. One or more resources participate in a transaction, so the `TransactionItem` feature was defined to represent

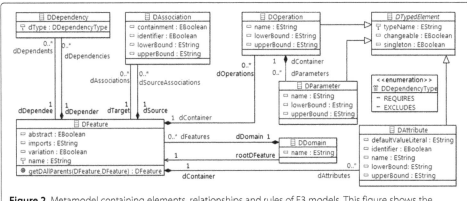

Figure 2 Metamodel containing elements, relationships and rules of F3 models. This figure shows the metamodel whose metaclasses and relationships define how F3 models can be created.

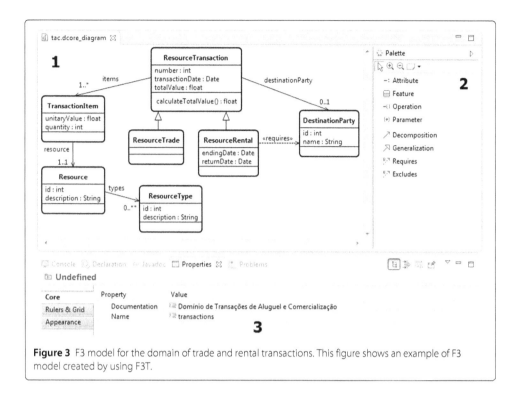

Figure 3 F3 model for the domain of trade and rental transactions. This figure shows an example of F3 model created by using F3T.

that. A resource can have classifications, so the `ResourceType` feature can be extended many times in an application to define any type of classification, such as category, genre, location and so on.

3.2 Framework module

Despite their graphical notation, F3 models actually are XML files, which makes them more accessible to other tools, such as generators. Therefore, Framework Module (FM) has been designed as a Model-to-Text (M2T) generator that transforms an F3 model into framework source-code and DSML.

FM has been developed with the support of Java Emitter Templates (JET) in the Eclipse IDE (The Eclipse Foundation Eclipse Modeling Project). JET contains a framework that works as a generic generator and a compiler that translate templates into Java files. These templates are XML files, in which tags are instructions to generate an output based on input information and text is a fixed content inserted in the output independently of the input. The Java files originated from the JET templates reuse the JET framework to compose a domain-specific generator. Thus, FM depend on the JET plug-in to work.

The hierarchy of the FM templates is shown in Figure 4. These templates are organized in two groups: one related to framework source-code (DSC); and the other related to framework DSML. Both groups are invoked from the Main template. The DSC template invokes the templates that originate the framework classes. Part of the JET template that generates Java classes in the framework source-code from the features found in the F3 models are seen as follows:

```
public <c:if test="($feature/@abstract)">abstract </c:if>
class <c:get select="$feature/@name"/> extends
<c:choose select="$feature/@variation">
   <c:when test="'true'">DVariation</c:when>
```

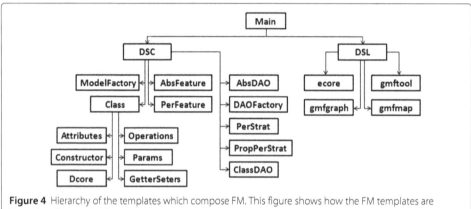

Figure 4 Hierarchy of the templates which compose FM. This figure shows how the FM templates are hierarchically organized.

```
<c:otherwise>
    <c:choose>
        <c:when test="$feature/dSuperFeature">
            <c:get select="$feature/dSuperFeature/@name"/>
        </c:when>
        <c:otherwise>DObject</c:otherwise>
    </c:choose>
</c:otherwise>
</c:choose> { ... }
```

Framework classes are generated according to F3 patterns (Viana et al. 2013). For instance, FM generates a class for each feature found in an F3 model. The reason is that, since a white-box framework is generated, these classes are directly extended by the application classes. These classes also contain the attributes and operations, as specified in its correspondent feature. Besides the classes that represent features, others are also generated to provide code flexibility and to implement non-functional requirements, such as the `DObject` class that is, directly or indirectly, extended by all feature classes in order to provide data persistence functionality to them. Generalization relationships result in inheritances, whereas decomposition relationships result in associations between the involved classes. Additional operations are included in framework classes to implement feature variations and constraints defined in F3 models. For instance, according to the *Variant Decomposition* F3 pattern, the `getResourceTypeClasses` operation was included in the code of the `Resource` class (Figure 3) so that the framework recognizes which classes implement the `ResourceType` feature in applications. Part of the `Resource` class code is presented as follows:

```
public abstract class Resource extends DObject {

    private int id;

    private Sting name;

    private List<ResourceType> types;

    public abstract Class<?>[] getResourceTypeClasses();
```

The DSML template invokes a set of templates that originate EMF/GMF models to the framework DSML. An example of these models is illustrated in Figure 5a, which was generated from the F3 model shown in Figure 3. Then, DSML source-code is be generated by EMF/GMF in three steps: 1) using the EMF generator from the *genmodel* file (Figure 5a); 2) using the GMF generator from the *gmfmap* file (Figure 5b); and 3) using the GMF generator from the *gmfgen* file (Figure 5c). After that, the DSML will be composed of 5 plug-in projects in the Eclipse IDE. The projects that contain the framework source-code and the DSML plug-ins for the domain of trade and rental transactions are shown in Figure 5d. The Java project in which the framework source-code was generated is identified by the domain name and the suffix ".framework". The others are DSML plug-ins.

3.3 Application module

Application Module (AM) has also been developed with the support of JET. It generates application source-code from an application model created from a framework DSML. The AM templates generate classes that extend framework classes and override operations that configure framework hot spots. After the DSML plug-ins are installed in the Eclipse IDE, AM recognizes the model files created from the DSML. An application model created with the DSML of the framework for the domain of trade and rental transactions is shown in Figure 6. This application is intended for a small store that trades products. Therefore, the `ProductTrade` application class extends the `ResourceTrade` framework class. `TradeItem` represents the products in a trade transaction, so it extends `TransactionItem`. `Product` is the resource in this application. Each product in the store may be classified by `Category` and by `Manufacturer`. As this store keeps no register of its customers, the `DestinationParty` feature was not used in this application.

The application source-code is generated in the source folder of the project, in which the application model is. AM generates a class for each feature instantiated in the application model. Since the framework is a white box, the application classes extend the framework classes indicated by the stereotypes in the model. It is expected that most of the class attributes requested by the application requirements have already been defined in the domain. Thus, these attributes are in the framework source-code and they must not be defined in the application classes again. Part of the code of the `Product` class is presented as follows:

Figure 5 Generation of the DSML plugins. This figure shows how DSML plug-ins are generated by F3: **a)** EMF/GMF models generated by F3T to create DSML plug-ins; **b)** Gmfmap model is used to create generator model; **c)** Generator model (gmfgen) is used to create the DSML graphical editor plug-in; **d)** all DSML plug-ins and the framework source-code project (trade.framework).

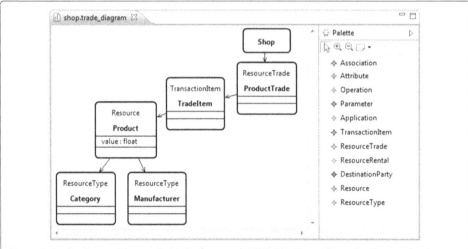

Figure 6 Application model created with the framework DSML. This Figure shows the Shop application model created with the DSML of trade and rental transactions.

```
public class Product extends Resource {

  private float value;

  public Class<?>[] getResourceTypeClasses() {
    return new Class<?>[] {
      Category.class, Manufacturer.class };
  }
}
```

4 Evaluation

In this section, two experiments are presented: one to evaluate the advantages of using F3T to develop frameworks; and the other to compare F3T with Pure::variants (Pure::Variants 2013). These experiments were conducted by following all steps described by Wohlin et al. 2000.

4.1 Experiment 1

In the first experiment, the use of F3T for framework development has been evaluated, since framework reuse supported by DSML was evaluated in a previous paper (Viana et al. 2012). This experiment was defined as: (*i*) **analysis** of F3T, described in Section 3; (*ii*) **for the purpose of** evaluation; (*iii*) **with respect to** time spent and number of problems; (*iv*) **from the point of view of** the developer; and (*v*) **in the context of** MSc and PhD Computer Science students.

4.1.1 Planning

The experiment was planned to answer two research questions:

- **RQ$_1$: Does F3T reduce the effort to develop a framework?**
- **RQ$_2$: Does F3T result in a outcome framework with a fewer number of problems?**

All of the subjects had to develop two frameworks applying the F3 approach. One of them should be done manually and the other by using F3T. In order to answer the first question, the time spent to develop each framework was measured. To answer the second question, the frameworks developed by the subjects have been analyzed and the problems found in their source-code have been identified. The planning phase was divided into seven parts, as follows:

Context selection The subjects of this experiment were 26 MSc and PhD students of Computer Science. All of them had prior experience in software development, Java programming, patterns and framework reuse.

Formulation of hypotheses The experiment questions have been formalized as follows:

- **RQ$_1$, Null Hypothesis, H1$_0$:** Considering the F3 approach, there is no significant time difference when developing frameworks with the support of F3T or manually. Thus, F3T does not reduce the time spent to develop frameworks. This hypothesis may be formalized as: **H1$_0$:** $\tau_{F3T} = \tau_{manual}$
- **RQ$_1$, Alternative Hypothesis 1, H1$_1$:** The time spent to develop frameworks by applying the F3 approach with the support of F3T is significantly lower than when applying the F3 approach manually. Thus, F3T reduces the time spent to develop frameworks. This hypothesis is formalized as: **H1$_1$:** $\tau_{F3T} < \tau_{manual}$
- **RQ$_1$, Alternative Hypothesis 2, H1$_2$:** The time spent to develop frameworks by applying the F3 approach with the support of F3T is significantly greater than when applying the F3 approach manually. Thus, F3T does not reduce the time spent to develop frameworks. This hypothesis is formalized as: **H1$_1$:** $\tau_{F3T} > \tau_{manual}$
- **RQ$_2$, Null Hypothesis, H2$_0$:** There is no significant difference in the number of problems found in the frameworks developed manually or using F3T. Thus, F3T does not reduce the number of mistakes made by the subjects during framework development. This hypothesis is formalized as: **H2$_0$:** $\rho_{F3T} = \rho_{manual}$
- **RQ$_2$, Alternative Hypothesis 1, H2$_1$:** The number of problems found in the frameworks developed with the support of F3T is significantly lower than when applying the F3 approach manually. Thus, F3T reduces the number of mistakes made by the subjects during framework development. This hypothesis is formalized as: **H2$_1$:** $\rho_{F3T} < \rho_{manual}$
- **RQ$_2$, Alternative Hypothesis 2, H2$_2$:** The number of problems found in the frameworks developed by with the support of F3T is significantly greater than when applying the F3 approach manually. Thus, F3T increases the number of mistakes made by the subjects during framework development. This hypothesis is formalized as: **H2$_1$:** $\rho_{F3T} > \rho_{manual}$

Variable selection The dependent variables of this experiment were:

- **time spent to develop a framework**;
- **number of problems found in the frameworks**.

The independent variables were:

- **Application**: Each subject had to develop two frameworks: one (Fw1) for the domain of trade and rental transactions and the other (Fw2) for the domain of automatic vehicles. Both Fw1 and Fw2 had 10 features.

- **Development Environment**: Eclipse 4.2.1, Astah Community 6.4, F3T.
- **Technologies**: Java version 6.

Selection of subjects The subjects were selected through a non probabilist approach by convenience. Therefore, the probability of all population elements belong to the same sample is unknown.

Experiment design The subjects were grouped in two groups of 13 subjects:

- **Group 1**, development of Fw1 manually and development of Fw2 with the support of F3T;
- **Group 2**, development of Fw2 manually and development of Fw1 with the support of F3T.

We have chosen to use groups in order to reduce the effects of the subjects experience. In order to measure this, the subjects answered a form about their level of experience in software development. This form was given to the subjects one week before the pilot experiment herein described. The goal of this pilot experiment was to ensure that the experiment environment and materials were adequate and the tasks could be properly executed.

To use the F3 approach manually, the subjects had to model the domain by using the class diagram of Astah and apply the F3 patterns on this model to implement framework source-code. On the other hand, to develop the frameworks by using F3T, the subjects had to create the F3 model of the domain using the editor provided by the tool and generate the framework source-code.

Design types The design type of this experiment was **one factor with two treatments paired** (Wohlin et al. 2000). The **factor** in this experiment is the way how the F3 approach was used to develop a framework and the **treatments** are the support of F3T in contrast with the manual development.

Instrumentation All the necessary materials used during the execution of this experiment were given to the subjects beforehand. These materials consisted of forms for collecting experiment data, domain requirements, F3 approach documentation and test units code. In the end of the experiment, all subjects received a questionnaire, in which they should report about the F3 approach and F3T.

4.2 Operation

The operation phase was divided into two parts, Preparation and Execution, as described in the subsections Preparation and Execution.

Preparation Firstly, the subjects received a characterization form, containing questions on their knowledge about Java programming, Eclipse IDE, patterns and frameworks. Then, the subjects were introduced to the F3 approach and F3T.

Execution Initially, the subjects signed a consent form and then answered the characterization form. After this, they watched a presentation about frameworks, which included the description of some popular examples and their hot spots. The subjects were also trained on how to develop frameworks using the F3 approach with and without the support of F3T.

After the training, the pilot experiment was executed. The subjects were split into two groups considering the results of the characterization forms. The subjects were not told about the nature of the experiment, but were verbally instructed on the F3 approach and its tool. The pilot experiment was intended to simulate the real one, except that the applications were different, however equivalent. Beforehand, all subjects were given ample time to read the approach and to ask questions on the experimental process. This could affect the experiment validation, therefore, this data was only used to balance the groups.

During the experiment execution, the subjects who had to develop the framework manually used a class diagram of the Astah Community to create the F3 model of the domain. Then, they used the documentation of the F3 patterns to apply them and implement the framework based on the features they defined in the F3 model. On the other hand, the subjects who had access to F3T had to create the F3 model and generate the framework source-code by using the resources of this tool. In both cases, after finishing the implementation, the subjects had to pause the chronometer and ran the test units to verify whether their code was correct or not. In case of success, their task was done. Otherwise, they had to continue measuring the time and fix the problems of the framework.

4.3   Analysis of data

This section presents the experimental findings. The analysis is divided into two subsections: (*1*) Descriptive Statistics and (*2*) Hypotheses Testing.

Descriptive statistics   The time each subject spent to develop a framework and the number of problems found in the outcome frameworks are shown in Table 2. From this table, one may notice that the subjects spent more time to develop the frameworks when they were doing it manually (M) then when using F3T, 72.5% against 27.5%, respectively. This result was expected, since F3T generates framework source-code from F3 models. However, it is worth highlighting that most of the time spent in the manual framework development was due to the framework implementation and the effort to fix the problems found in the frameworks, while in the framework development supported by F3T it was due to domain modeling. The dispersion of time spent by the subjects are also represented graphically in a boxplot on the left side of Figure 7.

In Table 2, the four types of problems that were analyzed in the outcome frameworks are presented: (*i*) incoherence, (*ii*) structure, (*iii*) bad smells, (*iv*) interface.

The incoherence problem indicates that, during the experiment, the subjects did not model the domain of the framework as expected. In other words, the subjects did not develop the frameworks with the correct domain features and constraints (mandatory, optional, and alternative features). As the ability to model the framework domains depend more on the subject skills than on tool support, incoherence problems could be found in equivalent proportions, approximately 50%, when the framework was developed either manually or with the support of F3T.

The structure problem indicates that the subjects did not implement the frameworks properly during the experiment. For instance, either they implemented classes with no constructor and with incorrect relationships or they forgot to declare the classes as

Table 2 Data obtained from framework development applying two approaches: Manual(M) and F3T

Subject	Time spent		Number of problems									
			Incoherence		Structure		Bad smells		Interface		Total	
	M	F3T	M	F3T	M	F3T	M	F3T	M	F3T	M	F3T
S1	72	26	1	1	0	0	1	0	0	0	2	1
S2	74	32	1	2	1	0	1	0	1	0	4	2
S3	83	31	3	3	1	1	1	0	1	0	6	4
S4	78	29	1	1	2	0	1	0	2	0	6	1
S5	67	26	0	1	0	0	0	0	0	0	0	1
S6	81	32	4	3	3	1	2	0	3	0	12	4
S7	79	24	3	3	1	0	1	0	0	1	5	4
S8	73	23	1	0	0	0	0	0	0	0	1	0
S9	79	26	1	2	2	0	1	0	1	0	5	2
S10	69	27	2	1	0	0	1	0	1	0	4	1
S11	71	29	1	2	1	0	0	0	1	0	3	2
S12	83	31	3	2	1	0	3	0	1	0	8	2
S13	74	26	1	0	1	0	1	0	0	0	3	0
S14	72	29	1	2	0	0	0	0	1	0	2	2
S15	76	31	3	4	2	0	1	0	2	0	8	4
S16	68	26	1	1	0	0	0	0	0	0	1	1
S17	80	33	5	4	4	1	3	0	4	1	16	6
S18	75	27	1	1	2	0	2	0	2	0	7	1
S19	73	29	0	1	1	0	1	0	0	0	2	1
S20	81	32	2	1	3	0	2	0	1	0	8	1
S21	86	35	3	4	3	0	3	0	2	0	11	4
S22	76	28	2	1	1	0	1	0	1	0	5	1
S23	83	31	4	3	3	1	2	0	3	1	12	5
S24	79	28	2	2	1	0	1	0	1	0	5	2
S25	77	29	3	2	1	0	1	0	1	0	6	2
S26	78	33	2	3	2	0	1	0	3	0	8	3
AVG	76.42	28.96	1.96	1.92	1.38	0.15	1.19	0	1.23	0.12	5.77	2.19
%	72.52	27.48	50.50	49.50	90	10	100	0	91.43	8.57	72.46	27.54

abstract. This kind of problem occurred when the subjects did not properly follow the instructions provided by the F3 patterns. From Table 2, one may observe that F3T helped the subjects to develop frameworks with less structure problems, i.e., 10% in opposition to 90%.

The bad smell problem indicates design weaknesses that do not affect functionality, however it makes the frameworks harder to maintain. In the experiment, this kind of problem occurred when the subjects forgot to apply some of the F3 patterns related to the organization of the framework classes, such as the *Modular Hierarchy* F3 pattern. In Table 2, one can notice F3T made a design with higher quality than the manual approach, i.e, 0% against 100%, because F3T automatically identified which patterns should be applied from the F3 models.

The interface problem indicates absence of getter/setter operations and also of operations that allow the framework to access the application-specific classes. Frequently, this kind of problem is a consequence of structure problems, hence the results of these two problems are quite similar. As shown in Table 2, the subjects designed a better framework interface when using F3T, i.e., 8.6% against 91.4%.

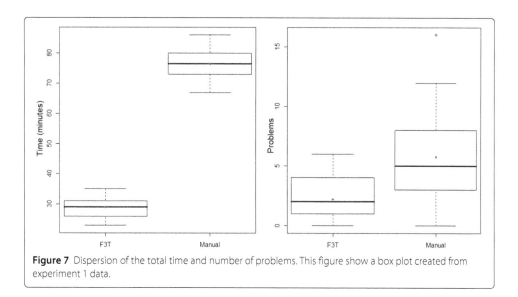

Figure 7 Dispersion of the total time and number of problems. This figure show a box plot created from experiment 1 data.

In the last two columns of Table 2, one may observe that F3T reduced the total number of problems found in the frameworks developed by the subjects. This is also graphically represented in the boxplot on the right side of Figure 7.

Testing the hypotheses The objective of this section is to verify, based on the data obtained in the experiment, whether it is possible to reject the null hypotheses in favor of the alternative hypotheses. All the tests were applied in the experiment data by using the software Action (Portal Action 2015). Since some statistical tests are applicable only in case the population follows a normal distribution, we applied the Shapiro-Wilk test and created a Q-Q chart to verify whether or not the experiment data departs from linearity before choosing a proper statistical test. When the p-value of this Shaphiro-Wilk test is greater than 0.05, it means that data is normally distributed and we can apply the Paired T-Test to verify which hypothesis is valid. Otherwise, the Paired Wilcoxon Signed Rank test is used. More details about these tests are found in the site of Action (Portal Action 2015). The tests have been carried out as follows:

- **Time**: The Shapiro-Wilk test has been applied to the experiment data that represents the time spent by each subject to develop a framework manually or using F3T, as shown in Table 2. Considering that the p-values were 0.8780 (Manual) and 0.6002 (F3T), the Shapiro-Wilk test confirmed that the time spent in framework development is normally distributed, as illustrated in the Q-Q charts (a) and (b) in Figure 8. Then, the Paired T-Test was applied to verify which hypothesis is accepted for RQ_1. The Paired T-Test resulted in a p-value 1,11E-28. It means that the chance of $H1_0$ to be accepted is lesser than 5% and the average values in columns "Time Spent" in manual development and F3T in Table 2 are valid. Therefore, when the F3 approach is applied, one spends less time developing a framework by using F3T than doing it manually.

- **Problems**: Similarly, the Shapiro-Wilk test has been applied to the experiment data shown in the last two columns of Table 2, which represent the total number of problems found in the outcome frameworks. The resulting p-values were 0.1522 in

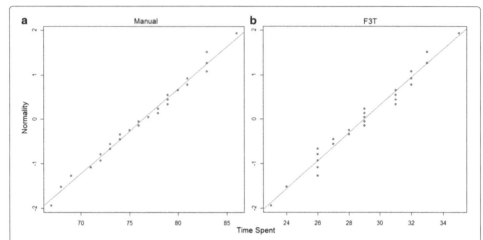

Figure 8 QQ-Plots of the normality tests applied to the time spent in framework development when **(a)** the manual approach was applied and when **(b)** F3T was used. This figure shows 2 QQ Plots illustrating the result of normality tests applied to the time spent on framework development.

manual development and 0.0075 with F3T, as represented by the QQ-Plots in Figure 9. Thus, the data related to manual development is normally distributed, but the same does not happen with the data related to F3T. Therefore, the Wilcoxon Signed Rank test was applied to verify whether the null hypothesis of RQ_2 may be accepted or not. As a result, the p-value was 2.87E-05, which means that the chance of $H2_0$ to be accepted is lesser than 5% and the average values in column "Number of Problems - Total" in Table 2 are valid. It reinforces that F3T reduces the number of problems found in the outcome frameworks.

Opinion of the subjects The opinion of the subjects has been in order to evaluate the impact of using F3T. After the experiment operation, all subjects received a questionnaire, in which they could report their perception about applying the F3 approach manually or supported by F3T. As shown in Figure 10, when asked if they encountered difficulties in

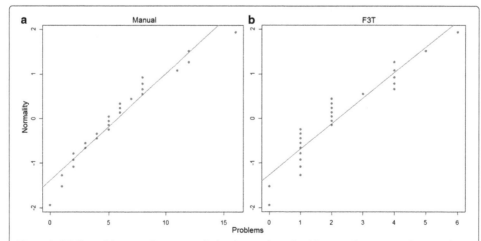

Figure 9 QQ-Plots of the normality tests applied to the number of problems on the outcome frameworks when **(a)** the manual approach was applied and when **(b)** F3T was used. This figure shows 2 QQ-Plots illustrating the result of normality tests applied to the number of problems on the outcome frameworks.

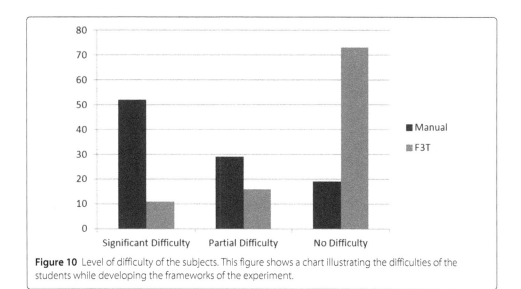

Figure 10 Level of difficulty of the subjects. This figure shows a chart illustrating the difficulties of the students while developing the frameworks of the experiment.

framework development by applying the F3 approach manually, approximately 52% of the subjects reported having significant difficulty, 29% mentioned partial difficulty and 19% had no difficulty. In contrast, when asked the same question with concerning the use of F3T, 73% subjects reported having no difficulty, 16% mentioned partial difficulty and only 11% had significant difficulty.

The subjects also specified the kind of difficulties they faced during framework development. The most common difficulties pointed out in the manual task were: 1) too much effort spent on coding; 2) mistakes they made due to lack of attention; 3) lack of experience for developing frameworks; and 4) time spent identifying the F3 patterns in F3 models. In contrast, the most common difficulties faced by the use of F3T were: 1) lack of practice with the tool; and 2) some actions in the tool interface, for instance, there are many steps in order to open the F3 model editor. The subjects said that the F3 patterns helped them to identify the necessary structures to implement the frameworks manually. They also said F3T automatized the tasks of identifying which F3 patterns should be used as well as of implementing the framework source-code. Thus, they could focus on domain modeling.

4.4 Experiment 2

In the second experiment, F3T has been compared to Pure::variants in a software product line environment. Pure::variants (Pure::Variants 2013) is a tool that supports the development of application variants. From the application source-code, Pure::variants generates a feature model, that specifies the features found in the application, as well as a family model, which defines the components that implement these features. Then, applications, variants of the base one, may be generated by selecting a subset of features of the feature model. Although these tools are based in different approaches, they have been chosen since both of them can be used to generate several applications in a domain. However, due to the differences of the tools, only the time to perform Domain and Application Engineering steps was taken into consideration in this experiment.

Therefore, this second experiment was defined as: (*i*) **analyse** F3T; (*ii*) **for the purpose of** evaluation; (*iii*) **with respect to** time spent; (*iv*) **from the point of view of** the developer; and (*v*) **in the context of** MSc and undergraduate Computer Science students.

4.4.1 Planning

The experiment aimed to answer the following research question:

- **RQ$_1$: Which tool allows a more efficient development of Domain and Application Engineering steps in terms of time?**

In this experiment, all the subjects had to carry out Domain Engineering (DE) and Application Engineering (AE) steps of software product lines by using F3T and Pure::variants. In order to answer the research question, the time spent in carrying out DE and AE steps with each tool were measured. The planning phase was divided into seven parts, which are described as follows.

Context selection The subjects of this experiment were 32 MSc and undergraduate students of Computer Science. All of them had prior experience in software development, Java programming, patterns and framework reuse.

Formulation of hypotheses The experiment questions have been defined as follows:

- **RQ$_1$, Null Hypothesis, H1$_0$:** There is no significant difference in the time spent carrying out DE and AE steps using F3T or Pure::variants. Thus, using F3T is not more efficient than Pure::variants. This hypothesis may be formalized as: **H$_0$:** $\tau_{F3T} = \tau_{pure}$
- **RQ$_1$, Alternative Hypothesis 1, H1$_1$:** The time spent to carry out DE and AE steps by using F3T is significantly lower than by using Pure::variants. Thus, it is more efficient to use F3T than Pure::variants. This hypothesis may be formalized as: **H$_1$:** $\tau_{F3T} < \tau_{pure}$
- **RQ$_1$, Alternative Hypothesis 2, H1$_2$:** The time spent to carry out DE and AE steps by using F3T is significantly greater than by using Pure::variants. Thus, it is more efficient to use Pure::variants than F3T. This hypothesis may be formalized as: **H$_1$:** $\tau_{F3T} > \tau_{pure}$

Variable selection The dependent variables of this experiment were:

- **time spent to carry out DE and AE steps**;
- **usability, related to the opinion of the subjects**.

The independent variables were as follows:

- **Domain**: Each subject had to develop two software product lines: in the first, they had to develop the artifacts for the domain of trade and rental transactions (DE1) and a library application (AE1); and in the second, they had to develop the artifacts for the domain of medical care (DE2) and a veterinary clinic application (AE2). These domains had 10 features each and the applications presented a similar complexity level.
- **Development Environment**: Eclipse 4.2.1 with F3T, Pure::variants evaluation version 3.2.
- **Technologies**: Java version 6.

Selection of subjects The subjects were selected through a non probabilist approach by convenience, so that the probability of all population elements belong to the same sample is unknown.

Experiment design The subjects were grouped in two groups of 16 subjects:

- **Group 1**, development of DE1/AE1 using F3T and development of DE2/AE2 using Pure::variants;
- **Group 2**, development of DE1/AE1 using Pure::variants and development of DE2/AE2 using F3T;

As in Experiment 1, the subjects were grouped in groups according to the level of experience, which was measured from a form in which they had to inform the software development techniques they had already used. This form was given to the subjects one week before the pilot experiment. The goal of this pilot experiment was to ensure that the experiment environment and materials were adequate and that the tasks could be properly executed.

While using F3T in DE, the subjects should create an F3 model based on the domain requirements, generate the framework source-code and DSML plug-ins from this model and install the DSML plug-ins in the Eclipse IDE. In AE, the subjects should create an application model by using the framework DSML according to the application requirements.

Pure::variants creates software product line artifacts from the source-code of a base application. Therefore, while using this tool, the first thing the subjects had to do was to implement this base application. Then, in DE they should generate the feature and the architectural models of the domain and define its variant environment. Finally, in AE the subjects should select the domain featured according to the application requirements and generate this application source-code.

Design types The design type of this experiment was **one factor with two treatments paired** (Wohlin et al. 2000). The **factor** was the tool used to carry out DE and AE steps and the **treatments** were the tool used in this experiment: F3T and Pure::variants.

Instrumentation All the necessary materials to assist the subjects during the execution of this experiment were given to the subjects beforehand, including tool manuals and domain/application requirements and models. They also received a form for collecting experiment data, in which the subjects have to report the time spent to carry out DE and AE steps and their opinion about the tools. All the subjects were also trained in the use of F3T and Pure::variants.

4.5 Operation

The operation phase was divided into two parts, Preparation and Execution, as described in the subsections Preparation and Execution.

Preparation Firstly, the subjects received a characterization form, containing questions on their knowledge about Java programming, Eclipse IDE, patterns, frameworks, F3T and

Pure::variants. A pilot experiment had also been previously performed so that the subjects could get more used to the experiment activities.

Execution In the first activity, the subjects should carry out DE for trade and rental transactions domain and develop an application for a library in AE. The subjects in Group 1 used F3T while the ones in Group 2 used Pure::variants. Each subject measured the time spent using the tools to carry out DE and AE steps. The subjects who were using Pure::Variants also measured the time spent on the implementation of the base application. The second activity was carried out in a similar way. However, in this activity, the subjects of the two groups should work with the domain of medical care in DE and with the veterinary clinic application in AE. Besides, the subjects in Group 1 were using Pure::variants and those in Group 2 were using F3T.

4.6   Analysis of data

This section presents the experimental findings. The analysis is divided into two subsections: (*1*) Descriptive Statistics and (*2*) Hypotheses Testing.

Descriptive statistics The time spent by each subject to develop the base Application Implementation (AI), Domain Engineering (DE) and Application Engineering (AE) is shown in Table 3. Considering DE and AE, one can observe that the subjects spent 45.27% of the total time using Pure::variants and 54.73% using F3T. The main reason for this is that most of the models in Pure::variants are generated from the base application code. Only in EA, the subjects had to decide which domain features should be included in the outcome application. While using F3T, they had to interpret domain requirements in order to create an F3 model and interpret the application requirements to create its model by using the framework DSML. The time spent by the subjects is also represented graphically in the boxplot in Figure 11.

Testing the hypotheses As in Experiment 1, the software Action has been used to verify whether it was possible to reject the null hypotheses in favor of the alternative hypotheses (Portal Action 2015). The Experiment 2 tests have been carried out as follows:

- **Time**: The Shapiro-Wilk test has been applied to the data that represents the time spent with each tool, as shown in columns "DE+AE" of Pure::variants and F3T in Table 3. Considering that the p-values were 0.6133 for Pure::variants and 0.4990 for F3T, the test confirmed that the time spent to carry out DE and AE steps was normally distributed, as shown in the Q-Q charts (a) and (b) in Figure 12. Then, the Paired T-Test was applied to verify which hypothesis would be accepted for RQ1. The Paired T-Test resulted in a p-value 1.19E-3. It means that the chance of H1_0 to be accepted is lower than 5% and the average values in columns "DE+AE" of Pure::variants and F3T in Table 3 are valid. Therefore, the time spent to carry out a software product line is lower with Pure:variants than with F3T.

Positive and negative characteristics of each tool After each experiment, the subjects had to write their opinion on Pure::variants and F3T and highlight positive and negatives

Table 3 Data obtained from using Pure::variants and F3T

Domain		Time spent (min.)							
		Pure::variants					F3T		
	Sub.	AI	DE	AE	DAE	Sub.	DE	AE	DAE
Medical	S1	35	19	10	29	S17	39	19	58
Care	S2	13	32	16	48	S18	20	8	28
	S3	31	30	8	38	S19	26	21	47
	S4	32	18	14	32	S20	18	10	28
	S5	15	15	9	24	S21	31	19	50
	S6	18	20	12	32	S22	36	26	62
	S7	28	31	11	42	S23	23	14	37
	S8	30	27	14	41	S24	35	22	57
	S9	17	26	18	44	S25	36	24	60
	S10	14	30	9	39	S26	32	18	50
	S11	17	23	13	36	S27	28	12	40
	S12	10	18	11	29	S28	23	16	39
	S13	19	22	10	32	S29	26	13	39
	S14	26	25	11	36	S30	31	22	53
	S15	22	21	15	36	S31	21	15	36
	S16	19	29	13	42	S32	24	19	43
Trans.	S17	21	30	10	40	S1	33	18	51
	S18	9	14	11	25	S2	25	20	45
	S19	14	24	12	36	S3	38	18	56
	S20	6	33	10	43	S4	30	12	42
	S21	15	20	8	28	S5	30	9	39
	S22	25	28	15	43	S6	26	13	39
	S23	16	24	12	36	S7	31	20	51
	S24	22	33	16	49	S8	28	17	45
	S25	30	18	10	28	S9	20	11	31
	S26	31	32	17	49	S10	21	10	31
	S27	16	30	9	39	S11	24	13	37
	S28	32	29	15	44	S12	24	14	38
	S29	18	23	10	33	S13	27	16	43
	S30	19	25	12	37	S14	35	22	57
	S31	13	19	13	32	S15	29	17	46
	S32	17	22	14	36	S16	32	14	46
AVG		20.31	24.69	12.13	36.81		28.19	16.31	44.50
%		35.56	43.22	21.23	45.27		63.34	36.66	54.73

characteristics of each tool. Most of the subjects mentioned that the models in both Pure::variants and F3T demand too many steps to be created. The reason is that both tools are based on the Eclipse IDE, in which every file/model is created through a set menu items and wizard forms.

The subjects also mentioned that the main positive characteristic of Pure: variants is that all DE models are generated from the base application source-code, whereas in F3T, an F3 model is created manually. However, each of the Pure::variants models is generated in a sequence of 4-5 steps. Therefore, the subjects argued that they needed to consult the manual tool very often to know how to proceed.

About F3T, the subjects mentioned the following positive characteristics: an application source-code is not needed to develop ED models; the number of models to be

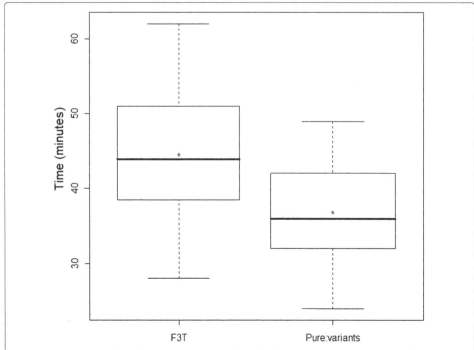

Figure 11 Dispersion of sum the time spent in DE and AE. This figure shows a box plot created from sum the time spent in DE and AE in experiment 2 data.

created in F3T ED (1 model) is smaller if compared with Pure::variants (4 models); the DE step in F3T results in a framework that may be reused in any Java environment besides the Eclipse IDE; and it is easier to customize the outcome applications in AE. The subjects also mentioned that they had some difficulties in creating F3 models. However, this may be attributed to two factors: 1) their lack of experience with domain modeling; and 2) the difficulty in interpreting the domain requirements used in the experiment.

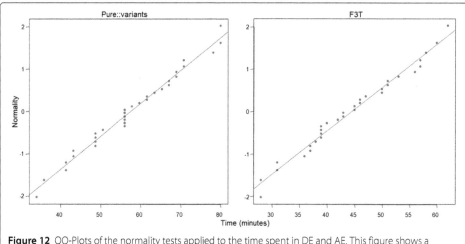

Figure 12 QQ-Plots of the normality tests applied to the time spent in DE and AE. This figure shows a QQ-Plot illustrating the result of normality tests applied to the time spent in DE+AE.

4.7   Threats to the validity of the experiments

Internal validity:

- Experience level of the subjects: the subjects had different levels of knowledge and it could affect the data collected. To mitigate this threat, the subjects were divided into two balanced groups considering their level of knowledge and the groups were rebalanced considering the preliminary results. Moreover, all the subjects had prior experience in application development by reusing frameworks, but no experience in developing frameworks. Thus, the subjects were trained with common framework implementation techniques and how to use the F3 approach and F3T.
- Productivity under evaluation: this might have influenced the experiment results since subjects tend to think they are being evaluated by experiment results. In order to mitigate this, the subjects were told that no one was being evaluated and their participation was considered anonymous.
- Facilities used during the study: different computers and installations could affect the recorded timings. Thus, the subjects used the same hardware configuration and operating system.

Validity by construction:

- Hypothesis expectations: the subjects already knew the researchers and that F3T was supposed to ease framework development, which reflects one of our hypothesis. These issues could affect the data collected and cause the experiment to be less impartial. In order to keep impartiality, the participants were asked to keep a steady pace during the whole study.

External validity:

- Interaction between configuration and treatment: there is a chance that the exercises performed in the experiment are not accurate for every framework development for real world applications. Only two frameworks were developed and they had the same complexity. To mitigate this threat, the exercises were designed considering framework domains based on real world.

Conclusion validity:

- Measure reliability: it refers to metrics used to measure the development effort. To mitigate this threat, only the time spent was used, which was obtained in forms filled out by the subjects;
- Low statistic power: the ability of a statistic test in revealing reliable data. To mitigate this threat, two tests were applied: T-Tests to statistically analyze the time spent to develop the frameworks and the Wilcoxon signed-rank test to statistically analyze the number of problems found in the outcome frameworks.

5   Related work

In this section, some work related to F3T and the F3 approach are presented.

Amatriain and Arumi 2011 proposed a method for the development of a framework and its DSL through iterative and incremental activities. In this method, the framework has its domain defined from a set of applications and it is implemented by applying a series of refactorings in the source-code of these applications. The advantage of this method is a small initial investment and the reuse of the applications. Although it is not mandatory, the F3 approach may also be applied in iterative and incremental activities, starting from a small domain and then adding features. Applications may also be used to facilitate the identification of the features of the framework domain. However, the advantage of the F3 approach is that the design and the implementation of the frameworks are supported by the F3 patterns and it is automatized by F3T.

Oliveira et al. 2011 presented the ReuseTool, which assists framework reuse by manipulating UML diagrams. The ReuseTool is based on the Reuse Description Language (RDL), a language created by these authors to facilitate the description of framework instantiation processes. Framework hot spots may be registered in the ReuseTool with the use of RDL. In order to instantiate the framework, application models may be created based on the framework description. Application source-code is generated from these models. Thus, RDL works as a meta language that registers framework hot spots and the ReuseTool provides a more friendly interface to develop applications by reusing the frameworks. In comparison, F3T supports framework development through domain modeling and application development through framework DSML.

Common Variability Language (CVL) is an Object Manager Group (OMG) standardization used for specifying and resolving domain variability (Rouille et al. 2012). Like F3 models in F3T, CVL is an extended feature model. However, CVL uses a mechanism similar to OCL to implement domain constraints. In comparison, F3 models define domain constraints through relationships and properties. Moreover, since F3 models and F3T focus on framework development, the features in this kind of model may contain attributes and operations.

6 Conclusions

F3T supported framework development and reuse through the generation of code from models. This tool provided an F3 model editor for developers to define the features of the framework domain. Then, framework source-code and DSML may be generated from F3 models. Framework DSML may be installed in the F3T to allow developers to model and to generate the source-code of applications that reuse the framework.

F3T has been created to semi-automatize the application of the F3 approach. Here, domain features are defined in F3 models in order to separate the framework elements from the complexities involved when developing them. F3 models incorporate elements and relationships from feature models and properties and operations from metamodels.

Framework source-code is generated based on patterns that propose solutions to design and implement domain features defined in F3 models. A DSML is generated along with the framework source-code and it includes all domain features. Developers may create models by mapping application requirements to these features to configure framework hot spots. Thus, F3T supports both Domain Engineering and Application Engineering, which improves productivity and the quality of the outcome frameworks and applications. Apart from this, F3T may be used to help the construction of software production lines. It provides an environment to model domains as well as to create frameworks that may be used as core assets for application development.

In addition to the advantages of the F3 approach, F3T improves the framework efficiency and the application development, since the implementation steps of the approach are executed through code generation. It also results in better quality artifacts, due to the model validations provided by the tool and to the fact that code generated is less likely to contain defects.

The first experiment has shown that, besides the gain of efficiency, F3T reduces the complexities surrounding framework development, since, by using this tool, developers are more concerned about defining framework features in a graphical model. F3T generates classes that provide flexibility to the framework and allows it to be instantiated in several applications.

In the second experiment, F3T was compared to Pure::variants. Each tool applies different approaches and artifacts to carry out DE and AE and both tools present pros and cons. In conclusion, F3T is more useful when there is no previous artifact and when the domain architecture is needed as a software artifact, such as a framework. Pure::variants is more useful when variations of an existing application need to be developed.

The current version of F3T only generates the model and persistent layers of frameworks and applications. As future work, it is intended to include the generation of a complete multi-portable Model-View-Controller architecture.

Competing interests
The authors declare that they have no competing interests.

Authors' contributions
MV developed the F3 approach and F3T and wrote most of the manuscript and carried out the experiments. RD participated in the planning of the experiments and performed the statistical analysis. RD was also responsible to write about the experiments in the manuscript. RP helped to execute the experiments. RP and AP helped in the design of the manuscript. All authors read and approved the final manuscript.

Acknowledgments
We would like to thank CAPES and FAPESP for sponsoring our research. We also want to thank all students who participated in the experiments presented in this article.

Author details
[1] Federal Institute of Sao Paulo, Campus Sao Carlos, Rod. Washington Luis, km 235, Block AT6, 13565-905 Sao Carlos, Brazil.
[2] Department of Computing, Federal University of Sao Carlos, Rod. Washington Luis, km 235, 13565-905 Sao Carlos, Brazil.
[3] Institute of Mathematical and Computer Sciences, University of Sao Paulo, Av. Trabalhador Sao Carlense, 400, 13566-590, Sao Carlos, Brazil.

References
Abi-Antoun M (2007) Making Frameworks Work: a Project Retrospective. In: ACM SIGPLAN Conference on Object-Oriented Programming Systems and Applications. ACM, New York, NY, USA. pp 1004–1018
Amatriain X, Arumi P (2011) Frameworks Generate Domain-Specific Languages: A Case Study in the Multimedia Domain. IEEE Trans Softw Eng 37(4):544–558
Antkiewicz M, Czarnecki K, Stephan M (2009) Engineering of Framework-Specific Modeling Languages. IEEE Trans Softw Eng 35(6):795–824
Bayer J, Flege O, Knauber P, Laqua R, Muthig D, Schmid K, Widen T, DeBaud J (1999) PuLSE: a Methodology to Develop Software Product Lines. In: Symposium on Software Reusability. ACM, New York, NY, USA. pp 122–131
Fowler M (2003) Patterns. IEEE Software 20(2):56–57
Frakes W, Kang K (2005) Software Reuse Research: Status and Future. IEEE Trans Softw Eng 31(7):529–536
Gomaa H (2004) Designing Software Product Lines with UML: From Use Cases to Pattern-Based Software Architectures. Addison-Wesley, Boston, MA, USA. p 736
Gronback RC (2009) Eclipse Modeling Project: A Domain-Specific Language (DSL) Toolkit. Addison-Wesley, New York. p 736
Hibernate. http://www.hibernate.org
Jezequel JM (2012) Model-Driven Engineering for Software Product Lines. ISRN Softw Eng 2012:1–24
Johnson RE (1997) Frameworks = (Components + Patterns). Commun ACM 40(10):39–42
Kang KC, Cohen SG, Hess JA, Novak WE, Peterson AS (1990) Feature-Oriented Domain Analysis (FODA): Feasibility Study. Technical report, Carnegie-Mellon University Software Engineering Institute, Pittsburgh, Pennsylvania, USA
Kim SD, Chang SH, Chang CW (2004) A Systematic Method to Instantiate Core Assets in Product Line Engineering. In: 11th Asia-Pacific Conference on Software Engineering. IEEE Computer Society, Los Alamitos, CA, USA. pp 92–98

Kirk D, Roper M, Wood M (2007) Identifying and Addressing Problems in Object-Oriented Framework Reuse. Empir Softw Eng 12(3):243–274

Lee K, Kang KC, Lee J (2002) Concepts and Guidelines of Feature Modeling for Product Line Software Engineering. In: 7th International Conference on Software Reuse: Methods, Techniques and Tools. Springer, London, UK. pp 62–77

Liem I, Nugroho Y (2008) An Application Generator Framelet. In: 9th International Conference on Software Engineering, Artificial Intelligence, Networking, and Parallel/Distributed Computing (SNPD'08). pp 794–799

Lolong S, Kistijantoro AI (2011) Domain Specific Language (DSL) Development for Desktop-Based Database Application Generator. In: International Conference on Electrical Engineering and Informatics (ICEEI). IEEE Computer Society, Los Alamitos, CA, USA. pp 1–6

Oliveira TC, Alencar P, Cowan D (2011) Design Patterns in Object-Oriented Frameworks. ReuseTool: An Extensible Tool Support for Object-Oriented Framework Reuse 84(12):2234–2252

OMG's MetaObject Facility. http://www.omg.org/mof

Parsons D, Rashid A, Speck A, Telea A (1999) IEEE Computer Society. In: Technology of Object-Oriented Languages and Systems, Los Alamitos, CA, USA. pp 141–151

Portal Action. http://www.portalaction.com.br/en

Pressman RS (2009) Software Engineering: A Practitioner's Approach, 7th edn. McGraw-Hill Science, New York. p 928

Pure::Variants. http://www.pure-systems.com/pure_variants.49.0.html

Rouille E, Combemale B, Barais O, Touzet D, Jezequel J-M (2012) Leveraging CVL to Manage Variability in Software Process Lines. In: 19th Asia-Pacific Software Engineering Conference (APSEC) Vol. 1. pp 148–157

Sarasa-Cabezuelo A, Temprado-Battad B, Rodríguez-Cerezo D, Sierra JL (2012) Building XML-Driven Application Generators with Compiler Construction. Comput Sci Inform Syst 9(2):485–504

Shiva SG, Shala LA (2007) IEEE Computer Society. In: Fourth International Conference on Information Technology, Los Alamitos, CA, USA. pp 603–609

Spring Framework. http://www.springsource.org/spring-framework

Srinivasan S (1999) Design patterns in object-oriented frameworks. ACM Comput 32(2):24–32

Stanojevic V, Vlajic S, Milic M, Ognjanovic M (2011) Guidelines for Framework Development Process. In: 7th Central and Eastern European Software Engineering Conference. IEEE Computer Society, Los Alamitos, CA, USA. pp 1–9

The Eclipse Foundation Eclipse Modeling Project. http://www.eclipse.org/modeling/

Viana M, Penteado R, do Prado A (2012) Generating Applications: Framework Reuse Supported by Domain-Specific Modeling Languages. In: 14th International Conference on Enterprise Information Systems. doi:10.5220/0003990000050014

Viana M, Durelli R, Penteado R, do Prado A (2013) F3: From Features to Frameworks. In: 15th International Conference on Enterprise Information Systems. doi:10.5220/000441770110011

Weiss DM, Lai CTR (1999) Software Product Line Engineering: A Family-Based Software Development Process. Addison-Wesley, New York. p 448

Wohlin C, Runeson P, Höst M, Ohlsson MC, Regnell B, Wesslén A (2000) Experimentation in Software Engineering: an Introduction. Kluwer Academic Publishers, Norwell, MA, USA

Xu L, Butler G (2006) Cascaded Refactoring for Framework Development and Evolution. ASWEC, Australian Software Engineering Conference. pp 319-330, doi:10.1109/ASWEC.2006.19

4

Personalized architectural documentation based on stakeholders' information needs

Matias Nicoletti*, Jorge Andres Diaz-Pace, Silvia Schiaffino, Antonela Tommasel and Daniela Godoy

*Correspondence:
matias.nicoletti@isistan.unicen.edu.ar
ISISTAN Research Institute,
CONICET-UNICEN, Paraje Arroyo
Seco, Campus Universitario, Tandil,
Argentina

Abstract

Background: The stakeholders of a software system are, to a greater or lesser extent, concerned about its software architecture, as an essential artifact for capturing the key design decisions of the system. The architecture is normally documented in the Software Architecture Document (SAD), which tends to be a large and complex technical description, and does not always address the information needs of every stakeholder. Individual stakeholders are interested in different, sometimes overlapping, subsets of the SAD and they also require varying levels of detail. As a consequence, stakeholders are affected by an information overload problem, which in practice discourages the usage of the architectural knowledge and diminishes its value for the organization.

Methods: This work presents a semi-automated approach to recommend relevant contents of a given SAD to specific stakeholder profiles. Our approach assumes that SADs are hosted in Wikis, which not only favor communication and interactions among stakeholders, but also enable us to apply User Profiling techniques to infer stakeholders' interests with respect to particular documents.

Results: We have built a recommendation tool implementing our approach, which was tested in two experiments with Wiki-based SADs. The experiments aimed at assessing the performance reached by our tool when inferring stakeholders' interests. To this end, precision and recall metrics were used.

Conclusions: Although preliminary, the results have shown that the recommendations of the tool help to find the architectural documents that best match the stakeholders' interests.

Keywords: Stakeholders; Architectural documentation; Software architecture; Wikis; Personalization; Recommender systems

1   Contents

This article is organized as follows. Section 2 presents the introduction of this article. Section 3 discusses related work on architecture documentation. Section 4 provides background information about the V&B method, and then presents the details of our approach in terms of user profiles, NLP tools and similarity metrics. Section 5 is devoted to the experiments used to evaluate the approach. Section 6 discusses the results of the experiments of this study. Finally, Section 7 gives the conclusions and discusses future lines of work.

2 Background

Software Architecture is a useful model for describing the high-level structure of a system in terms of components, responsibilities allocated to those components, and relationships among them (Bass et al. 2012). The software architecture plays an important role in early development stages as the container of the main design decisions for satisfying the stakeholders' concerns. An example of decisions is the use of certain patterns, such as layers or client-server, to meet modifiability or performance qualities. In a development project, the software architecture is typically captured by the Software Architecture Documentation (SAD), which acts as a channel of communication and knowledge sharing among the stakeholders of the project (Clements et al. 2010). Along this line, a SAD must be clear in explaining: i) how the main functional requirements are addressed by the different software components, and ii) how the component structure satisfies the quality-attribute requirements of the system (e.g., performance, availability, modifiability). As indicated in the ISO Standard (ISO/IEC/IEEE 2011), a challenging aspect of the SAD is that is targeted to multiple readers (i.e., stakeholders such as managers, developers, architects, customers, testers, sub-contractors), which might have different backgrounds and information needs. Generally, each reader needs the architectural knowledge in order to understand specific parts of the system and perform tasks related to the project.

A common problem that stakeholders face when they consume information from a SAD is that of *information overload*. For instance, recent studies (Koning and Vliet 2006; Su 2010) have shown that many individual stakeholder's concerns are addressed by a fraction (less than 25%) of the SAD, but for each stakeholder a different (sometimes overlapping) SAD fraction is needed. In practice, the process of creating and maintaining a SAD tends to be a low-priority or underestimated activity in many projects (due to budget constraints, tight schedules, or pressures on developing features, among other reasons). A common approach is to produce a generic document loaded with development-oriented contents. However, this approach is not the most convenient solution from a multiple-stakeholder perspective. In addition, generic SADs are often extensive and complex, and therefore, stakeholders have difficulties in accessing the information needed for their tasks.

In this work, we aim at improving the ways by which stakeholders access and find relevant information in architectural documents, in the context of Wiki environments. In particular, we have investigated techniques to infer the interests of a user[a] as he/she works with a Wiki-based SAD, and then generate specific recommendations of SAD sections (i.e., Wiki documents) that might be relevant to that user. These kind of recommendations are useful when the size of the documentation is large, as it is common in architectural documentation. To this end, the techniques should determine the relevance of a given SAD section for each user by analyzing the characteristics of the SAD sections and the work context of the users. In other words, we need to characterize (or model) users' interests, preferences and goals with respect to the SAD. Our approach is based on the construction of *user profiles* (Schiaffino and Amandi 2009; Castro-Herrera et al. 2009). Initially, profiles for different stakeholder types are derived from the Views and Beyond (V&B) method for architectural documentation (Clements et al. 2003). As stakeholders browse the SAD, their profiles are enriched with information coming from Wiki documents via Natural Language Processing (NLP) techniques (Baeza-Yates and Ribeiro-Neto 2011) and implicit interest indicators (Al halabi et al. 2007; Claypool et al. 2001). We apply the NLP techniques to perform a semantic analysis of the SAD textual contents through concept and tag mining (Nicoletti et al. 2012; Nicoletti et al. 2013a).

Our approach was initially presented in a previous work (Nicoletti et al. 2013b), and we employed a similarity function based on TF.IDF for matching Wiki documents against user profiles. We have extended that work by developing a recommendation tool for our approach, which works integrated into a Wiki-based system (DokuWiki[b]). In this article, we additionally investigate alternative similarity functions and assess their performance empirically. The preliminary results discussed in (Nicoletti et al. 2013b) for a given SAD are complemented with an additional experiment that uses a different SAD and different test subjects. The results of this second experiment confirmed the trends of the first experiment regarding the performance of our approach and usefulness of the recommendations. The results also shed light on the selection of similarity metrics (according on their performance) for a future deployment of our tool in real-life software development environments.

3   Related work

Several documentation methods for architectural knowledge have been proposed in the literature. Relevant examples include: *Kruchten's 4+1 View Model, Software Systems Architecture, Siemens 4 Views*, and *SEI Views & Beyond* (Clements et al. 2010). These methods prescribe a structure for the SAD (i.e., a template) and promote the use of separate architectural views. These methods provide few or no guidelines for generating the documentation corpus, and the *documenters* (in general, the architecture team) need to determine the *right contents* for each section of the template.

In particular, Views & Beyond (V&B) (Clements et al. 2003) is an appealing method for our work, since it proposes a role-based personalization of the SAD contents (a role here is a stakeholder type). The basic V&B principle states that documenting a software architecture involves documenting the *relevant views*, and then documenting information that applies to more than one view. A view is deemed as relevant if some stakeholder cares about it, or if the view addresses a key quality-attribute aspect of the system. Also, this method defines some documentation guidelines, such as the combination of views or the adjustment of the detail level for each view.

However, V&B still presents some drawbacks in practice. The method assumes that the stakeholder profiles are static (in time) and that their interests can be inferred just using the project role. In our opinion, the stakeholders' interests might change during the project lifetime, and they might be influenced by other factors, in addition to the stakeholder's role. A conditioning factor is the stakeholder's background. For instance, two stakeholders who share the developer role but work in different sub-systems might have different architectural interests (and thus, require different subsets of the SAD). Another factor is the stakeholder's reading history through the SAD (Su 2010). Also, V&B is often viewed by practitioners as a heavy-duty method, due to the amount of documentation to be generated in order to fulfill the SAD template. A contribution of our approach to fosters the applicability of V&B is the provision of more accurate profiles of interests regarding architectural documentation, thanks to the usage of User Profiling techniques. Furthermore, in our proposal, the contents of user profile can be adjusted as the user's working context changes during project life cycle.

To the best of our knowledge, only a few previous works (Castro-Herrera et al. 2009; Su 2010) have considered User Modeling techniques for architectural documentation. Su 2010 proposed an automated approach to deal with chunks of architectural information. These chunks are the result of specific exploration paths followed by a stakeholder (or user) when reading a SAD. The relevance of a given chunk is determined by factors such as the time spent by a reader on a section, or the access frequency of a section. The idea is that, when a new user is about to navigate the SAD, a tool can assist him/her to find relevant information by reusing previous similar exploration paths (from other users). A prototype tool has been recently developed (Su et al. 2011). Unfortunately, this approach still lacks an empirical performance evaluation, in contrast with our approach.

Related to (Su et al. 2011), de Boer and van Vliet (de Boer and van Vliet 2008) investigated the application of Latent Semantic Analysis (LSA) techniques to software documentation with auditing purposes. LSA is used for helping auditors in the search of specific architectural topics (e.g., terms like architecture, scenario, performance, SOA, etc.) across several documents by creating a "reading guide". In background, the LSA algorithm constructs a vector-space model for the documents. In this approach, the auditors must explicitly indicate the terms of interest (or "search query"), so as to steer the navigation through potentially-relevant documents. This approach is related to ours in the sense that documents are modeled with term-based representations. A difference with our approach is that we do not require explicit queries, because the user interests are inferred semi-automatically to generate personalized recommendations.

Castro-Herrera et al. 2009 proposed a user modeling approach to support the requirements elicitation process. A recommendation system is used to link relevant forums with the project stakeholders. For this task, the system builds user profiles by combining a term-based model (extracted with the help of NLP techniques) with context information, such as the stakeholder's role or his/her preferences for specific requirements or quality attributes. This technique is of particular interest for our work, since it is a possible strategy to solve the problem when the SAD is supported by collaborative tools.

The nature of the software architecting process makes it suitable for employing collaborative web-based tools, such as Wikis. In the last years, several successful experiences of Wiki-based tools applied to architecting tasks have been reported (Farenhorst and van Vliet 2008; Unphon and Dittrich 2010). A Wiki is an effective communication channel that improves the sharing of architectural knowledge among stakeholders. From the perspective of User Profiling, an advantage of hosting the documentation (e.g., a SAD) in a Wiki is that users' interactions can be monitored in order to gather information to build user profiles.

Graaf et al. 2012 presented an empirical study on semantic Wikis. In this research, there is a SAD based on a Wiki that supports semantic annotations and, in particular, includes an ontology of Software Architecture concepts. The authors argued that ontology-based SADs are more effective than traditional file-based approaches. Effectiveness here refers to the ability of user to find relevant information according to his/her interests. In a controlled experiment with a small group of software professionals, the authors showed evidence supporting their hypothesis. Although the objectives of this research are different to ours, our approach shares the usage of a Software Architecture ontology. which is part of a semantic dictionary (explained in Section 4.1).

4   Our approach

In order to share the architecture knowledge among the stakeholders, it must be adequately documented and communicated. The Software Architecture Document (SAD) is the usual artifact for capturing this knowledge. The SAD format can range from Word documents to a collection of Web pages hosted in a Wiki. The latter format is becoming common nowadays (de Graaf et al. 2012; Farenhorst and van Vliet 2008; Jansen et al. 2009). The SAD is generally structured around the concept of *architectural views*, which represent the many structures that are simultaneously present in software systems. A view presents an aspect or viewpoint of the system (e.g., static aspects, runtime aspects, allocation of software elements to hardware, etc.). Therefore, the SAD consists of a collection of documents (according to predefined templates) whose contents include views (e.g., module views, components-and-connectors views, allocation views) plus textual information about the views (e.g., system context, architectural drivers, key decisions, intended audience).

Stakeholders are important actors in the documentation process as they are the main consumers of the SAD. By *stakeholder* (Mitchell et al. 1997), we mean any person, group or organization that is interested in or affected by the architecture (e.g., managers, architects, developers, testers, end-users, contractors, auditors). We argue that the value of a SAD strongly depends on how its contents satisfy the *stakeholders' information needs*. As we mentioned in Section 3, the V&B method proposes a stakeholder-based strategy for organizing the SAD views and their contents (Clements et al. 2003). V&B characterizes several types of stakeholders and then links them to specific architectural views, based on the anticipated usage of the views by the stakeholders and their preferred level of detail for the views. This information is summarized in the matrix of Figure 1.

We see the V&B characterization of stakeholders as a basic form of *user profiles*, and then propose a semi-automated approach that leverages on these profiles (and enriches

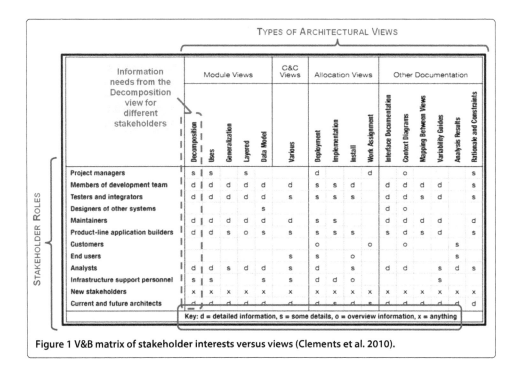

Figure 1 V&B matrix of stakeholder interests versus views (Clements et al. 2010).

them) for establishing links with relevant SAD documents. From this perspective, the SAD is personalized according to the stakeholders' information needs, as captured in his/her profile. The process requires a certain time to learn the user interests and build accurate profiles. This situation is known as the "cold start" problem (Schiaffino and Amandi 2009). Initially, the profiles are only based on the V&B matrix of stakeholders' preferences for architectural views. The "cold start" phase lasts until the system is able to gather additional information about stakeholders' interests so as to enrich the profiles. The user's browsing activity over a Web-based SAD is an example of such an information.

A key aspect of our approach is the granularity of SAD contents when mapped to Wiki pages. This granularity defines the "unit of recommendation" of our tool. In particular, we used one Wiki page per architectural view, plus one Wiki page per additional section (documentation beyond views) of the SEI's V&B template, as it has been suggested by other Wiki-based SADs based on V&B^c (Clements et al. 2003). However, this mapping choice is not mandatory.

A general schema of our profile-based recommendation approach is depicted in Figure 2. The design consists of a pipeline of processing units that: i) generates user profiles, ii) generates document representations, and iii) computes matching relationships among users and SAD documents. We refer to these relationships as *relevance links*, which are actually the recommendations provided by our tool. The relevance links are computed on the basis of the similarity between the user profiles and the document representations. A detailed description of our pipeline can be found on Section 4.3.

4.1 Inputs of the approach

The inputs needed to perform the analysis of stakeholders and construct their profiles are the following:

- *SAD textual contents*: The plain text from SAD documents (or sections) is automatically processed using NLP techniques (see Section 4.5) in order to generate documents models.
- *Interest indicators:* When users interact with Web pages, several interest indicators can be recorded (Al halabi et al. 2007; Claypool et al. 2001). In particular, we analyzed

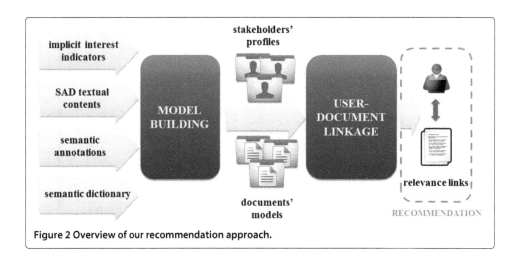

Figure 2 Overview of our recommendation approach.

indicators such as: time spent on reading a page, number of visits, mouse scrolls, mouse clicks, and the ratio between scrolls and time (which represents the frequency of scrolls while reading of Web page), among others (Claypool et al. 2001).

- *Semantic dictionary:* We considered a dictionary composed of a hierarchy of concepts and categories. Categories are concepts with a higher level of abstraction. This kind of semantic source of knowledge is derived from a previous work (Nicoletti et al. 2013a). Instead of using a general-purpose dictionary, we here customized it to consider only Software Architecture concepts along with their corresponding categories. This dictionary was built by combining concepts from an existing ontology for software architectures (de Graaf et al. 2012) with concepts described by the SEI's software architecture bibliography (Bass et al. 2012). We should note that thesauri commonly used for NLP tasks, such as WordNet or Wikipedia (Nicoletti et al. 2013a), are not specific enough in the Software Architecture domain of knowledge.

- *Semantic annotations:* Our approach needs to build a model (or representation) of each SAD document. We argue that these models can be enriched with explicit annotations provided by an expert (e.g., a member of the software architecture team), who, in general, will also generate the SAD contents. This expert is able to select those concepts or categories that best describe the semantics of each document. The annotations are considered part of the document representations. Moreover, the annotations are helpful to model documents/sections of the SAD template that are partially completed (or even empty), or to refine the representation of documents that are not accurately described by their textual contents (e.g., documents that contain many images and little text).

Our approach is regarded as semi-automated because the intervention of experts is required to input semantic annotations in the SAD documents. The expert also makes annotations on role types and, thus, incorporates V&B-related information. The initial stakeholders' profiles are mainly filled in with these annotations. For both annotation tasks, the expert uses the semantic dictionary as a "label catalog". The rest of the tasks and computations can be performed automatically.

4.2 Modeling users and documents

Both user profiles and documents are represented by the same structure. This structure comprises two parts: i) a set of semantic concepts and categories, which are extracted from the dictionary mentioned above, and ii) a set of tags (or keywords) (Schiaffino and Amandi 2009; Nicoletti et al. 2013a). For each item (i.e., concept, category or tag), the number of occurrences is recorded as the item frequency.

In our context, tags are keywords or non-trivial words often extracted with NLP techniques. Trivial words, such us pronouns or prepositions, are usually excluded. Concepts are basic units of meaning that serves humans to organize and share their knowledge. For instance, the English Wikipedia articles have been used as a source of concepts. Categories are concepts with a higher level of abstraction, which might be link to concrete concepts or to other categories with different level of abstraction. In our dictionary, for instance, *performance*, *fault tolerance* and *security* are examples of concepts within the category *quality atributes*, which, in turn, is linked to the high-level category *requirements*.

A user profile or a document model is a triple $M = < CON, CAT, TAG >$, in which:

- $CON = \{con_1, \ldots, con_n\}$ is a set of concepts, where con_i $(1 \leq i \leq n)$ is a pair $< C, F >$ with C as the concept and F as its frequency.
- $CAT = \{cat_1, \ldots, cat_m\}$ is a set of categories, where cat_i $(1 \leq i \leq m)$ is a pair $< C, F >$ with C as the category and F as its frequency.
- $TAG = \{tag_1, \ldots, tag_t\}$ is a set of tags, where tag_i $(1 \leq i \leq t)$ is a pair $< T, F >$ with T as the tag and F as its frequency.

This representation is convenient to calculate similarities between users and documents, as well as for quickly describing the interests of a given user or the contents of a given document. For instance, Figure 3 shows how the model of user interests might look like. We also decided to combine both concepts and tags, since the SAD is generally composed of general concepts and problem-specific concepts. Some examples of problem-specific concepts are: names of software components, specific stakeholders' names, and tactics and patterns that are not included in the common catalogs, among others. The general concepts are defined in our semantic dictionary, whereas the problem-specific concepts are mined from the text.

4.3 The processing procedure

The process is divided into three main stages, as depicted in Figure 4. First, the *document representation generation* is performed. This stage runs a NLP semantic analysis of the documents (hosted in the Wiki), and afterwards merges the semantic annotations with the partial representation of those documents. We refer to a model (of a document or a user) as being "partial" when its constituents (e.g., tags) must be refined by running one or more processing units. First, the document annotations are included in the partial models of documents. A prefixed value (parameter N) denotes the weight (or frequency) that each annotation would have in the document model. Second, a NLP analysis of documents is performed. To this end, we have configured a sub-pipeline of NLP tasks that

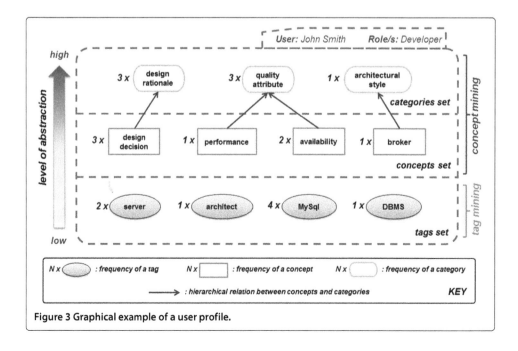

Figure 3 Graphical example of a user profile.

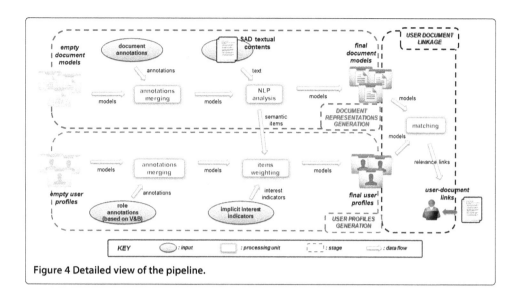

Figure 4 Detailed view of the pipeline.

produces a term-based representation of the documents. The details of this sub-pipeline are described in Section 4.5.

Second, the *user profiles generation* stage takes place. The initial user profiles, which are empty at this point, are enriched with semantic annotations coming from the roles (or stakeholder types) associated to each user. The role annotations and the user profiles are merged as described in the previous stage. Next, we perform what we call *semantic items weighting*: the semantic items that were extracted from the documents visited by a given user are added to that user profile. We assume that when a user accesses a SAD section, the contents of that section are likely to be relevant to that user. Therefore, we consider interest indicators from usage statistics to weight the relevance of the semantic items incorporated into user profiles. In particular, we used the number of visits as the frequency of the new items for the user profile. For example, if a user visited a given document N times, and that document contains a concept X and a tag T, then both X and T are incorporated to the user profile with a frequency of N. This indicator was prioritized over the others based on an empirical assessment of its relevance for inferring user interests (see Section 5).

Finally, the *user document linkage* stage is executed. In this stage, the models for both users and documents have already been generated. These two kinds of models are processed by an algorithm that determines the degree of matching (or similarity) between the models. In this article, we analyzed several metrics to compute the similarity between two models (see Section 4.4) and compared them empirically (see Section 5).

The output of the complete procedure is a set of weighted links between users and documents, in which the weights indicate the relevance of the documents for each user. The output is grouped by user and anked in descending order to select the most important links per user. A threshold k is used to establish the number of documents retrieved as relevant. For example, if we have N different sections in a SAD, with $k = 1/4$ we are considering the first $1/4N$ sections as relevant and the other $3/4N$ as irrelevant. Figure 5 shows an snapshot of our recommendation tool at work.

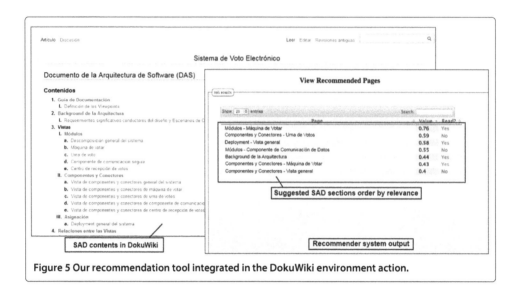

Figure 5 Our recommendation tool integrated in the DokuWiki environment action.

4.4   Computing similarity between models

In general, the strategies to compute the similarity (or distance) between two items map the similarity between the symbolic descriptions of two objects to a unique numerical value (Huang 2008). In this section we describe different strategies we used to compute the degree of matching between user profiles and documents models. For each strategy, we present a short description, its formal definition and, if necessary, some consideration for its usage. It is worth noting that for those strategies that compute the distance between two items, we consider the similarities as the inverse of such distance.

4.4.1   Euclidean distance

The Euclidean distance represents the distance between two points in space, given by the Phytagorean formula. It is one of the most widely used distances for numerical data (Deza and Deza 2006; 2009; Liu 2011). Equation 1 (Deza and Deza 2009) is the formal definition of this distance, where $\vec{t_a}$ and $\vec{t_b}$ are the vectors to be analyzed, and $w_{t,a}$ and $w_{t,b}$ are the weights associated to attributes t_a and t_b respectively. In this case, weights correspond to number of occurrences.

$$Euclidean\left(\vec{t_a}, \vec{t_b}\right) = \sqrt{\sum_{t=0}^{m}\left(w_{t,a} - w_{t,b}\right)^2} \tag{1}$$

4.4.2   Manhattan distance

This measure takes its name from its geometrical interpretation in the so called Taxicab geometry, in which the distance between two points is the sum of the absolute differences of their Cartesian coordinates. Its name allude to the grid layout of most streets on the island of Manhattan, which causes the shortest path a car could take between two intersections in the borough to have a length equal to the intersections distance in taxicab geometry. Equation 2 shows the formal definition of the Manhattan distance between two vectors $\vec{t_a}$ and $\vec{t_b}$.

$$Manhattan\left(\vec{t_a}, \vec{t_b}\right) = \sqrt{\sum_{k=0}^{n}\left|w_{t,a} - w_{t,b}\right|} \tag{2}$$

4.4.3 Chebyshev distance

This strategy defines the distance between two distributions considering the maximum difference between their attributes. It is a metric defined on a vector space where the distance between two vectors is the greatest of their differences along any coordinate dimension. Equation 3 shows its formal definition (Deza and Deza 2009).

$$Chebyshev\left(\overrightarrow{t_a}, \overrightarrow{t_b}\right) = max\left\{|w_{1,a} - w_{1,b}|, \ldots, |w_{m,a} - w_{m,b}|\right\} \tag{3}$$

4.4.4 Cosine similarity

The representation of distributions as vectors enables us to measure the similarity between them as the correlation between the corresponding vectors (Huang 2008). Such similarity can be quantified as the cosine of the angle between them. The strategy is independent of the length of the distributions, and it is one of the most widely used in information retrieval systems. Equation 4 presents the formal definition of the cosine similarity of vectors $\overrightarrow{t_a}$ and $\overrightarrow{t_b}$, where $\overrightarrow{t_a} \cdot \overrightarrow{t_b}$ represents the inner product of these vectors, and $\left\|\overrightarrow{t_a}\right\|$ and $\left\|\overrightarrow{t_b}\right\|$ represent their norms (Deza and Deza 2009; Liu 2011).

$$Cosine\left(\overrightarrow{t_a}, \overrightarrow{t_b}\right) = \frac{\overrightarrow{t_a} \cdot \overrightarrow{t_b}}{\left\|\overrightarrow{t_a}\right\| \left\|\overrightarrow{t_b}\right\|} = \frac{\sum_{t=0}^{m}\left(w_{t,a} * w_{t,b}\right)}{\sqrt{\sum_{t=0}^{m} w_{t,a}^2} * \sqrt{\sum_{t=0}^{m} w_{t,b}^2}} \tag{4}$$

4.4.5 Cosine distance

Given the previous equation, the cosine distance in Equation 5 shows how to adapt it to compute the distance between two distributions.

$$CosineDistance\left(\overrightarrow{t_a}, \overrightarrow{t_b}\right) = 1 - Cosine\left(\overrightarrow{t_a}, \overrightarrow{t_b}\right) \tag{5}$$

4.4.6 Kullback-Leibler divergence

This strategy is also known as information gain or relative entropy (Huang 2008), and it is defined as in Equation 6.

$$D_{KL}\left(\overrightarrow{t_a} \| \overrightarrow{t_b}\right) = \sum_{t=1}^{m}\left[w_{t,a} * log\left(\frac{w_{t,a}}{w_{t,b}}\right)\right] \tag{6}$$

The formula presents an indetermination condition when $\frac{w_{t,a}}{w_{t,b}}$, and returns 0, that is when $w_{t,a}$ or $w_{t,b}$ are equal to 0. To avoid this indetermination and be able to compute the formula correctly, a correction is applied to those value equal to 0. These values are replaced by 10^{-6}, so that it does not affect the original distributions. Additionally, the strategy is not symmetrical, that is $D_{KL}\left(\overrightarrow{t_a} \| \overrightarrow{t_b}\right) \neq D_{KL}\left(\overrightarrow{t_b} \| \overrightarrow{t_a}\right)$. In this context, it cannot be used to measure distances. To overcome this difficulty, the average divergence is computed using the formula in Equation 7, where $\pi_1 = \frac{w_{t,a}}{w_{t,a}+w_{t,b}}$, $\pi_2 = \frac{w_{t,b}}{w_{t,a}+w_{t,b}}$ and $wt = \pi_1 * w_{t,a} + \pi_2 * w_{t,b}$.

$$AverageKullback\left(\overrightarrow{t_a} \| \overrightarrow{t_b}\right) = \sum_{t=1}^{m}\left[\pi_1 * D_{KL}\left(w_{t,a} \| w_t\right) + \pi_2 * D_{KL}\left(w_{t,b} \| w_t\right)\right] \tag{7}$$

4.4.7 Dice-Sorensen similarity

The Dice-Sorensen coefficient is a statistic used for comparing the similarity of two samples (Dice 1945; Sørensen 1948). It is based on an analysis of the presence or absence of data in the samples considered. As compared to Euclidean distance, Sorensen distance retains sensitivity in more heterogeneous data sets and gives less weight to outliers. Its formal definition is given by Equation 8 (Deza and Deza 2009).

$$\text{Dice-Sorensen}\left(\vec{t_a}, \vec{t_b}\right) = \frac{2 * \left|\vec{t_a} \cdot \vec{t_b}\right|}{\left\|\vec{t_a}\right\|^2 + \left\|\vec{t_b}\right\|^2} \tag{8}$$

4.4.8 Jaccard distance

The Jaccard distance is a statistic used for comparing the similarity and diversity of sample sets. This strategy is very useful to analyze text similarity in huge collections (Rajaraman and Ullman 2012). Equation 9 shows the formal definition of this strategy where t_a and t_b represent the attributes of distributions $\vec{t_a}$ and $\vec{t_b}$ respectively.

$$Jaccard\left(\vec{t_a}, \vec{t_b}\right) = 1 - \frac{|t_a \cap t_b|}{|t_a \cup t_b|} = \frac{|t_a \cup t_b| - |t_a \cap t_b|}{|t_a \cup t_b|} \tag{9}$$

4.4.9 Overlap coefficient

The overlap coefficient, also known as Simpson similarity, is a similarity measure related to the Jaccard index that computes the overlap between two sets, which is defined as Equation 10 (Deza and Deza 2009).

$$Overlap\left(\vec{t_a}, \vec{t_b}\right) = \frac{|t_a \cap t_b|}{min\left\{\left|\vec{t_a}\right|, \left|\vec{t_b}\right|\right\}} \tag{10}$$

4.4.10 Pearson correlation coefficient

This strategy measures how related two distributions are. Equation 11 shows its formal definition, where $TF_a = \sum_{t=1}^{m} w_{t,a}$ and $TF_{ba} = \sum_{t=1}^{m} w_{t,b}$.

$$Pearson\left(\vec{t_a}, \vec{t_b}\right) = \frac{m * \sum_{t=1}^{m}\left(w_{t,a} \times w_{t,b}\right) - TF_a * TF_b}{\sqrt{\left[\left(m * \sum_{t=1}^{m} w_{t,a}^2 - TF_a^2\right) * \left(m * \sum_{t=1}^{m} w_{t,b}^2 - TF_b^2\right)\right]}} \tag{11}$$

This strategy gives as result a value in the range $[-1, +1]$, being 1 when $\vec{t_a} = \vec{t_b}$.

4.4.11 Pearson correlation coefficient distance

This strategy applies a change to Pearson correlation coefficient so that the value of the metric fits in the range $[0, +1]$ and hence, the strategy represents the distance between two distributions $\vec{t_a}$ and $\vec{t_b}$.

$$PearsonDistance\left(\vec{t_a}, \vec{t_b}\right) = \begin{cases} 1 - Pearson\left(\vec{t_a}, \vec{t_b}\right) & if\ Pearson\left(\vec{t_a}, \vec{t_b}\right) \geq 0 \\ \left|Pearson\left(\vec{t_a}, \vec{t_b}\right)\right| & if\ Pearson\left(\vec{t_a}, \vec{t_b}\right) < 0 \end{cases} \tag{12}$$

4.4.12 Tanimoto distance

The Tanimoto distance can be defined as a variation of Jaccard distance (Huang 2008). It compares the weights of shared attributes with the weights of those attributes that belong to one of the distributions but are not shared between them. The strategy calculates the similarity between two distributions $\vec{t_a}$ and $\vec{t_b}$ giving a value in the range $[0, 1]$, being 1 when $\vec{t_a} = \vec{t_b}$ and 0 when the distributions are completely different. The formula of the distance is shown in Equation 14.

$$TanimotoSem\left(\overrightarrow{t_a}, \overrightarrow{t_b}\right) = \frac{\overrightarrow{t_a} \cdot \overrightarrow{t_b}}{\left\|\overrightarrow{t_a}\right\|^2 + \left\|\overrightarrow{t_b}\right\|^2 - \overrightarrow{t_a} \cdot \overrightarrow{t_b}} \tag{13}$$

$$Tanimoto\left(\overrightarrow{t_a}, \overrightarrow{t_b}\right) = 1 - TanimotoSem\left(\overrightarrow{t_a}, \overrightarrow{t_b}\right) \tag{14}$$

4.4.13   TF.IDF-based similarity function

In addition to the previous similarity metrics, we propose a candidate function that specifically fits the problem of matching stakeholder profiles against architecture documents. Our function is based on the TF.IDF (Term Frequency x Inverse Document Frequency) metric of the Information Retrieval field (Baeza-Yates and Ribeiro-Neto 2011). The function is computed as indicated in Equation 15, in which U is a triple describing a user profile, D is a triple describing a document model (Section 4.2), N is the amount of concepts, M is the amount of categories, T is the amount of tags (all from the user profile), ConF.IDF(x) is the CF.IDF-value for user concept x, CatF.IDF(y) is the CF.IDF-value for user category y, and TF.IDF(t) is the TF.IDF-value for user tag t (Goossen et al. 2011; Nicoletti et al. 2012). This computation outputs a value in the range of $[0, +\infty]$, which is then normalized to the range $[0, 1]$. A high value represents a good similarity between the user and the document. If the value is close to 0, it means that there are few o none semantic items shared between the two models.

$$\text{TFIDF-based}(U, D) = \sum_{n \in N} \text{ConF.IDF}(con_n) + \sum_{m \in M} \text{CatF.IDF}(cat_m) + \sum_{t \in T} \text{TF.IDF}(tag_t) \tag{15}$$

4.5   NLP Semantic analysis

This analysis aims at extracting concepts and tags from a textual input. The analysis is executed on the raw text from the Wiki pages. This involves two processes: tag mining and concept mining. The sequence of tasks for tag mining is the following:

1. *Text parsing:* The input text from the SAD is parsed in order to remove custom annotations from the Wiki syntax as well as invalid characters.
2. *Sentence detection:* The parsed input text is split into a set of sentences. The OpenNLP[d] implementation was used for this task.
3. *Tokenizer:* The sentences are divided into tokens (terms). The OpenNLP implementation is again used here.
4. *Stop-words removal:* Frequently used terms are removed. We use approximately 600 words for this task (a mixture of commonly-used stop-words).
5. *Stemming:* The terms are reduced to their root form to improve the keyword matching. Porter's Stemming algorithm[e] is used here.

The sequence of tasks for concept mining is the following:

1. *Text parsing:* Similar as done in tag mining (above).
2. *Sentence detection:* Similar as done in tag mining (above).
3. *Concept matching:* A set of concepts is associated with each sentence. Since the size of the concept dictionary is relatively small, we process the complete dictionary and try to match concepts with sentences. We apply stop-words removal and stemming (Porter's algorithm) to both concept names and sentence

text alike, aiming at improving the string matching algorithm. In case the match is positive, the concept is associated with the sentence.

4. *Categories matching:* The category hierarchy tree is built for each concept. We associate a set of intermediate level categories to each concept, which is already associated with each sentence, based on our previous work (Nicoletti et al. 2013a). The process is repeated for the upper level categories. In the resulting profile, we register the matching categories and their frequency.

5   Evaluation: methods and results

Our approach was empirically evaluated in two experiments[f] with real users of SADs. The evaluation pursued two main goals. The first goal was to assess the performance of the pipeline in terms of correctness of the recommendations (i.e., the relevance links between users and documents). The second goal was to compare the candidate similarity functions to compute the user-document links and thus determine the functions with the best performance. Additionally, we analyzed the benefits regarding to the effort reductions in stakeholders' tasks, if the people would have been assisted by our recommendation tool. At last, we assessed whether the interest indicators were relevant for inferring stakeholders' interests by means of an Information Gain analysis.

To accomplish the goals above, we asked different groups of users to work with Wiki-based SADs and perform specific architecture-related tasks. In background, we monitored the browsing activity of these users and collected Wiki usage statistics. We also had information about the actual users' interests on the SAD, as they provided us feedback during the experiment. This feedback allowed us to check, *postmortem*, if the SAD documents recommended by our tool could have been useful to these users (note that these users did not receive recommendations while working with the SAD).

In this study, inferring the interests of a user on a given document can be seen as a binary-class classification problem. We used standard Machine Learning metrics such as: precision, recall, and F-measure (Baeza-Yates and Ribeiro-Neto 2011). In our context, precision represents the percentage of recommended documents that were actually relevant to the user. Recall is the fraction of relevant documents that were suggested. F-measure is considered as the harmonic mean (or weighted average) of precision and recall. In particular, we used $F_{0.5}$ *measure* that is a variation of the regular metric that prioritizes precision over recall. We conducted two experiments, each one with a different SAD and separate groups of subjects, in order to analyze whether our approach exhibits similar performance trends with different experimental configurations.

5.1   Experiment #1: Electronic voting system

For this first experiment, we employed 77 test subjects, who were undergraduate and graduate students from a Software Architecture course taught at UNICEN University (Tandil, Argentina). The graduate students were practitioners taking software development courses for their Master degree. We organized the participants into 11 groups: 10 groups of 7 undergraduate students each, plus an additional group of 7 practitioners.

The materials used in the experiment were: a SAD describing an Electronic Voting System according to the V&B template[g], and predefined question sets for evaluating the quality of the architectural documentation[h]. The SAD documents were hosted on DokuWiki, and described the main design decisions and architectural views for the system. The SAD contained 24 pages (documents) and 22 architectural diagrams, which are representative amounts of real-life SADs. After discarding those SAD pages containing general information, such us indexes, acronyms or definitions, the documentation corpus was reduced to 16 pages. The mapping of Wiki pages to SAD contents was as follows: one Wiki page per architectural view, and one Wiki page per additional section (i.e., documentation beyond views) of the V&B template.

The SAD contents were of acceptable quality, but still had some inconsistencies, omissions, and opportunities for improvement. The question sets were geared to discover these problems from the perspective of different types of stakeholders. A question set is a questionnaire designed with a specific stakeholder role in mind, so as to influence his/her navigation patterns through the Wiki. The questionnaire included: i) a set of quality-attribute scenarios to be evaluated with an ATAM-like design review (Bass et al. 2012), and ii) a set of role-specific questions (also ATAM-like) referring to the quality of the architectural descriptions (Nord et al. 2009). We decided to work with 4 common stakeholder roles, namely: manager, software architect, evaluator, end-user/client; and defined a question set for each role accordingly. Each person was asked to record the elapsed time per item, the difficulty of the task, and the SAD documents that supported his/her responses.

5.1.1 Experimental procedure

The experiment involved five main steps. First, an instance of DokuWiki with the SAD was deployed on a public-access server. This Wiki used a modified version of the software that included monitoring capabilities via PHP/JQuery scripts. Second, the subjects were asked to browse our Wiki for a week, so that they could familiarized with the software architecture of the Electronic Voting System as well as with the V&B templates. Then, we assigned a role to each user within the groups, and distributed the corresponding question sets. Third, the groups were given 3 weeks to go through their question sets and produce an assessment report. After the 3 weeks, we collected the usage statistics logged by the Wiki. Fourth, we generated a matrix with the real user interests on the SAD documents per group. That is, each user-document pair was labeled as relevant or not-relevant (1 or 0). These matrices of real interests were determined from: i) the question sets assigned to the user roles (indirect source), and ii) the answers of the users to those question sets (direct source). In the first source, each question set was designed in such a way it predetermined the types of SAD documents that a user should look at to answer it. Still, users playing the same role but in different groups might read different documents (of the same SAD). In the second source, each user explicitly said in his/her questionnaire what SAD documents he/she looked at. These matrices were actually the references for computing precision, recall, and F-measure (see Sections 5.1.3 and 5.2.2).

The explicit feedback reported by the subjects in their questionnaires also allowed us to analyze the difficulty and time required to solve each questionnaire item, which we called task-difficulty and resolution-time respectively (see Sections 5.1.4 and 5.2.3). Task-difficulty was measured in a categorical scale: low, medium and high. Resolution time was also binned in a categorical scale: low (0-20 minutes), medium (20-60 minutes) and high (more than 60 minutes). For each user-document pair, we recorded the maximum task-difficulty and the maximum resolution-time, which were computed as follows. If a user indicated that a given item had a difficulty-value D and a resolution-time T, then we labeled the SAD documents associated to that item with a difficulty D and a time T only when: i) the documents had not been labeled before, or ii) the documents had been labeled before with lower values. This procedure was repeated for each item of the questionnaire, for every user's report.

As regards the semantic annotations (inputs of our approach), each Wiki document was annotated with semantic concepts and tags by mutual agreement among the authors (simulating an expert's opinion). These annotations were not visible to the subjects during the experiments. We annotated the roles considering the V&B model (Clements et al. 2003) and the topics involved in the questionnaire for each role. These role annotations constituted the initial stakeholders' profiles, which were later enriched by interest indicators and items coming from the Wiki pages visited by the users.

5.1.2   Relevance of interest indicators

Prior to the evaluation of our approach, we conducted an Information Gain (IG) analysis (Mitchell 1997) in order to assess the importance of interest indicators for inferring relevance labels of documents for each user. This analysis measures the quality of a given independent variable (e.g., an indicator such as the number of visits) for predicting a target dependent variable (e.g., the relevance label). The IG value for an indicator is in the range $[0, 1]$. A value of 0 means that the indicator is irrelevant, whereas a value of 1 means that it is highly relevant.

In our study, we employed the Wiki usage statistics to build a dataset (with $\simeq 900$ samples) and computed the IG value of each interest indicator. The IG values for this experiment were: $IG_{visits} = 1$ (number of visits), $IG_{scroll\,time} = 0.80$ (scrolling time), $IG_{time} = 0.74$ (time spent reading a SAD document), which show that these 3 indicators are suitable to classify the user interests. Based on these results, we chose the number of visits as the main interest indicator in our NLP pipeline.

5.1.3   Performance of the recommender system (experiment #1)

We ran the NLP pipeline with the following inputs: i) the text contents from the SAD documents, ii) the number of visits for each SAD document, iii) the document annotations provided by experts, and iv) the role annotations for each user (i.e., the basic profiles per stakeholder type). We experimented with several values for the k parameter (see Section 4.3), in order to assess the performance of the recommender system. For each k-value, we firstly computed the measures per user, and then an average for the 77 users. In addition, we tested the 13 candidate similarity functions described in Section 4.4.

Figure 6 summarizes the precision, recall and F-measure in our approach for different configurations (i.e., k-values and similarity functions). Considering that we prioritized precision over recall, the best F-measure value was obtained for a k-value in the range $[0.3, 0.4]$ with very small variations depending on the similarity function being used. . In particular, the best performance was exhibited by the *Tanimoto* function with $k = 0.35$, with an F-measure of 0.66 that corresponded to a precision of 0.67 and a recall of 0.65). However, the maximum precision obtained was 0.7 for $k = 0.25$, but the recall dropped to 0.5 because of the natural trade-off between these metrics.

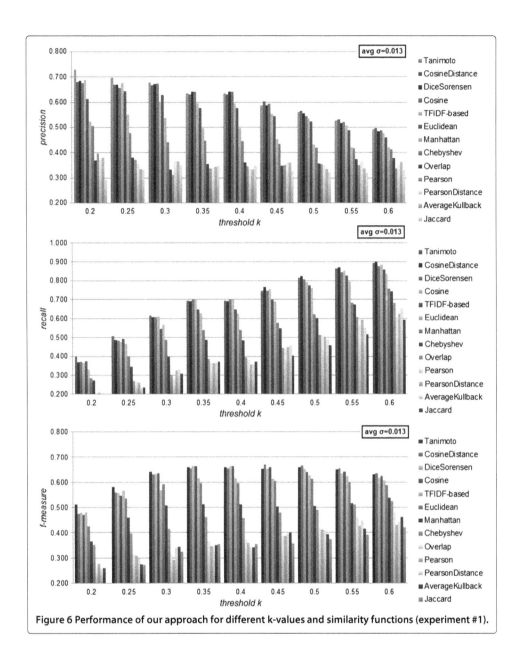

Figure 6 Performance of our approach for different k-values and similarity functions (experiment #1).

We additionally performed a statistical analysis of the similarity functions based on their F-measure values. To this end, we applied both the Student's t-test (two-sided) and the Mann-Whitney-Wilcoxon (MWW) test to the average F-measure obtained for the different 77 subjects. We used the MWW test in those cases in which normality of samples could not been verified with Shapiro-Wilk Normality test. For each pair of similarity functions, we tested the null hypothesis H_0 : *F-measure values of one function tend to be equal to those of the other function*, against the alternative hypothesis H_1 : *F-measure values of one function tend to be higher (or lower) than those of the other function*. For non-normal distributions, we used the notation H_0^* and H_1^*, respectively. In those cases were the Student's test was used (normal distributions), we were able to verify the homoscedasticity of the samples by using the F-test (two-samples) with a significance level of 0.95.

Figure 7 presents the results of this statistical analysis, in which each cell of the tablel represents the accepted hypothesis for each pair of functions with a significance level of 0.05. This table also includes the corresponding p-values for each statistical test. Notice that we can identify a subset of 3 functions (*Tanimoto, Cosine, andCosineDistance*) with the highest performance, which are also statistically different from the remaining functions, but similar to each other.

5.1.4 Usefulness of the recommendations (experiment #1)

To analyze the quality of the recommendations, we recorded the maximum of both task-difficulty and resolution-time associated with those SAD documents recommended by our tool. The set of recommended documents for a given user are those ranked in the first places (i.e., high similarity values), and the size of that set is determined by the k value. For example, if the system recommended N documents to a particular user, and they were linked to high-difficulty tasks, we categorized the recommendations as potentially useful. On the other hand, if the N sections were linked to tasks requiring little time to be solved, the recommendations were considered not as useful as in the previous case.

Figure 8 shows a comparative chart between the percentage of potentially useful recommendations (high or medium values) and the less useful ones (low values)regarding both task-difficulty and resolution-time. The results of this chart were computed with the *Cosine* function (one of the best performing functions) for the range of k values [0.3, 0.4]. The chart shows that a high percentage of the recommended documents are generally related to tasks with high or medium difficulty, as well as tasks requiring high or medium time to be solved.

In the case of task-difficulty, those tasks with high or medium difficulty were targeted by an average of 75% of the recommendations, whereas tasks with low difficulty were targeted by the remaining 25% recommendations. In the case of resolution time, those tasks requiring high or medium time (more than 20 minutes) were targeted by an average of 80%, whereas tasks that were quickly solved were targeted by the remaining 20%. Similar percentages were also observed for the other best performing functions, showing trend in the quality of recommendations, which seems independent of the similarity function chosen.

	TAN	COS	COSD	DICS	TFIDF	EUC	MAN	CHE	OVE	PEA	PEAD	KUL	JAC
TAN													
COS	p=0.277 (H_0)												
COSD	p=0.362 (H_0)	p=0.917 (H_0)											
DICS	p=0.011 (H_1*)	p≈0 (H_1*)	p≈0 (H_1*)										
TFIDF	p≈0 (H_1)	p≈0 (H_1)	p≈0 (H_1)	p≈0 (H_1*)									
EUC	p≈0 (H_1)	p≈0 (H_1)	p≈0 (H_1)	p≈0 (H_1*)	p=0.489 (H_0)								
MAN	p≈0 (H_1*)	p≈0 (H_1*)	p≈0 (H_1*)	p≈0 (H_1*)	p≈0 (H_1*)	p≈0 (H_1*)							
CHE	p≈0 (H_1)	p≈0 (H_1)	p≈0 (H_1)	p≈0 (H_1*)	p≈0 (H_1)	p≈0 (H_1)	p=0.085 (H_0*)						
OVE	p≈0 (H_1)	p≈0 (H_1)	p≈0 (H_1)	p≈0 (H_1*)	p≈0 (H_1)	p≈0 (H_1)	p≈0 (H_1*)	p≈0 (H_1)					
PEA	p≈0 (H_1*)	p≈0 (H_1*)	p≈0 (H_1*)	p≈0 (H_1*)	p≈0 (H_1*)	p≈0 (H_1*)	p≈0 (H_1*)	p≈0 (H_1*)	p=0.043 (H_1*)				
PEAD	p≈0 (H_1*)	p≈0 (H_1*)	p≈0 (H_1*)	p≈0 (H_1*)	p≈0 (H_1*)	p≈0 (H_1*)	p≈0 (H_1*)	p≈0 (H_1*)	p=0.005 (H_1*)	p=0.072 (H_0*)			
KUL	p≈0 (H_1)	p≈0 (H_1)	p≈0 (H_1)	p≈0 (H_1*)	p≈0 (H_1)	p≈0 (H_1)	p≈0 (H_1*)	p≈0 (H_1)	p=0.004 (H_1)	p≈0 (H_1*)	p=0.026 (H_1*)		
JAC	p≈0 (H_1)	p≈0 (H_1)	p≈0 (H_1)	p≈0 (H_1*)	p≈0 (H_1)	p≈0 (H_1)	p≈0 (H_1*)	p≈0 (H_1)	p=0.005 (H_1)	p≈0 (H_1*)	p=0.028 (H_1*)	p=0.821 (H_0)	

Figure 7 Accepted hypothesis and p-values of statistical tests for each pair of functions.

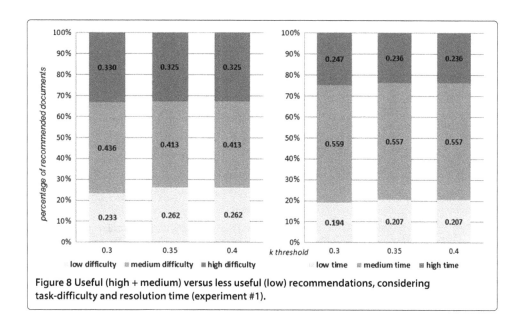

Figure 8 Useful (high + medium) versus less useful (low) recommendations, considering task-difficulty and resolution time (experiment #1).

5.2 Experiment #2: Clemson transit assistance system

This experiment was designed in a similar manner to the first experiment, but had a few differences. The participants were only 10 graduate students (who also were taking a Software Architecture post-graduate course at UNICEN University). As regard the materials, we used a different SAD hosted on DokuWiki, which materialized a solution for a model problem: the Clemson Transit Assistance System (CTAS)[i]. As this SAD was also open to improvements/suggestions, the students were asked to perform an ATAM-based evaluation activity. The matrix of real users' interests was computed similarly as in experiment #1. Despite the differences above, we were careful while designing the experiment #2 so as to make the results of both experiments comparable. According to Figure 2, we changed the following inputs of our approach: the interest indicators (different subjects browsing the Wiki), the SAD textual contents (we used a new SAD), and the semantic annotations. Actually, only those annotations related to problem-specific aspects of the new SAD were modified. The experimental procedure of experiment #2 was executed exactly in the same way as in experiment #1.

5.2.1 Relevance of interest indicators

An Information Gain analysis was performed with the Wiki-usage data from the new group of subjects. In this case, a dataset of $\simeq$ 300 samples was built. In particular, the IG values were the following: $IG_{visits} = 1$, $IG_{time} = 0.87$, $IG_{scroll\,time} = 0.72$. We notice that the same 3 interest indicators that showed the highest scores in experiment #1, were also the highest ones in this second experiment, although with some variations in IG_{time},and $IG_{scroll\,time}$. Like in experiment #1, we selected the number of visits as the main interest indicator for the NLP pipeline.

5.2.2 Performance of the recommender system (experiment #2)

The results of precision, recall and F-measure, derived from the matrix of users' interests are summarized in Figure 9. Similarly to experiment #1, we show a comparison across the candidate similarity functions. In this experiment, the *Cosine* function obtained the best

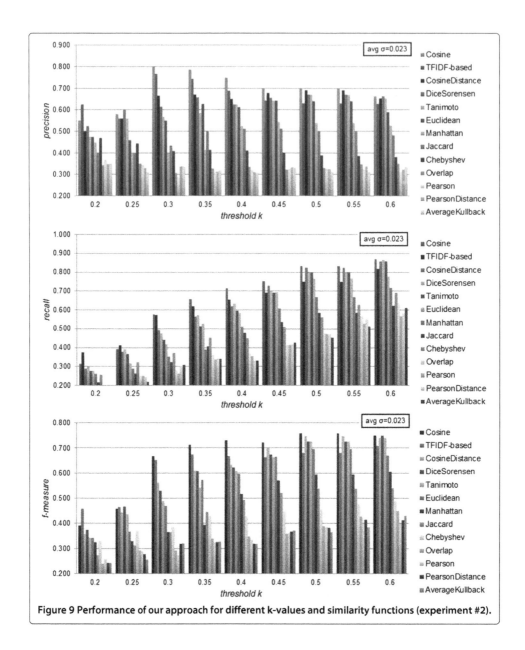

Figure 9 Performance of our approach for different k-values and similarity functions (experiment #2).

performance reaching an F-measure of $[0.73; 0.76]$ for $k = [0.4; 0.6]$, with a precision of $[0.70; 0.75]$ and a recall of $[0.75; 0.83]$. This performance was higher than the one obtained in experiment #1. Another interesting result is that the *TFIDF-based* function performed slightly better than in the previous experiment, with a F-measure of $[0.66; 0.68]$ for $k = [0.3; 0.4]$, reaching a precision of $[0.74; 0.76]$ and a recall of $[0.66; 0.7]$.

When comparing the performance results of both experiments, we observe that, in general, the overall performance of our approach does not significantly differ using a different set of inputs. This situation can be seen in Table 1, which shows the ranking of similarity functions for both experiments, using an average of F-measure (the standard deviation was ≈ 0.03). Although both rankings present several similarities, we may notice that the exact same ranking could not be verified. For instance, *Tanimoto* function moved from the first to the fifth place, whereas the *TFIDF-based* function (proposed by us) moved from the fifth to the second place.

Table 1 Rankings of performance (average F-measure) for the 13 similarity functions

Ranking for experiment #1	Ranking for experiment #2
Tanimoto (TAN)	**Cosine (COS)**
CosineDistance (COSD)	**TFIDF-based (TFIDF)**
Cosine (COS)	**CosineDistance (COSD)**
DiceSorensen (DICS)	**DiceSorensen (DICS)**
TFIDF-based (TFIDF)	**Tanimoto (TAN)**
Euclidean (EUC)	**Euclidean (EUC)**
Manhattan (MAN)	Manhattan (MAN)
Chebyshev (CHE)	Jaccard (JAC)
Overlap (OVE)	Chebyshev (CHE)
Pearson (PEA)	Overlap (OVE)
PearsonDistance (PEAD)	PearsonDistance (PEAD)
AverageKullback (KUL)	Pearson (PEA)
Jaccard (JAC)	AverageKullback (KUL)

We identified a subset of 6 out of 13 functions that exhibited twice a noticeably better performance than the rest (these 6 functions are highlighted in the table). This observation might indicate that certain functions are best suited to solve the profile similarity problem in our domain of study. Furthermore, we were able to confirm the statistical results of Section 5.1.3. However, only 2 of the functions with good performance could be verified, namely *Cosine* and *CosineDistance*. The *Tanimoto* function actually showed a considerably lower performance in experiment #2.

5.2.3   Usefulness of the recommendations (experiment #2)

Figure 10 presents results of the quality of recommendations of *Cosine* function for the range of best *k* values [0.4, 0.6]. We can appreciate that in average 72% of the recommendations targeted high or medium difficulty tasks, and that an average of 73% of recommendations targeted tasks requiring high or medium resolution time. These results are consistent with the ones of experiment #1, although the percentages of good-quality recommendations are slightly lower. However these minor differences might be explained

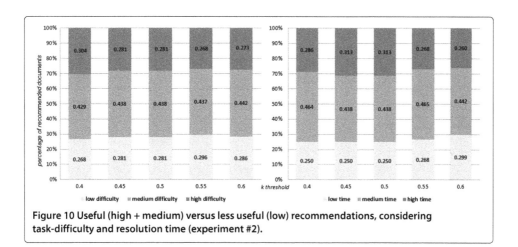

Figure 10 Useful (high + medium) versus less useful (low) recommendations, considering task-difficulty and resolution time (experiment #2).

by the judgment used by test subjects to classify questionnaire items regarding their difficulty. Also, the required time might differ according to the subjects' skills on architecture evaluation.

6 Discussion

From the analysis of the experiments above, we consider that our approach exhibited a good performance. For the Electronic Vote System (experiment #1), the best performances were obtained for values of k in the range $[0.3, 0.4]$ by the *Tanimoto* function with a F-measure of 0.66. The precision was 0.67, meaning that 67% of the recommendable documents were actually relevant to the users. The recall was 0.65, meaning that 65% of the documents actually relevant were effectively classified as relevant.

The second experiment (CTAS architecture) allowed us to verify the trends of the performance values measured in experiment #1. In fact, our pipeline performed even better than in the first experiment. For instance, the *Cosine* function achieved an F-measure of $[0.73; 0.76]$ for $k = [0.4; 0.6]$. We noticed that the highest performance was reached for higher k-values in experiment #2 with respect to the experiment #1. We lately associated this observation with the fact that the test subjects indicated a higher percentage of actually relevant documents in the experiment #2. The criterion for choosing k can not be generalized and depends on problem-specific settings.

For each experiment, we built a ranking that compared the 13 similarity functions based on their average performance. A statistical analysis allowed us to select 2 good-performance functions (*Cosine* and *CosineDistance*) with a confidence of 95%.

The results were also encouraging in terms of its potential for assisting stakeholders to deal with the information overload problem, since the recommended sections (in our experiments) were generally associated to difficult and time-consuming tasks. Anyway, a more rigorous evaluation on both usefulness of recommendations should be addressed in future experiments.

The results of this study, although preliminary, have important implications in the field of Software Architecture Documentation. First, our proposed approach was successfully evaluated with 2 experiments involving SAD users. To the best of our knowledge, there are not other similar approaches that had been empirically evaluated. Second, we proposed 2 alternative similarity functions to the function proposed in our previous work (Nicoletti et al. 2013b). These alternative functions have shown (statistically) higher performances values than the ones observed in previous results.

6.1 Threats to validity

We carefully designed the experiments in order to recreate a real software development scenario. However, there are still some threats to validity that should be considered (Wohlin et al. 2012).

6.1.1 Construct validity

To measure the time spent to solve each questionnaire item we let the subjects inform an approximate value, instead of recording the actual time between assignments. Although the categorical scale is a good approximation of resolution time, there are certainly more precise alternatives. The reason for our decision was that the experiments were not designed as a "quiet room"[j]. A resolution procedure based on a quiet room would differ from a real scenario, in which stakeholders performs several concurrent tasks. Also, executing the experiments in a quiet room style would have made it impractical to obtain a significant sample of data.

Test subjects were not aware of the experimental objectives. Therefore, we minimized the chance that they had behaved in any particular way that may had biased the results.

6.1.2 Internal validity

Both SADs (e-Vote and CTAS) and the question sets were not part of the actual "working context" (e.g., artifacts, project tasks) of the subjects, so the values reported for task-difficulty and resolution-time might be affected by this condition. We also should note that the evaluation of SADs is not a common case in many architecture-centric developments, although some experiences have been reported as part of ATAM evaluations with checklists (Nord et al. 2009). Furthermore, we argue that the activity of evaluating a SAD is not very different from that of searching through the SAD during normal development activities, so the threat effect is reduced.

Another threat is the possible bias caused by some subjects having prior knowledge of the software architectures (documented by the SADs) or having performed this kind of practical assignment before. We were careful when selecting the subjects to check that they had neither participated in similar activities nor worked with the SADs before.

The Wiki pages browsed by the subjects and the V&B stakeholder types provide an approximation to the user profiles, but they are not the only information sources at work. Inter-personal conversations, questionnaires or interactions with other artifacts/tools (not covered by our approach) can reveal additional information about the interests of a user. We are planning to explore new information sources in future studies.

6.1.3 External validity

We are aware of the fact that an experiment with students in an academic environment might not be the same as an industrial context with seasoned software practitioners. Therefore, we cannot generalize the results of our study to an industrial scenario. To mitigate this threat, we designed our experimental environment to be as realistic as possible. First, the architecture documentation was representative of real-life SADs. Second, the test subjects were not tested in a "quiet room" style (as mentioned above). On the contrary, the subjects were free to solve the questionnaires at the university or at their homes, even working in groups. We believe this latter scenario is the closest one to a real development environment. In addition, most students were actually software practitioners working for local industries with 1-3 years of experience.

6.1.4 Conclusion validity

In contrast with external validity, the use of graduate and undergraduate students instead of industry practitioners allowed us to obtain a good sample (87 subjects) to support the validity of the results. Indeed, it would have been harder to gather a similar number of industry professionals with the time availability required by the experiments. As a downside, the level of heterogeneity of the test groups was low, since most subjects shared similar levels of knowledge and technical background. This situation reduced threats to conclusion validity, but it trades off with external validity.

7 Conclusions and future work

In this work, we have proposed an approach for discovering stakeholders' interests in a Wiki-based SAD that relies on user modeling and NLP techniques. We capture the stakeholders' interests in user profiles, and then look for SAD documents whose contents match those profiles. All the SAD documents are preprocessed in advance by an NLP pipeline. In this context, our tool can recommend specific SAD documents for each stakeholder. The ultimate goal is to improve the stakeholders' access to relevant architectural information, and thus, make the SAD a more effective artifact for communicating architectural concerns. A preliminary evaluation with simulated recommendations has shown the potential of our approach. Also, we empirically identified 2 (out of 13) candidate similarity functions that achieved good performance, with a F-measure value around 0.73, and precision values of 0.7 and recall of 0.75 (depending on the k threshold used). Nonetheless, experiments with other SADs and sets of stakeholders are required in order to validate these claims.

This research opens several lines of future work. In addition to the browsing activity of users, another source for inferring interests are the interactions between users (e.g., chats rooms, instant messaging systems, or voice over IP). In the short term, we will add a chat mechanism to the Wiki infrastructure, so as to monitor user conversations with respect to the SAD and apply our NLP pipeline on these conversations. The mined information will be incorporated to the user profiles.

Managing architectural knowledge in a software project involves both production and consumption of SAD contents. However, as the amount of documentation increases (and also its production costs), its value for the stakeholders tends to decrease. We believe that our approach can help to deal with the production-side of the process, i.e., the ways in which a documenter writes (or updates) SAD documents. Based on the user profiles, the documenter could document "just enough" of the SAD, by prioritizing those documents that maximize the stakeholders' overall satisfaction. In fact, we have recently developed a prototype tool (Diaz-Pace et al. 2013) to assist the documenter in this activity, although yet without user profiles. Finally, as a long-term goal, we want to investigate the pros and cons of personalization techniques when applied to other types of documents within an architecture-centric development process (e.g., technical manuals, requirements specifications, or API documentation).

Endnotes

[a] The terms user and stakeholder are considered synonyms.

[b] The DokuWiki project official Website might be found at: http://www.dokuwiki.org/.

[c] A Wiki-based SAD example provided by the SEI (Pittsburgh, EEUU) might be found at: http://wiki.sei.cmu.edu/sad.

[d] The OpenNLP official Website might be found at: http://opennlp.apache.org/.

[e] The Porter's Stemming algorithm official Website might be found at: http://snowball.tartarus.org/.

[f] We acknowledge that the experiments are in compliance with the Helsinki Declaration and were approved by the Professors responsible for the involved academic courses. The participants were neither negatively affected nor harmed in any way during the execution of the experiments.

[g] Examples of V&B templates might be found at: http://wiki.sei.cmu.edu/sad.

[h] More information about the resources used in our experiments can be found at the following article Website: http://mnicoletti.sites.exa.unicen.edu.ar/jserd2013.

[i] A reference document that describes the CTAS might be found at: http://people.cs. clemson.edu/~johnmc/courses/cpsc875/resources/Telematics.pdf.

[j] A quiet room is a term referring to a place used for experimentation with human subjects in which there are no distractions that may bias the results of tests.

Competing interests
The authors declare that they have no competing interests.

Acknowledgements
This work was partially supported by ANPCyT (Argentina) through PICT Project 2011 No. 0366 and PICT Project 2010 No. 2247, and also by CONICET (Argentina) through PIP Project No. 112-201101-00078. The authors would like to thank to the reviewers for their valuable feedback to improve the quality of this manuscript.

References
Al halabi WS, Kubat M, Tapia M (2007) Time spent on a web page is sufficient to infer a user's interest. In: Proceedings of the IASTED European Conference: Internet and Multimedia Systems and Applications (IMSA IASTED). ACTA Press, Anaheim, CA, USA, pp 41–46

Baeza-Yates R, Ribeiro-Neto B (2011) Modern Information Retrieval: The Concepts and Technology Behind Search. 2nd edn. Addison-Wesley Professional, Boston, USA

Bass L, Clements P, Kazman R (2012) Software Architecture in Practice. 3rd edn. Addison-Wesley Professional, Boston, USA

Castro-Herrera C, Cleland-Huang J, Mobasher B (2009) Enhancing stakeholder profiles to improve recommendations in online requirements elicitation. In: 17th IEEE International Requirements Engineering Conference (RE), Atlanta, USA, pp 37–46

Claypool M, Le P, Wased M, Brown D (2001) Implicit interest indicators In: Proceedings of the 6th International Conference on Intelligent User Interfaces (ICIUI). IUI '01. ACM, New York, NY, USA, pp 33–40

Clements P, Bachmann F, Bass L, Garlan D, Ivers J, Little R, Nord R, Stafford J (2003) A practical method for documenting software architectures. In: Proceedings of the International Conference on Software Engineering (ICSE). Portland, USA

Clements P, Bachmann F, Bass L, Garlan D, Ivers J, Little R, Merson P, Nord R, Stafford J (2010) Documenting Software Architectures: Views and Beyond (2nd Edition). 2nd edn. Addison-Wesley Professional, Boston, USA

de Boer RC, van Vliet H (2008) Architectural knowledge discovery with latent semantic analysis: Constructing a reading guide for software product audits. J Syst Softw 81(9):1456–1469

de Graaf KA, Tang A, Liang P, van Vliet H (2012) Ontology-based software architecture documentation In: Proceedings of Joint Working Conference on Software Architecture & 6th European Conference on Software Architecture (WICSA/ECSA). WICSA 2012. IEEE Computer Society, Helsinki, Finland, pp 315–319

Deza E, Deza M (2006) Dictionary of Distances. North-Holland Elsevier, Amsterdam, Netherlands

Deza MM, Deza E (2009) Encyclopedia of Distances. Springer, New York, USA

Dice LR (1945) Measures of the amount of ecologic association between species. Ecology 26(3):297–302

Diaz-Pace JA, Nicoletti M, Schiaffino S, Villavicencio C, Sanchez L (2013) A stakeholder-centric optimization strategy for architectural documentation. In: Cuzzocrea A, Maabout S. (eds.) Model and Data Engineering. Lecture Notes in Computer Science, Springer, New York, USA, pp 104–117

Farenhorst R, van Vliet H (2008) Experiences with a wiki to support architectural knowledge sharing. In: Proceedings of the 3rd Workshop on Wikis for Software Engineering (Wiki4SE), Porto, Portugal

Goossen F, IJntema W, Frasincar F, Hogenboom F, Kaymak U (2011) News personalization using the cf-idf semantic recommender. In: Proceedings of the International Conference on Web Intelligence, Mining and Semantics (ICWIMS). WIMS '11. ACM, New York, NY, USA, pp 10–11012

Huang A (2008) Similarity measures for text document clustering. In: Proceedings of the 6th New Zealand Computer Science Research Student Conference (NZCSRSC2008). Christchurch, New Zealand, pp 49–56

ISO/IEC/IEEE (2011) ISO/IEC/IEEE 42010: Systems and Software Engineering - Architecture Description. ISO/IEC/IEEE. International Organization for Standardization, number: 42010. http://www.iso-architecture.org/.

Koning H, Vliet HV (2006) Real-life it architecture design reports and their relation to ieee std 1471 stakeholders and concerns. Automated Softw Eng 13:201–223

Jansen A, Avgeriou P, van der Ven JS (2009) Enriching software architecture documentation. J Syst Softw 82(8):1232–1248. SI: Architectural Decisions and Rationale

Liu B (2011) Web Data Mining: Exploring Hyperlinks, Contents and Usage Data. 2nd edn. Data-Centric Systems and Applications. Springer, New York, USA

Mitchell T (1997) Machine Learning, 1st edn. McGraw-Hill Science/Engineering/Math, New York, USA

Mitchell RK, Agle BR, Wood DJ (1997) Toward a theory of stakeholder identification and salience: Defining the principle of who and what really counts. Acad Manag Rev 22:853

Nicoletti M, Diaz-Pace JA, Schiaffino S (2012) Towards software architecture documents matching stakeholders interests. In: Cipolla-Ficarra F, Veltman K, Verber D, Cipolla-Ficarra M, Kammuller F (eds.) Advances in New Technologies, Interactive Interfaces and Communicability. Lecture Notes in Computer Science. Springer, New York, USA, pp 176–185

Nicoletti M, Schiaffino S, Godoy D (2013a) Mining interests for user profiling in electronic conversations. Expert Syst Appl 40(2):638–645

Nicoletti M, Diaz-Pace JA, Schiaffino S (2013b) Discovering stakeholders' interests in wiki-based architectural documentation. In: Diego Vallespir MdOB (ed.) Proceedings of CIbSE 2013 (former IDEAS). XVI Ibero-American

Conference on Software Engineering, Montevideo, Uruguay. Universidad ORT Uruguay, Universidad de la Republica, Antel, pp 5–18

Nord RL, Clements PC, Emery DE, Hilliard R (2009) Reviewing architecture documents using question sets In: Proceedings of Joint Working IEEE/IFIP Conference on Software Architecture & European Conference on Software Architecture (WICSA/ECSA). IEEE, Cambridge, UK, pp 325–328

Rajaraman A, Ullman JD (2012) Mining of Massive Datasets. Cambridge University Press, Cambridge

Schiaffino S, Amandi A (2009) Intelligent user profiling. In: Bramer M (ed.) Artificial Intelligence: An International Perspective. Lecture Notes in Computer Science. Springer, New York, USA, pp 193–216

Su MT (2010) Capturing exploration to improve software architecture documentation. In: Proceedings of the 4th European Conference on Software Architecture (ECSA). ECSA '10. ACM, New York, NY, USA, pp 17–21

Su MT, Hosking J, Grundy J (2011) Capturing architecture documentation navigation trails for content chunking and sharing. In: 2011 9th Working IEEE/IFIP Conference on Software Architecture (WICSA), Boulder, USA, pp 256–259

Sørensen T (1948) A method of establishing groups of equal amplitude in plant sociology based on similarity of species and its application to analyses of the vegetation on danish commons. Biol Skr 5:1–34

Unphon H, Dittrich Y (2010) Software architecture awareness in long-term software product evolution. J Syst Softw 83(11):2211–2226

Wohlin C, Runeson P, Höst M, Ohlsson M, Regnell B (2012) Experimentation in Software Engineering, Vol. 978-3-642-29043-5. Springer, New York, USA

5

Assessing the benefits of search-based approaches when designing self-adaptive systems: a controlled experiment

Sandro S Andrade[1,2]*[†] and Raimundo J de A Macêdo[1][†]

*Correspondence: sandros@ufba.br
[†]Equal contributors
[1]Distributed Systems Laboratory (LaSiD), Federal University of Bahia (UFBa), Institute of Mathematics, Department of Computer Science, Av Adhemar de Barros, s/n, Ondina, 40.170-110 Salvador-BA, Brazil
[2]GSORT Distributed Systems Group, Federal Institute of Education, Science, and Technology of Bahia (IFBa), Department of Computer Science, Av. Araújo Pinho, 39, Canela, 40.110-150 Salvador-BA, Brazil

Abstract

Background: The well-orchestrated use of distilled experience, domain-specific knowledge, and well-informed trade-off decisions is imperative if we are to design effective architectures for complex software-intensive systems. In particular, designing modern self-adaptive systems requires intricate decision-making over a remarkably complex problem space and a vast array of solution mechanisms. Nowadays, a large number of approaches tackle the issue of endowing software systems with self-adaptive behavior from different perspectives and under diverse assumptions, making it harder for architects to make judicious decisions about design alternatives and quality attributes trade-offs. It has currently been claimed that search-based software design approaches may improve the quality of resulting artifacts and the productivity of design processes, as a consequence of promoting a more comprehensive and systematic representation of design knowledge and preventing design bias and false intuition. To the best of our knowledge, no empirical studies have been performed to provide sound evidence of such claim in the self-adaptive systems domain.

Methods: This paper reports the results of a quasi-experiment performed with 24 students of a graduate program in Distributed and Ubiquitous Computing. The experiment evaluated the design of self-adaptive systems using a search-based approach proposed by us, in contrast to the use of a non-automated approach based on architectural styles catalogs. The goal was to investigate to which extent the adoption of search-based design approaches impacts on the effectiveness and complexity of resulting architectures. In addition, we also analyzed the approach's potential for leveraging the acquisition of distilled design knowledge.

Results: Our findings show that search-based approaches can improve the effectiveness of resulting self-adaptive systems architectures and reduce their design complexity. We found no evidence regarding the approach's potential for leveraging the acquisition of distilled design knowledge by novice software architects.

Conclusion: This study contributes to reveal empirical evidence on the benefits of search-based approaches when designing self-adaptive systems architectures. The results presented herein increase our belief that the systematic representation of distilled design knowledge and the adoption of search-based design approaches indeed lead to improved architectures.

Keywords: Self-adaptive systems; Software architecture; Software modeling; Search-based software engineering; Empirical software engineering

1 Background

Modern software-intensive systems are becoming increasingly complex and the fulfillment of requirements for performance, flexibility, dependability, and energy-efficiency in uncertain and dynamic environments is still a quite challenging task (Huebscher and McCann 2008). Elastic data storage services, energy-aware mobile systems, self-tuning databases, and reconfigurable network services are some of the application domains in which self-adaptive mechanisms play a paramount role (Patikirikorala et al. 2012). Such scenarios are usually characterized by incomplete knowledge about user requirements, workloads, and available resources. As a consequence, committing to a particular solution in design time may yield suboptimal architectures, which easily degrade the service when conditions deviate from those previously defined. Establishing the foundations that enable the systematic design, development, and evolution of systems with self-management capabilities has been the focus of many research efforts in areas such as self-adaptive systems, autonomic computing, and artificial intelligence (Salehie and Tahvildari 2009).

A self-adaptive (SA) system continuously monitor its own behavior and its operating environment, adapting itself whenever current conditions prevent it from delivering the expected quality of service (Salehie and Tahvildari 2009). SA systems usually comprise two parts: a managed element and a managing element (Huebscher and McCann 2008). The managed element provides functional services to the user, operating in a potentially dynamic and uncertain environment. The managing system is responsible for adapting the managed element, mostly by using a particular implementation of an adaptation loop. The MAPE-K approach (Kephart and Chess 2003) is a widely accepted reference architecture for adaptation loops. It defines the basic components for the loop's tasks of **M**onitoring, **A**nalyzing, **P**lanning, and **E**xecuting; performed with the support of a **K**nowledge Base.

The many approaches for self-adaptation available nowadays employ different mechanisms for the aforementioned tasks. Reflexive middleware platforms (Ogel et al. 2003), graph grammars (Bruni et al. 2008), intelligent agents (Benyon and Murray 1993), policy-based approaches (Georgas and Taylor 2008), self-organizing structures (Georgiadis et al. 2002), and control theory (Tilbury et al. 2004) are some of the currently adopted underpinnings for enabling self-adaptation. Becoming familiar with the most prominent modeling dimensions for SA systems is crucial for specifying relevant adaptation requirements; making unbiased and well-informed decisions about alternative architectures; and accurately evaluating the resulting system's quality attributes.

Although some previous work have already tackled this issue (Andersson et al. 2009; Brun et al. 2009; de Lemos et al. 2010; Patikirikorala et al. 2012), representing such dimensions by using ill-structured notations – such as natural language, ad-hoc architectural styles catalogs, and informally depicted reference architectures – makes it harder and time-consuming for novice architects to grasp the architectural tactics that lead to particular adaptation quality attributes. As a consequence, effective subtle architectures for an adaptation problem at hand may not be considered because of design bias, limited knowledge about the solution domain, or time constraints. Furthermore, the lack of flexible, expressive, and automated mechanisms for performing the usual decide-design-evaluate cycles hampers the eliciting of relevant insights about quality attributes trade-offs.

Over the past twelve years, Search-Based Software Engineering (SBSE) (Harman et al. 2012) has provided promising approaches for tackling the aforementioned issues in areas such as requirements engineering, design, testing, and refactoring, just to mention a few. SBSE claims that the majority of issues in such areas are indeed optimization questions and that the software's virtual nature is inherently well suited for search-based optimization (Harman 2010). In particular, substantial work towards search-based software design (Räihä 2010) advocates the benefits of SBSE in finding out subtle effective designs and providing well-informed means to reveal quality attributes trade-offs.

To the best of our knowledge, the first effort in applying search-based approaches to the design of SA systems is that proposed by us in (Andrade and de Araújo Macêdo 2013a,b). In such work, we provide a meta-modeling infrastructure for defining domain-specific design spaces which systematically capture the domain's prominent design dimensions, their associated variation points (alternative solutions), and the architectural changes required to implement each solution. The goal is to support the automated redesign of an initial model, endowing it with additional capabilities from the application domain at hand. Each domain-specific design space entails a set of quality metrics that evaluate each candidate architecture regarding different attributes. We have been using such an approach to enable the automated design of managing elements for initial (non-adaptive) systems such as web servers and MapReduce distributed architectures (Dean and Ghemawat 2008). Since even small input models usually span huge design spaces, we also provide a domain-independent multi-objective optimization engine. Such engine currently relies on the NSGA-II (Non-dominated Sorting Genetic Algorithm II) algorithm (Deb et al. 2002) to find out a set of Pareto-optimal (Deb and Kalyanmoy 2001) candidate architectures. All these solutions represent optimal architectures, differing only in which quality metric they favor.

In (Andrade and de Araújo Macêdom 2014), we report the results of a quasi-experiment which investigated the benefits of search-based approaches when designing SA systems architectures. In this paper, we extend such a report by providing a more accurate description of involved treatments, analysis of resulting data, and threats to validity. The study was performed with 24 students of a graduate program in Distributed and Ubiquitous Computing and evaluated the design of SA systems using our search-based approach, in contrast to using a style-based non-automated approach. The experiment aimed at evaluating the impact of the adopted design method on three dependent variables: the effectiveness and complexity of resulting architectures, as well as the method's potential for leveraging the acquisition of distilled design knowledge by novice architects. All the material used in the experiment is available at http://wiki.ifba.edu.br/tr-ce012014.

The remainder of this paper is organized as follows. Section 2 presents the foundations of SA systems and feedback control. Section 3 describes the automated software architecture design approach proposed by us and adopted as one of the experiment treatments. Section 4 presents an overview of the experiment. Section 5 explains the experiment objects, the hypotheses being investigated, the adopted measurement approach, and the experiment design. In Section 6, we analyze and discuss the experiment results. Threats to validity are identified in Section 7 and related work is discussed in Section 8. Finally, conclusions and venues for future work are presented in Section 9.

2 Self-adaptive systems and feedback control

A SA system is defined in (DARPA 1997) as "a software that evaluates its own behavior and changes behavior when the evaluation indicates that it is not accomplishing what the software is intended to do, or when better functionality or performance is possible". We adopt a slightly broader perspective by defining a SA system as a system which presents some on-line infrastructure which allows moving a specific development process stage (e.g.: design, implementation, or deployment) – usually undertaken off-line – to runtime. Such definition entails from simple adaptive algorithms to more sophisticated solutions such as self-optimization by automated redeployment (Malek et al. 2010) and self-organization enabled by dynamic architectures (Parunak and Brueckner 2011). Feedback control is a well-established technology for handling dynamic electromechanical systems in areas such as avionics, chemical processes, and factory automation. Under such perspective, the use of feedback control considering software applications as the system under control (Tilbury et al. 2004) is still on its early days, albeit the large number of recent work towards this topic (Patikirikorala et al. 2012).

Figure 1 presents the common elements of a feedback control system. The *target system* is a software system with a *system output* – $y(t)$ – which represents the quality attribute (e.g.: average service response time or CPU utilization) intended to be controlled. Such attribute is directly influenced by a *system input* signal – $v(t)$, which manipulates, for instance, buffer sizes or the number of threads in a pool. The goal is to retain the system output as close as possible to a *reference input*, which represents the desired service level specified by the administrator. Uncertainties in the operating environment (e.g.: changing workloads or hardware failures) introduce a *disturbance input* signal – $d(t)$ – which makes it harder to derive accurate models for system input-output relationships. *Noise input* signals – $n(t)$ – produced by sensors with high stochastic sensitivity may further complicate the control goals. Dealing with unmodeled and unforeseen disturbances and noises has motivated the idea where the *measured output* – $m(t)=y(t)+n(t)$ – is fed back to the controller. By calculating how much the measured output deviates from the reference input (*control error* – $e(t)$), the feedback controller makes use of some specific control law to decide about the *control input* signal – $u(t)$ – to be applied in the target system. A transducer is commonly used in cases demanding unit conversion and/or delay handling.

It is worth mentioning that, in contrast to frameworks for steady-state analysis such as queue theory, control theory provides the means to design controllers that systematically exhibit particular behavior for both steady-state and transient responses. That allows for characterizing the resulting system (controller + target system) in terms of the so-called SASO properties (Tilbury et al. 2004): **S**tability, **A**ccuracy, **S**ettling time, and **O**vershoot.

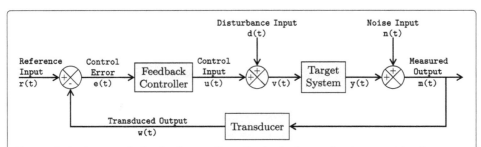

Figure 1 Basic elements of a feedback control loop. The feedback controller aims at retaining the target system's output $y(t)$ as close as possible to the reference input $r(t)$, irrespective of the presence of unforeseen disturbance and noise signals.

Among several definitions of stability available today (Slotine and Li 1991), one widely used in feedback control is that of BIBO-stability (Hayes 2011). A system is BIBO-stable if for any bounded input signal $v(t)$ the output $y(t)$ is bounded.

Being the resulting system stable, the remaining SASO properties can be investigated. As depicted in Figure 2a, the smaller the steady-state error e_{ss} (difference between the reference input and measured output), the more accurate is the resulting system. The settling time K_s is the time elapsed from the change in input to when the measured output is within some variation range (usually 2%) of its steady-state value. Finally, the maximum overshoot M_p is the normalized maximum amount by which the system output exceeds its steady-state value.

The systematic design of control architectures which exhibit intentionally chosen values of accuracy, settling time and overshoot is imperative if we are to conceive effective self-adaptive systems. Disregarding such an aspect may lead to over/under provisioning of resources (due to inaccurate convergence), violations of service level agreements (due to slower responses), or excessive use of resources during transient response as a consequence of large overshoots. Figure 2b depicts the step response (dynamics exhibited by the target system when the reference input changes from 0 to 1) for systems with different controllers. The controller 3 presents an ideal response, with no overshoot, high accuracy, and small settling time.

A large body of knowledge regarding control laws and methods for designing controllers is currently available (Patikirikorala et al. 2012). Currently adopted control-theoretic approaches for endowing systems with self-adaptation capabilities include the use of PID control, state-space models, MIMO (Multiple-Input Multiple-Output) control, gain scheduling, self-tuning regulators, fluid flow analysis, and fuzzy control (Tilbury et al. 2004). As a consequence, designing effective architectures for SA systems requires architects become familiar with the intricacies of both the problem space (so that accurate and realistic self-adaptation requirements can be elicited) and solution space (in order to adopt the most effective adaptation strategy/mechanism for the problem at hand). That involves deciding on self-adaptation goals; system and environment monitoring mechanisms; measurement noises and uncertainties; unanticipated/unforeseen adaptations; diverse control robustness degrees; change enacting mechanisms; and adaptation

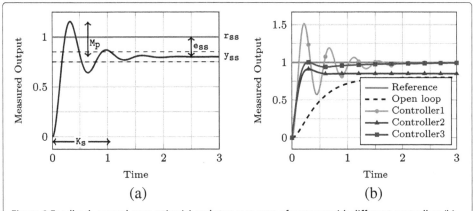

Figure 2 Feedback control properties (a) and step response of systems with different controllers (b). Properties such as settling time (K_s), steady-state error (e_{ss}), and overshoot (M_p) are commonly affected by the control law and tuning techniques chosen for the feedback controller managing the target system.

temporal predictability, just to mention a few (Andersson et al. 2009; Brun et al. 2009; Patikirikorala et al. 2012).

3 Searching for effective self-adaptive systems architectures

A number of efforts from the software engineering for SA systems community (de Lemos et al. 2010) have addressed the issue of providing principled engineering approaches for such an application domain, leveraging the systematic capture of design knowledge and enabling the early reasoning of self-adaptation quality attributes. In previous work (Andrade and de Araújo Macêdo 2013a,b), we presented an infrastructure for systematically representing distilled architecture design knowledge for a given application domain (design space), along with a domain-independent architecture optimization engine as the underlying mechanism for explicitly eliciting design trade-offs (conflicting quality attributes). Such an infrastructure, depicted in Figure 3, provides the underpinnings of our search-based approach for designing self-adaptive systems architectures. The ultimate goal is to support the automatic extension of an initial UML (Unified Modeling Language) model – describing the managed element – with new architectural elements (which implements the managing system), searching for those solutions that exhibit desired control properties.

A concrete design space and its quality attributes are specified by experts once per n domain (*design space inception* stage) by using a modeling language – namely DuSE – we have designed for such a purpose. A supporting UML profile is also defined for that domain, enabling the annotations that drive the automated design process. A *design space* (e.g.: for networked and concurrent systems) is defined as a set of *n design dimensions*

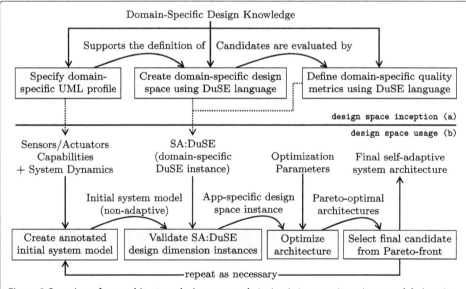

Figure 3 Overview of our architecture design approach. In the *design space inception* stage **(a)**, domain experts use the DuSE's constructs for specifying a domain-specific design space (degrees of freedom, their corresponding alternative solutions, and the architecture extensions required to implement each solution). Henceforth – in the *design space usage* stage **(b)** – architects submit initial models to the optimization engine, which searches for those (near-)optimal extensions revealing design trade-offs. A particular design space instance – SA:DuSE – enables the use of such an infrastructure in the self-adaptive systems domain.

representing specific design concerns in such a domain (e.g.: concurrency strategy and event dispatching model).

Definition 1. *A **design space** is a tuple ds=⟨DD, QM, P⟩, where DD is a non-empty totally ordered set of design dimensions, QM is a non-empty totally ordered set of quality metrics, and P is the accompanying UML profile for such an design space.*

Each design dimension entails a set of *variation points*, representing alternative solutions for such a concern (e.g.: leader-followers or half-sync/half-async; for the concurrency strategy dimension).

Definition 2. *A **design dimension** is a tuple dd=⟨VP, targetElementsExp⟩, where VP is a non-empty totally ordered set of variation points and targetElementsExp is an OCL (Object Constraint Language) expression which returns – when evaluated on an initial UML architectural model M – the elements of M that demand a decision about the architectural concern represented by dd. Such elements are named **target elements** of dd with respect to M and denoted by targetElements(dd, M).*

The *targetElementsExp* expression relies on the associated UML profile's annotations to detect, in the initial model, the architectural *loci* that demand decisions about such concern. For instance, an initial model may require the choice of particular control strategies for two different service components. Therefore, two instances of the control strategy design dimension are created to capture the decisions for those architectural *loci*.

Definition 3. *A **design dimension instance** is a tuple ddi=⟨M, dd, te⟩, where M is an initial UML architectural model, dd is a design dimension, and te is a target element of dd with respect to M.*

A variation point describes the elements (architectural extensions) that must be added to the initial model in order to implement such particular solution.

Definition 4. *A **variation point** is a tuple vp=⟨C, postConditionExp⟩, where C is a totally ordered set of architectural changes and postConditionExp is an OCL expression evaluated after all changes in C are applied in the initial model. Such an expression must return true for valid architectures or false otherwise.*

Definition 5. *An **architectural change** c is a single indivisible operation that, when applied to a model M, results in a model M′ ≠ M. An architectural change c may represent an element addition, element removal or element's property change.*

The set of all design dimension instances generated by *ds*, when evaluated in *M*, provides the underlying infrastructure of our search-based approach for automating the architecture design process.

Definition 6. *An **application specific design space** is a tuple asds=⟨M, ds, DDI⟩, where M is an initial UML architectural model, ds is a design space, and DDI is a partially ordered set of design dimension instances, defined as:*

$$DDI = \bigcup^{dd \in ds.DD} \left(\bigcup^{te \in dd.targetElements(M)} ddi = \langle M, dd, te \rangle \right) \tag{1}$$

The ultimate decision space may then be specified in terms of an application specific design space.

Definition 7. *The **architectural decision space** $\mathcal{D}_{asds}$ for a given application specific design space asds is the Cartesian product of all variation point indexes of design dimensions associated to each design dimension instance in asds.DDI:*

$$\mathcal{D}_{asds} = \{1, 2, \ldots, |asds.DDI_1.dd.VP|\} \times \tag{2}$$
$$\{1, 2, \ldots, |asds.DDI_2.dd.VP|\} \times$$
$$\ldots$$
$$\{1, 2, \ldots, |asds.DDI_{|DDI|}.dd.VP|\}$$

*A vector $\mathbf{x} \in \mathcal{D}_{asds}$ is named **candidate vector**. The architectural model resulting from the valid application of all changes of variation points whose indexes are described in $\mathbf{x}$ is named **candidate architecture**. The subset of $\mathcal{D}_{asds}$ formed only by those candidate vectors resulting in valid architectures is named **architectural feasible space** ($\mathcal{F}_{asds}$).*

Therefore, a candidate architecture (a location in such n-dimensional space) is formed by the initial model extended with the merge of all architectural extensions provided by all involved variation points.

Finally, a quality metric may be defined for a given design space.

Definition 8. *A **quality metric** is a tuple $qm = \langle \Phi, g \rangle$. Φ is a function $\Phi \colon \mathcal{F}_{asds} \to \mathcal{V}$, where $\mathcal{F}_{asds}$ is an architectural feasible space and $\mathcal{V}$ is a set supporting measurements at least in interval scale (Stevens 1946). g must take the value 1 or -1 indicating, respectively, whether the metric should be maximized or minimized. The **architectural objective space** $\mathcal{O}_{asds}$ is defined as the Cartesian product $\mathcal{V}_1 \times \mathcal{V}_2 \times \ldots \times \mathcal{V}_n$, where $\mathcal{V}_i$ is the image of the function Φ_i (evaluation of the i-th metric of asds.ds.QM).*

As a consequence of such an infrastructure, huge design spaces may easily be spawned even for small input models, motivating the adoption of meta-heuristics and multi-objective optimization approaches. The number of different candidate vectors in $\mathcal{D}_{asds}$ (including those resulting in invalid architectures) is given by:

$$\prod_{dd \in ds.DD} |dd.VP|^{|dd.targetElements(M)|} \tag{3}$$

Once a concrete design space is defined, architects can submit initial models to manual design space exploration or rely on the multi-objective optimization engine we provide (*design space usage* stage). The domain-independent optimization engine we provide handles all required steps to forge candidate architectures for a given set of design space locations, evaluate their quality regarding the attributes defined for the design space, and find out a set of Pareto-optimal architectures.

Let $\Phi_{asds.ds.QM}(M_c)$ be the function that evaluate all quality metrics in *asds.ds.QM* with respect to a candidate architecture M_c:

$$\Phi_{QM} : \mathcal{F}_{asds} \to \mathcal{O} \tag{4}$$

$$\Phi_{QM}(M_r) \mapsto (-g_1 \cdot \Phi_1(M_r), -g_2 \cdot \Phi_2(M_r), \ldots, -g_n \cdot \Phi_n(M_r))$$

Let $\mathcal{T} : \mathbf{x}' \to M_c$ be the function that produces the candidate architecture M_c associated to a candidate vector $\mathbf{x}' \in \mathcal{F}_{asds}$. The optimization problem may then be stated as:

$$\overset{\prec}{\min_{\mathbf{x}' \in \mathcal{F}_{asds}}} \Phi_{QM}(\mathcal{T}(\mathbf{x}')) \tag{5}$$

where $\overset{\prec}{\min}$ denote minimization for Pareto optimality (Deb and Kalyanmoy 2001). Further information about the DuSE meta-model and its architecture optimization engine may be found in (Andrade and de Araújo Macêdo 2013a,b).

The aforementioned infrastructure provides the underpinnings of our SA systems design approach. We have specified a particular DuSE instance (SA:DuSE) that captures the most prominent degrees of freedom and quality attributes when designing adaptation loops based on feedback control (Tilbury et al. 2004). Currently, SA:DuSE yields architectural extensions regarding seven different control laws (Tilbury et al. 2004) (Proportional, Integral, Proportional-Integral, Proportional-Derivative, Proportional-Integral-Derivative, Static State Feedback, and Dynamic State Feedback), seven empirical tuning approaches (Wang 2005) (four Chien-Hrones-Reswick variations, Ziegler-Nichols, Cohen-Coon, and Linear Quadratic Regulator), five mechanisms for control adaptation (Landau et al. 2011) (fixed gain, gain scheduling, model-reference, model-identification, and reconfiguring control), and six different multiple loops arrangements (Weyns et al. 2010) (no cooperation, information sharing, coordinated control, regional planning, master/slave, and hierarchical).

In addition, four quality metrics (objective functions) evaluate the resulting architectures regarding the average settling time, average overshoot, control overhead, and control robustness. The first three metrics are intended to be minimized, while the last one is intended to be maximized. It is well-known from studies (Tilbury et al. 2004) in control theory field that settling time and average overshoot represent conflicting control goals (as presented in Figure 2b). The same has been observed for control overhead and control robustness metrics. One of our research goals was to investigate to which extent the proposed SA:DuSE design space captures such trade-offs when automating the design of SA systems architectures (as discussed below). Moreover, the architectural decision space produced by SA:DuSE exhibited 8,643,600 candidate vectors for an input model with two controllable ports. For models with four controllable ports, such number rapidly increases to 7.4711821e13, further motivating the need for effective search-based approaches. Further information about the SA:DuSE design dimensions, its corresponding variation points, and the adopted quality metrics may be found in (Andrade and de Araújo Macêdo 2013a).

Our approach has been fully implemented in a supporting tool named DuSE-MT (http://duse.sf.net), developed using the C++ programming language and the Qt cross-platform toolkit (http://www.qt.io). DuSE-MT is a meta-model agnostic tool we develop in order to support general software modeling activities and, in particular, the automated design process we propose. The NSGA-II evolutionary algorithm (Deb et al. 2002) is currently used as optimization back-end, but other approaches can be easily adopted in the future thanks to the DuSE-MT's plugin-based architecture and the optimization engine's internals we have designed.

Figure 4 depicts the scatter plot matrix for the population of architectures resulting from one optimization run using a web server architecture (presented in Section 5.1) as initial model. The matrix's main diagonal presents – for each quality metric – the histograms of solutions in the Pareto-front and of dominated solutions. The remaining cells present the projection of the final population with respect to the quality metrics indicated at the cell's row and column. For instance, the scatter plot at the first column and second row depicts solutions using average settling time values in the abscissa and average overshoot values in the ordinate. Solutions in the Pareto-front

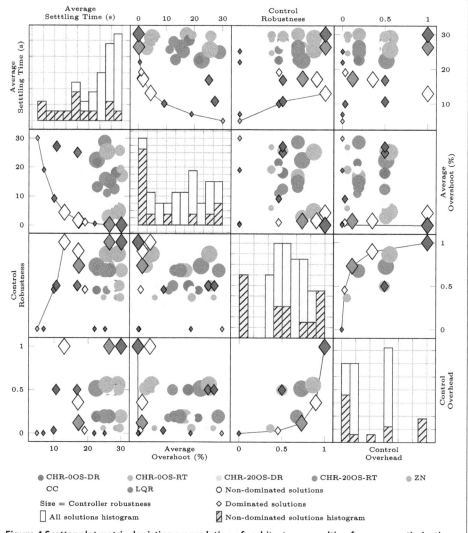

Figure 4 Scatter plot matrix depicting a population of architectures resulting from one optimization run using a web server initial model. The four charts at the matrix's main diagonal present the histograms of solutions in the Pareto-front and of dominated solutions. The remaining cells present the projection of the population for every pair of quality metrics.

are presented as diamonds, while the dominated ones are depicted as circles. A partial Pareto-front – regarding only the two quality metrics involved in a given cell – is shown as diamonds connected by a line. As indicated in the figure's legend, the solution color represents the controller tuning approach adopted by such an architecture. Finally, the solution size denotes the architecture's control robustness (the bigger, the more robust).

The outcome of our approach provides useful insights and supports the self-adaptive systems architect in several aspects. First, we observe that architectures exhibiting short average settling times are quite rare in the final population, making it harder for novice architects to find out such effective solutions by manually scouring the design space or by performing random searches. Second, the outcome reveals pronounced trade-offs between two pairs of quality attributes: *i)* average settling time and average overshoot (first column, second row); and *ii)* control robustness and control overhead (third column, fourth row). The Pareto-fronts for such combinations are smooth, providing alternative solutions regarding the fulfillment of such quality attributes. No significant trade-offs have been found in other quality metric pairs. Third, the rigorous identification of Pareto-optimal solutions prevents novice architects from adopting those combinations of control law, tuning technique, and control adaptation mechanism that lead to inferior architectures. Finally, the metric values presented by solutions in the Pareto-front allow for the early analysis of the dynamics exhibited by real prototypes implementing such architectures.

As part of the activities we have been conducting for evaluating our approach, in this work we look for any empirical evidence supporting the claim that search-based approaches improve the effectiveness and reduce the complexity of SA systems architectures. Furthermore, we want to know whether search-based approaches leverage the acquisition of distilled design knowledge by novice architects.

4   Methods

The goal of the experiment we report herein was to **analyze** the design of SA systems, **for the purpose of** evaluating the search-based design approach we propose and a design process based on architecture styles catalogs, **with respect to** the effectiveness and complexity of resulting architectures, as well as the method's potential for leveraging the acquisition of distilled design knowledge by novice SA systems architects, **from the viewpoint of** researchers, and **in the context of** graduate students endowing systems with self-adaptation capabilities.

The quasi-experiment (Wohlin et al. 2012) is characterized as a blocked subject-object study with a paired comparison design. Two UML models representing a web server and a MapReduce distributed architecture are used as experiment objects and two treatments (search-based approach and style-based approach) are considered for the design method factor (independent variable). We use the Generational Distance metric (Deb and Kalyanmoy 2001; Van Veldhuizen and Lamont 2000) to assess effectiveness in terms of how far the architectures designed by the subjects are from a previously determined Pareto-optimal set of architectures. Design complexity is evaluated by using the Component Point approach (Wijayasiriwardhane and Lai 2010) while a questionnaire with multiple choice questions evaluates the method's potential for leveraging the acquisition of design knowledge.

5   Experiment planning

The experiment took place as part of a 32 hours course on Software Engineering for Distributed Systems, arranged in eight classes (four hours each) along four weeks. As presented in Table 1, the course was split in three parts: lectures, exam and training, and experiment. In the first four classes, students were exposed to the foundations of SA systems and feedback control, as well as to the SISO (Single-Input Single-Output) and MIMO (Multiple-Input Multiple-Output) feedback control strategies (Tilbury et al. 2004) more widely adopted in SA systems. It is worth mentioning that all students had previously undertaken a 32 hours course on Software Architecture and Software Modeling.

Roughly half of the students work as software developers/designers, while the remaining have a stronger background in network administration. We try to insulate the effect of this factor by using blocking techniques as described in Section 5.4. Furthermore, no explicit guidance about self-adaptation quality attributes trade-offs was given during the lectures, since such an aspect is part of the hypotheses investigated herein. In the 5th day, we conducted an one hour discussion about the matter, followed up by a three hours exam where students used pen and paper to answer open-ended questions. In the 6th day, we discussed the exam results and presented a 3 hours training session about the DuSE-MT tool and the architecture styles catalog for SA systems we developed for this experiment.

The experiment took place in the last two days of the course. Students were randomly assigned to two equal size groups, blocked by their stronger technical background (see Section 5.4). Since we undertook the experiment as a blocked subject-object study with three objects (web server initial model, MapReduce architecture initial model, and questionnaire) and two treatments (search-based approach and style-based approach), a total of twelve tests were undertaken (presented in Table 2 and discussed later in Section 5.4). Each group experienced every combination of an experiment object and a treatment, exchanging the first experienced combination at the second day in order to minimize maturation threats. All design tests aimed at extending an initial model with a SA mechanism which regulates a performance metric, while yet minimizing the settling time, maximum

Table 1 Overview of the 32 h course in which the experiment was undertaken

Part	Day	Activity
Lectures	1	Self-adaptive systems foundations (motivation, MAPE-K reference architecture, current approaches, challenges)
	2	Feedback control introduction (control goals, control properties, fixed gain SISO approaches)
	3	Feedback control (MIMO and adaptive approaches)
	4	Self-adaptive systems - case studies
Exam and training	5	First hour: discussion
		Next 3 hours: Pen and paper exam
	6	First hour: exam discussion
		Next 3 hours: Training (DuSE-MT and architectural styles catalog)
Experiment	7	First 110 minutes: Tests #1 and #2
		Next 110 minutes: Tests #3 and #4
		Next 20 minutes: Tests #5 and #6 (questionnaire)
	8	First 110 minutes: Tests #7 and #8
		Next 110 minutes: Tests #9 and #10
		Next 20 minutes: Tests #11 and #12 (questionnaire)

Table 2 Tests defined for the experiment

#Test	Object	Treatment	Subjects
1	Web server	Style-based approach	Group 1
2	MapReduce architecture	Search-based approach	Group 2
3	MapReduce architecture	Style-based approach	Group 1
4	Web server	Search-based approach	Group 2
5	Questionnaire	Style-based approach	Group 1
6	Questionnaire	Search-based approach	Group 2
7	MapReduce architecture	Search-based approach	Group 1
8	Web server	Style-based approach	Group 2
9	Web server	Search-based approach	Group 1
10	MapReduce architecture	Style-based approach	Group 2
11	Questionnaire	Search-based approach	Group 1
12	Questionnaire	Style-based approach	Group 2

overshoot, and control overhead. Both groups used DuSE-MT as the design tool, but all functionalities regarding design space navigation and architecture optimization were turned off when using the style-based approach as treatment. Conversely, students had no access to the style catalog when using the search-based approach. We would like to emphasize that the experiment was not intended to investigate design productivity and fault density, since those aspects are obviously favored when adopting automated design approaches.

5.1 Design objects

The experiment's design tests aimed to create managing elements (adaptation loops) for two distinct managed elements: a web server and a MapReduce distributed architecture (Dean and Ghemawat 2008). Such managed elements were used as experiment objects and are depicted in Figure 5a and 5b as elements with the *"input model elements"* key. Experiment subjects were expected to extend such input models with a particular feedback loop design that produces short settling times, minimum overshoot, and low control overhead. Figure 5 shows two examples of such loops as elements with the *"added elements"* key. We chose these experiment objects because they constitute two self-adaptation scenarios widely investigated nowadays and pose different design challenges: MIMO local control for the web server case study vs. SISO nested control in a distributed environment for the MapReduce architecture case study.

The web server model (WS) – depicted in Figure 5a – entails a single component providing four interfaces: two for monitoring purposes (IAvgCPUUtilization and IAvgMemUtilization) and two for adjusting parameters that directly impacts the measured outputs (IKeepAliveTimeout and IMaxRequestWorkers). The goal is to retain web server's CPU and memory utilization as close as possible to the specified reference values, by simultaneously adjusting the number of threads serving HTTP requests (via IMaxRequestWorkers interface) and the amount of time the server must wait for subsequent requests on a given connection (via IKeepAliveTimeout interface).

The MapReduce architecture model (MR) – depicted in Figure 5b – describes a distributed computing infrastructure (cluster) where an array of n nodes stores and analyzes huge datasets. The cluster infrastructure orchestrates the parallel execution of a Map function for each data block stored in cluster's nodes and combines all

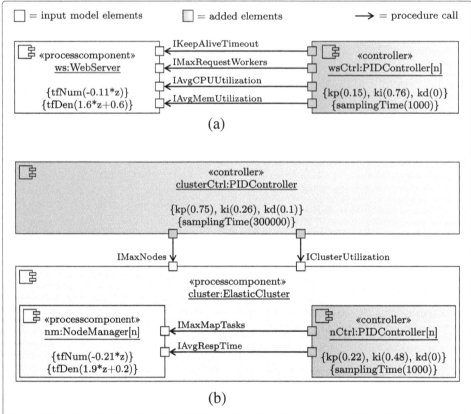

Figure 5 Experiment objects (input model elements only): web server model (a) and MapReduce architecture model (b). The added elements exemplify the architectural extensions to be designed by the experiment subjects, either by applying the architectural styles catalog (reference approach) or by adopting our automated design space exploration mechanism (intervention approach).

Map's outputs to form the Reduce function's input (Dean and Ghemawat 2008). Apache Hadoop (White 2009) is a well-established open source implementation of the MapReduce programming model, whose performance may be fine-tuned through nearly 190 configuration parameters. Although default values for such parameters are already provided by Hadoop, improvements of 50% in performance have been observed in properly configured setups (Jiang et al. 2010). In spite of that, Hadoop provides no services for parameter self-optimization or feedback control loops. The model we present in Figure 5b entails two nested controllable components: `NodeManager` and `ElasticCluster`. Each cluster machine runs the `NodeManager` service, which may have its partial job's average response time (measured via `IAvgRespTime` interface) regulated by adjusting the maximum number of map tasks simultaneously executing in that host (Hadoop's `mapreduce.tasktracker.map.tasks.maximum` parameter, changed via `IMaxMapTasks` interface). Additionally, the overall cluster utilization (measured via `IClusterUtilization` interface) may also be regulated by adjusting the number of cluster hosts serving the job (via `IMaxNodes` interface).

5.2 Variables selection

In this quasi-experiment, we are interested in analyzing the impact of the adopted design method on three dependent variables: the effectiveness of the resulting managing element, the complexity of managing element's architecture, and the method's potential for promoting the acquisition of insights and refined experience about quality attributes trade-offs involved in SA systems design. This subsection describes the metrics we adopted to quantify such variables.

5.2.1 Measuring effectiveness (Generational distance)

We quantify the effectiveness of resulting feedback control loops in terms of how close their quality attributes are from a set of Pareto-optimal solutions previously obtained. Since meta-heuristics-based approaches – like ours – do not guarantee global optimality, we performed a set of 50 optimization runs and calculated the reference Pareto-front P^* of the union of all runs' outputs. A Pareto-front is a set of solutions for which it is impossible to make any other architecture better off without make at least another one worse. We assume that P^* (triangle path in Figure 6) is a nice representative of the most effective solutions and constitutes a reasonable reference value for evaluating how effective are the architectures designed by the experiment subjects. We have done such procedure for both the objects (WS and MR) used in the experiment, producing the P^*_{WS} and P^*_{MR} reference Pareto-fronts.

The Generational Distance (GD) (Deb and Kalyanmoy 2001; Van Veldhuizen and Lamont 2000) is a widely used metric to evaluate closeness between two Pareto-Fronts Q and P^*. The metric finds an average distance of the solutions of Q (or r) from P^*, as follows:

$$GD = \frac{\left(\sum_{i=1}^{|Q|} d_i^p\right)^{1/p}}{|Q|}; \quad \text{where } d_i^2 = \min_{k=1}^{|P*|} \sqrt{\sum_{m=1}^{M} \left(f_m^{(i)} - f*_m^{(k)}\right)^2} \qquad (6)$$

$f_m^{(i)}$ is the m-th objective function value of the i-th member of Pareto-front Q. d_i^2 calculates the shortest distance between $f_m^{(i)}$ and $f*_m^{(k)}$: the m-th objective function value of the k-th member of Pareto-front P^*. Any L^p-norm can be used in Generational Distance. For $p = 2$ as described above, d_i^2 is the Euclidean distance between the solution $i \in Q$ and the nearest member of P^*. We chose the Generational Distance because it is more suitable

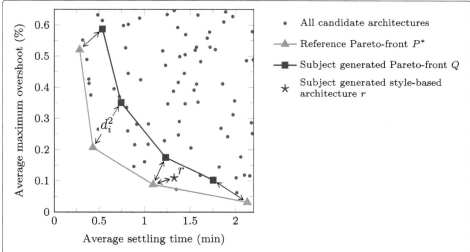

Figure 6 Example of reference Pareto-front P* and Generational Distance (GD) metric. *GD finds the average Euclidean distance from each i-th solution in Q to the nearest solution in P*. The lower the GD value, the more effective are the architectures regarding self-adaptation quality attributes. The style-based architecture r is shown as more effective than those produced by the search-based approach. That is one of the null hypotheses investigated herein.*

than alternatives like Error Ratio and Set Coverage (Deb and Kalyanmoy 2001) when comparing disjoint Pareto-fronts. Furthermore, its evaluation can be performed with lower computational costs when compared to metrics such as Hypervolume (van Veldhuizen and Lamont 1999) and Attainment Surface Based Statistical Metric (Fonseca and Fleming 1996).

As for designs produced with the style-based approach (e.g.: solution r in Figure 6), their corresponding location in objective space (quality metrics values) were first calculated and then compared to the reference Pareto-front using Generational Distance. Note that a Pareto-front Q obtained with the search-based approach (e.g.: square path in Figure 6) is not necessarily as effective as the reference Pareto-front P^*, because of the inherent randomness in the adopted evolutionary multi-objective optimization approach (NSGA-II).

Although r is shown, in Figure 6, more effective than any solution in Q, we believe that this is unlikely to happen in designs undertaken by architects with no previous experience in SA systems. Therefore, in this experiment, we look for any evidence that supports/rejects our claim that search-based approaches may improve the effectiveness of such designs.

5.2.2 Measuring complexity (Component Point)

The second dependent variable we focus in this experiment is design complexity, since it directly impacts the development effort required to implement the proposed architectures. We used the Component Point (CP) approach (Wijayasiriwardhane and Lai 2010) to quantify such an aspect, motivated by its original conception towards the measurement of UML models and by the existence of empirical evidence regarding its validity and usefulness (Wijayasiriwardhane and Lai 2010). CP provides the means to measure design complexity in terms of component's interfaces complexity and component's interaction complexity. We define the complexity CC_c for a component c as:

$$CC_c = IFCI_c + ITCI_c = \frac{IFC_c}{n_c} + \frac{ITC_c}{m_c} \tag{7}$$

$IFCI_c$ is the Interface Complexity per Interface, defined as the component's Interface Complexity (IFC_c) divided by the number of component's provided interfaces (n_c). Similarly, the Interaction Complexity per Interaction ($ITCI_c$) is defined as the component's Interaction Complexity (ITC_c) divided by the number of component's interactions (m_c). IFC_c and ITC_c, in their turn, are defined as follows.

The first step when calculating IFC_c is classifying each interface of a component into two types: ILF (Internal Logical Files) or EIF (External Interface Files). ILF interfaces are those whose operations change attributes of other interfaces, while the remaining interfaces as classified as EIF. The CP approach also specifies how a complexity level (Low, Average, High) should be assigned to each interface, based on the number of operations and number of operation's parameters it presents. Hence, IFC_c is defined as:

$$IFC_c = \sum_{j=1}^{2} \sum_{k=1}^{3} I_{jk} \times W_{jk} \tag{8}$$

I_{jk} is the number of interfaces of type j (1=ILF and 2=EIF) with complexity level k (1=Low, 2=Average, and 3=High). W_{jk} is the weight, given by the CP approach, for the interface type j with complexity level k.

ITC_c is evaluated in terms of the Interaction Frequency (IF_{ij}) of the j-th operation of the i-th interface and the Complexity Measure (CM_{ijk}) of the k-th data type involved in the execution of the j-th operation of the i-th interface. IF_{ij} is defined as a ratio of the number of interactions (N_O) performed by the operation and the number of interactions (N_I) performed by all operations of the interface. CM_{ijk}, in its turn, is defined as:

$$CM_{ijk}(D,L) = L + \sum_{n=1}^{m} CM(DT_n, L+1) \tag{9}$$

D is the data type under measurement, L is the number of the level where the data type D occurs in the component data type graph (initially 1), DT_n is the data type of the n-th D's data member and m is the number of data members in D. Finally, ITC_c can be defined as:

$$ITC_c = \sum_{i=1}^{p} \sum_{j=1}^{q} \left(IF_{ij} \times \sum_{k=1}^{r} CM_{ijk} \right) \tag{10}$$

p is the number of interfaces provided by component c, q is the number of operations that the i-th interface provides, and r is the number of data types involved in the execution of the j-th operation of the i-th interface. The overall architecture complexity AC is defined as the sum of the CC_i of every component i comprising the solution.

5.2.3 Measuring the acquisition of distilled design knowledge (post-experiment questionnaire)

The third dependent variable we investigated herein is the method's potential for leveraging the acquisition of distilled design knowledge. For that purpose, we prepared a questionnaire with 10 multiple choice questions related to refined knowledge about quality attribute trade-offs in the SA systems domain. Students answered such questionnaire at the end of each experiment day and we assigned grades according to the number of correctly answered questions. The goal was to evaluate to which extent the adopted design approach may leverage the acquisition of distilled knowledge about such design trade-offs. The questionnaire is available at the experiment website.

5.3 Hypotheses formulation

In the quasi-experiment we report herein, we compare the use of a search-based architecture design approach and a style-based design approach with respect to the effectiveness and complexity of resulting architectures, as well as to the method's potential to promote the acquisition of distilled design knowledge. Such goal has been stated in three null hypotheses (H_0) and their corresponding alternative hypotheses (H_1):

- H_0^1: there is no difference in *design effectiveness* (measured in terms of the Generational Distance GD) between a feedback control loop design created using the style-based approach (reference approach: RA) and a feedback control loop design created using the search-based approach (intervention approach: IA).

$$H_0^1 : \mu_{GD_{RA}} = \mu_{GD_{IA}}$$
$$H_1^1 : \mu_{GD_{RA}} > \mu_{GD_{IA}}$$

- H_0^2: there is no difference in *design complexity* (measured in terms of the Architectural Complexity AC) between a feedback control loop design created using the style-based approach and a feedback control loop design created using the search-based approach.

$$H_0^2 : \mu_{AC_{RA}} = \mu_{AC_{IA}}$$
$$H_1^2 : \mu_{AC_{RA}} > \mu_{AC_{IA}}$$

- H_0^3: there is no difference in the *acquisition of distilled design knowledge* (measured in terms of applied questionnaire's grade *QG*) between designing a feedback control loop using the style-based approach and designing a feedback control loop using the search-based approach.

$$H_0^3 : \mu_{QG_{RA}} = \mu_{QG_{IA}}$$
$$H_1^3 : \mu_{QG_{RA}} < \mu_{QG_{IA}}$$

5.4 Experiment design

The experiment was undertaken as a blocked subject-object study, which means that each subject exercises both treatments and that effects can be compared in pairs. Since the experiment students had a stronger technical background in two different fields (14 devoted to software development and 10 devoted to network administration), we used such an information as a blocking factor. By doing that, we eliminate the undesired effect of student's technical background on the dependent variables, increasing the precision of the experiment.

Students from each technical background partition were randomly and equally assigned to groups 1 and 2, yielding a similar proportion of developers and network administrators in each group. As presented in Table 2, a total of eight design tests and four questionnaire answering tests were conducted in the experiment. Each group experienced every combination of an object (WS model, MR model, or the questionnaire) and a treatment (style-based approach or search-based approach). In the first experiment day, group 1 applied the style-based approach, initially in the WS model and then in the MR model, while group 2 adopted the search-based approach with the opposite object order. At the end of the day, both groups answered the questionnaire based on their experience with the corresponding approach. In the second experiment day, groups exchanged the treatments and experienced the objects in the opposite order to the one conducted by them in the previous day. The same questionnaire was applied again at the end of the second day.

To minimize the effect of subjects gaining information from previous assignments, we systematically balanced which object-treatment combination is first experienced in each group. The tests' operation order is presented in Table 1. To reduce hypotheses guessing and other social threats, students did not receive any feedback and were not aware of the experiment until its completion.

The architecture styles catalog we developed for this experiment documents the same design knowledge present in the SA:DuSE design space as a group of eleven architectural styles. Table 3 presents one of such styles. We describe each solution using a schema that documents the style's prominent components, connectors, and data elements, the resulting architecture topology, induced qualities, typical uses, and potential cautions, among other aspects.

Table 3 One of the eleven architectural styles for self-adaptive systems described in the catalog

Style #2 – P(ID) Feedback control with system identification	
Summary	A separate component (controller) measures system output and acts accordingly to drive the system to the expected output (feedback)
Components	System, controller, effector, sensor, transducer/QoS subsystem (optional, if output not directly delivered by the system itself)
Connectors	(Remote) procedure call, event bus or data access
Data elements	Reference value(s), input values, output values, transduced values (optional)
Topology	Circular with one entry point: (reference input → controller → system → measured output [→ transducer/QoS subsystem] → ...)
Variants	#2.1: PID-SI with Precompensation - (PID-SI/PC)
	#2.2: PID-SI with Sensor Delay - (PID-SI/SD)
	#2.3: PID-SI with Filtering - (PID-SI/F)
Qualities yielded	Reactive behavior; adaptation to unmodeled disturbances; no need for an accurate system model; can make stable an unstable system
Typical uses	When a good enough system model is available, disturbance modeling is quite complicated, target system is unstable but linear or with identifiable linear operating regions
Cautions	When disturbance spans over a wide range; when system is primary non-linear or have dynamics that are difficult to be modeled; when structural reconfiguration is needed
Example	...

As for the operation stage, we commit the participants by presenting some real cases demanding self-adaptation capabilities and explaining how the myriad of available approaches makes things harder for novice architects. Grades have been assigned to all tests as a form of inducement. Some instrumentation was required in order to enable/disable the search features in DuSE-MT and collect the resulting architectures from each participant. After the experiment operation, 20 subjects provided usable data for paired comparison of Generational Distance and Architecture Complexity. Questionnaire answers were restrict to those provided by such 20 subjects.

6   Results and discussion

With the support of DuSE-MT, all UML models resulting from the design tests were serialized in XML (eXtensible Markup Language) files, along with their corresponding quality attributes values (objective-space location). Such values were used to compute the Generational Distance for all resulting models. The Architecture Complexity value was also calculated for each resulting UML model.

6.1   Analysis

Table 4 and Figure 7 summarize the measured values of all dependent variables, as well as their paired difference with respect to the adopted treatment. The first step we undertook in the analysis stage was to investigate whether the usual assumptions for the use of parametric tests – preferable because of their enhanced power – hold in the collected data. Such assumptions are: *i)* data is taken from an interval or ratio scale (held for all experiment's dependent variables); *ii)* observations are independent (enforced by experiment design); *iii)* measured values are normally distributed in the populations; and *iv)* population variances are equal between groups (homoscedasticity).

Table 4 Descriptive statistics for the experiment's dependent variables

	Generational distance (GD)		
	Mean(μ)	Median	Std. dev.
Search-based approach (IA)	2.40	2.45	1.08
Style-based approach (RA)	2.59	2.41	1.03
Difference (IA−RA)	-0.19	-0.62	1.32
	Architecture complexity (AC)		
	Mean(μ)	Median	Std. dev.
Search-based approach (IA)	6.46	6.65	2.77
Style-based approach (RA)	7.02	7.05	2.70
Difference (IA−RA)	-0.57	-1.90	3.47
	Questionnaire grade (QG)		
	Mean(μ)	Median	Std. dev.
Search-based approach (IA)	6.85	7.00	1.43
Style-based approach (RA)	7.04	7.25	1.27
Difference (IA−RA)	-0.19	-0.50	1.51

We used the Anderson-Darling test (Corder and Foreman 2009) to evaluate to which extent the paired differences are normally distributed. The Brown-Forsythe test (Good 2005) was applied to investigate the null hypothesis of homoscedasticity between the intervention approach and reference approach groups. Table 5 presents such a results. With a significance level (α) of 0.05, we observed that only the Questionnaire Grade (QG) paired difference could be considered normally distributed (Anderson-Darling p-value > 0.05). In addition, for all dependent variables, the null hypothesis of homoscedasticity could not be rejected (Brown-Forsythe p-value > 0.05). Since all assumptions must hold, only hypothesis H_0^3 was evaluated by using a parametric test. The paired differences of Generational Distance (GD) and Architecture Complexity (AC) were not considered normally distributed (p-value $< \alpha = 0.05$) and, as such, hypotheses H_0^1 and H_0^2 were evaluated by using a non-parametric test. As presented in Table 6, we used the Wilcoxon Signed-Rank test (Gibbons and Chakraborti 2003; Wohlin et al. 2012) to investigate H_0^1 and H_0^2 and the Paired t-test (Wohlin et al. 2012) to investigate H_0^3. With a significance level (α) of 0.05, H_0^1 and H_0^2 were rejected while no evidence could be found about H_0^3.

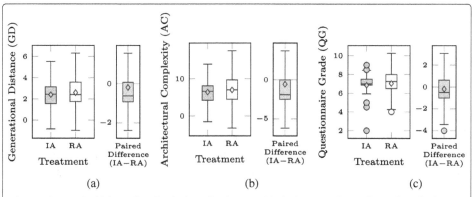

Figure 7 Box and whiskers plots for design effectiveness (a), design complexity (b), and method's potential for leveraging the acquisition of distilled knowledge (c). For each dependent variable it is shown the values for the search-based approach (IA: intervention approach), the style-based approach (RA: reference approach), as well as the values of the paired difference (IA−RA).

Table 5 Results of Anderson-Darling normality test and Brown-Forsythe heteroscedasticity test ($\alpha = 0.05$)

Dependent variable	Anderson-Darling p-value	Brown-Forsythe p-value
Generational distance	1.29814505086953E-007	0.9009324909
Architecture complexity	2.88672812219819E-010	0.7207666486
Questionnaire grade	0.635529605	0.7167840476

6.2 Discussion

The descriptive statistics and results of hypotheses tests show that there are improvements in the dependent variables, except for the Questionnaire Grade (QG). Actually, students who first exercised the search-based approach got slightly smaller grades (6.85) than other ones (7.04). Since both the architecture style catalog and the design space used in the experiment contain the same information, two possible reasons for such difference remain. First, students exposed to the search-based approach may have experienced a larger set of candidate architectures, which would contribute to obfuscate some quality trade-offs evaluated in the questionnaire. Second, the quality trade-offs may actually be not too difficult to grasp without the use of structured design spaces and automated architecture optimization, so that the difference is actually by chance. Further experiments are needed to better investigate such an aspect.

Generational Distance (adopted measure for effectiveness) is, on average, 7% lower with the search-based approach (2.40) when compared to the style-based approach (2.59). Architecture Complexity is, on average, 7% lower with the search-based approach (6.46) when compared to the style-based approach (7.02). While such values already indicate some improvements in the resulting architectures, we still lack further investigation about the boundaries that such enhancements may present.

7 Threats to validity

This section presents the threats to validity (Wohlin et al. 2012) we identified for the experiment.

7.1 Threats to construct validity

Construct Validity is the degree to which the objects and measurements reflect their associated constructs in the real world. We have identified three such threats: inadequate pre-operational explication of constructs, hypothesis guessing, and objects representativeness.

First, since the theory behind feedback control loops encompasses areas such as systems and signals, modeling of dynamic behavior, and analysis in frequency domain, students may have had no enough time to get a firm grasp about such mathematical background. To reduce this threat, we focused on requiring minimum knowledge about such as aspect and tried to leverage tool support regarding this issue in DuSE-MT. Second, students

Table 6 Results of statistical tests ($\alpha = 0.05$)

H_0^i	Test	Criteria	Conclusion
1	Wilcoxon signed-rank	T(410) > T-critical(378)	Rejected
2	Wilcoxon signed-rank	T(367) > T-critical(361)	Rejected
3	Paired t-test	p-value=0.5488018266	Not rejected

may have tried to perform better when using the search-based approach because it is the treatment proposed by the course holders. Moreover, authors involvement with the intervening approach may have lead to better training on the use of the search-based mechanism. To mitigate this issue, students were not aware of the experiment and were graded on all tests. Third, the objects used in the experiment may not actually reflect the kind of problems routinely faced in the SA systems domain. Since the two adopted self-adaptation scenarios have been repeatedly investigated in a number of recent papers, we believe they constitute interesting and representative examples of current practice.

7.2 Threats to internal validity

Internal Validity concerns in analyzing to which extent unknown factors may affect the dependent variables with respect to causality. We have identified two such threats. The first one is maturation, where subject gain insights from previous experiment sessions. To reduce this threat, we alternately assigned such objects during the two experiment days. The second is related to instrumentation. Since a new modeling tool was adopted in the experiment (DuSE-MT), that may have impacted in some extent the student's abilities for developing the required models.

7.3 Threats to external validity

External Validity is related to the ability of generalizing the experiment results to other settings. Since we used students of a graduate program in Distributed and Ubiquitous Computing, they may not represent the expected background in current industry practice.

7.4 Threats to conclusion validity

Conclusion Validity is related to the ability of generalizing the results to the overall concept or theory which supports the experiment. Since the experiment objects were created by us, there is a potential threat that such objects do not actually represent the problem under investigation. Such threat could have been reduced by relying on external SA systems experts to design such objects.

8   Related work

To the best of our knowledge, no controlled experiments regarding the use of search-based approaches when designing SA systems have been undertaken so far. However, we identified one experiment regarding SA systems design and a number of papers reporting on controlled experiments about software architecture design.

In (Weyns et al. 2013), the authors report the results of a quasi-experiment that investigates whether the use of external feedback loops (when compared with internal adaptation mechanisms) improves the design of SA systems. The design was evaluated with respect to design complexity (in terms of activity complexity and control flow complexity), fault density, and design productivity. The experiment shows that external feedback loops reduce the number of adopted control flow primitives, increasing the design's understandability and maintainability. They also observed improvements in design productivity when using external feedback loops, but found no significant effects on design complexity in terms of activity complexity. The experiment we present herein tackles a similar design issue but with different treatments, objects, measurements, and hypotheses. While their experiment reveals evidence about the decoupling and reusability benefits of external feedback loops, we believe our experiment contributes by revealing the potential benefits of systematic design knowledge representation and search-based automated design approaches in such a domain.

A controlled experiment aimed at evaluating the impact of design rationale documentation techniques on effectiveness and efficiency of decision-making in the presence of requirements changing is presented in (Falessi et al. 2006). The results show that the use of such documentation technique significantly improves effectiveness but with no impacts on efficiency. In (Bratthall et al. 2000), the authors present a controlled experiment which evaluates the impact of the use of design rationale documentation on software evolution. They conclude that there are improvements in correctness and productivity when such documentation is available. Our search-based design approach – under evaluation herein – supports rationale documentation in terms of domain-specific design spaces. The experiment we report in this paper is ultimately assessing the impact of having such rationale documented in a structured and systematic way, in contrast to ad-hoc styles catalogs or unstructured rationale documents.

In (Golden et al. 2005), a controlled experiment was performed to evaluate the usefulness of architectural patterns when evolving architectures to support specific usability concerns. The authors conclude that usability concerns are amenable to be handled in architectural level and that architectural patterns can significantly leverage such an aspect. In the SA systems domain, architecture-centric approaches with explicit (first-class) representation of feedback loops have been advocated as a promising research direction (Brun et al. 2009; Hebig et al. 2010; Müller et al. 2008), due to their generality and support for early reasoning of self-adaptation quality attributes. The experiment we describe in this paper evaluates how search-based design approaches impact such first-class representation of feedback loops.

A controlled experiment about the impact of the use of design patterns on the productivity and correctness of software evolution activities is described in (Vokác et al. 2004). They conclude that each design pattern presents a specific impact on such dependent variables and, therefore, claim that design patterns should not be characterized as useful or harmful in general. In contrast, our experiment compares the use of two distinct representations of such distilled design knowledge: architectural styles vs. structured design spaces. Furthermore, we are interested in evaluating whether search-based design automation improves the effectiveness of SA systems.

With respect to software engineering mechanisms for SA systems, (Weyns et al. 2012) present FORMS (FOrmal Reference Model for Self-adaptation): an unifying reference model for formal specification of distributed SA systems. Their approach provides a small number of modeling elements capturing key design concerns in the SA systems domain. In contrast to our approach, FORMS provides no means for automated design of feedback loops and a steep learning curve may be experienced because of its rigorous formal underpinnings.

(Vogel and Giese 2012) propose a new modeling language for explicitly describing feedback control loops as runtime megamodels (multiple models@runtime). In contrast, our approach builds on top of widely accepted standards for modeling languages, like MOF (Meta Object Facility) and UML. Although our approach has been used as an off-line design mechanism, future work includes moving such an infrastructure to runtime, providing a models@runtime approach for Dynamic Adaptive Search-Based Software Engineering (Harman et al. 2012).

A UML profile for modeling feedback control loops as first-class entities is presented in (Hebig et al. 2010). In our mechanism, we go a step further towards the use of UML profiles as the underlying mechanism for identifying *loci* of architectural decisions, enabling automated design, and detecting invalid candidate architectures. (Cheng et al. 2006) present an adaptation language which relies on utility theory for handling self-adaptation in the presence of multiple objectives. *A priori* preference articulation methods – like utility functions – convert a multi-objective optimization problem into a single-objective one, but its effectiveness highly depends on an well-chosen preference vector. Our approach, on the other hand, accommodates the multi-objective nature of SA systems design as an essential aspect by using *a posteriori* preference articulation.

An on-line learning-based approach for handling unanticipated changes at runtime is presented in (Esfahani et al. 2013). Whilst we have considered in this work only feedback control as the enabling mechanism for self-adaptation, other strategies may be modeled as new variation points. (Křikava et al. 2012) propose a models@runtime approach which represents adaptation logic as networks of messaging passing actors. Our work, in contrast, leverages design reuse by requiring the use of highly distilled design knowledge only once – when designing a domain-specific DuSE design space. Thereafter, novice architects have better support for designing effective architectures and getting insights from the search activities.

9 Conclusions

This paper presented a quasi-experiment aimed at evaluating whether search-based architecture design approaches improve the effectiveness and complexity of SA systems when compared to style-based design approaches. To the best of our knowledge, this is the first endeavor in evaluating how search-based automated design impacts the quality of SA systems. The results reveal that the use of systematically structured design spaces and architecture optimization mechanisms indeed provide enhanced support to the evaluation of quality trade-offs, for the experiment objects considered herein.

Some insights have been identified from the experiment results. We found no evidence that search-based approaches leverage the acquisition of distilled design knowledge in the SA systems domain. Alternative instruments for evaluating such an aspect may be adopted in future research, enabling the eliciting of more elucidative conclusions. However, search-based design approaches do contribute in revealing architectures which indeed exhibit a near-optimal trade-off between quality attributes. In contrast, architects using the style-based approach are more likely to design sub-optimal architectures. Improved effectiveness results in managing elements with lower overhead and enhanced use of resources, leveraging the overall SA behavior. Moreover, designs with lower complexity were also obtained when using the search-based approach, fostered by the systematic representation of the architecture changes required to implement the involved feedback loops. As a consequence, one should expect positive effects in understandability, maintainability, and testability of development artifacts implementing such architectures.

A lot of current research are driving their efforts towards the establishment of principled and well-founded underpinnings for engineering software-intensive systems, specially in particular application domains like SA systems. The organization of software design knowledge for routine use is mandatory if we are to realize the upcoming generation of software-intensive systems.

Competing interests
The authors declare that they have no competing interests.

Authors' contributions
Both authors planned the experiment. SSA carried it out, analyzed its results, and prepared the initial draft of the manuscript. Corrections and reviews were made by RJAM. Both authors read and approved the final manuscript.

References
Andersson J, Lemos R, Malek S, Weyns D (2009) Software engineering for self-adaptive systems. In: Cheng BH, Lemos R, Giese H, Inverardi P, Magee J (eds). Software Engineering for Self-Adaptive Systems. Springer, Berlin, Heidelberg. pp 27–47. Chap. Modeling Dimensions of Self-Adaptive Software Systems doi:10.1007/978-3-642-02161-9_2

Andrade SS, de Araújo Macêdo RJ (2013) A search-based approach for architectural design of feedback control concerns in self-adaptive systems. In: 7th IEEE International Conference on Self-Adaptive and Self-Organizing Systems, SASO 2013, Philadelphia, PA, USA, September 9-13, 2013. IEEE Computer Society, Washington, DC, USA. pp 61–70. doi:10.1109/SASO.2013.42. http://dx.doi.org/10.1109/SASO.2013.42

Andrade SS, de Araújo Macêdo RJ (2013) Architectural design spaces for feedback control concerns in self-adaptive systems (S). In: The 25th International Conference on Software Engineering and Knowledge Engineering, Boston, MA, USA, June 27-29, 2013. Knowledge Systems Institute Graduate School, Skokie, Illinois, USA. pp 741–746

Andrade SS, de Araújo Macêdom RJ (2014) Do search-based approaches improve the design of self-adaptive systems? A controlled experiment. In: 2014 Brazilian Symposium on Software Engineering, Maceió, Brazil, September 28 - October 3, 2014. IEEE, Washington, DC, USA. pp 101–110. doi:10.1109/SBES.2014.17. http://dx.doi.org/10.1109/SBES.2014.17

DARPA (1997) Self-adaptive software. Technical Report 98-12, Defense Advanced Research Projects Agency

Bratthall L, Johansson E, Regnell B (2000) Is a design rationale vital when predicting change impact? A controlled experiment on software architecture evolution. In: Bomarius F, Oivo M (eds). Product Focused Software Process Improvement, Second International Conference, PROFES 2000, Oulu, Finland, June 20-22, 2000, Proceedings. Lecture Notes in Computer Science. Springer, New York, NY, USA Vol. 1840. pp 126–139. doi:10.1007/978-3-540-45051-1_14. http://dx.doi.org/10.1007/978-3-540-45051-1_14

Benyon D, Murray D (1993) Adaptive systems: from intelligent tutoring to autonomous agents. Knowledge Based Systems 6(4):179–219. doi:10.1016/0950-7051(93)90012-I

Bruni R, Bucchiarone A, Gnesi S, Melgratti H (2008) Modelling dynamic software architectures using typed graph grammars. Electronic Notes in Theoretical Computer Science 213(1):39–53. doi:10.1016/j.entcs.2008.04.073. Proceedings of the Third Workshop on Graph Transformation for Concurrency and Verification (GT-VC 2007)

Brun Y, Serugendo GDM, Gacek C, Giese H, Kienle HM, Litoiu M, Müller HA, Pezzè M, Shaw M (2009) Engineering self-adaptive systems through feedback loops. In: Cheng BHC, de Lemos R, Giese H, Inverardi P, Magee J (eds). Software Engineering for Self-Adaptive Systems [outcome of a Dagstuhl Seminar]. Lecture Notes in Computer Science. Springer, New York, NY, USA Vol. 5525. pp 48–70. doi:10.1007/978-3-642-02161-9_3. http://dx.doi.org/10.1007/978-3-642-02161-9_3

Cheng S-W, Garlan D, Schmerl B (2006) Architecture-based self-adaptation in the presence of multiple objectives. In: Proceedings of the 2006 International Workshop on Self-Adaptation and Self-Managing Systems. SEAMS 2006. ACM, New York, NY, USA. pp 2–8. doi:10.1145/1137677.1137679. http://doi.acm.org/10.1145/1137677.1137679

Corder GW, Foreman DI (2009) Nonparametric Statistics for Non-Statisticians: A Step-by-Step Approach. Wiley, Hoboken, NJ, USA

de Lemos R, Giese H, Müller HA, Shaw M, Andersson J, Litoiu M, Schmerl BR, Tamura G, Villegas NM, Vogel T, Weyns D, Baresi L, Becker B, Bencomo N, Brun Y, Cukic B, Desmarais R, Dustdar S, Engels G, Geihs K, Göschka KM, Gorla A, Grassi V, Inverardi P, Karsai G, Kramer J, Lopes A, Magee J, Malek S, Mankovski S, et al (2010) Software engineering for self-adaptive systems: A second research roadmap. In: de Lemos R, Giese H, Müller HA, Shaw M (eds). Software Engineering for Self-Adaptive Systems II - International Seminar, Dagstuhl Castle, Germany, October 24-29, 2010 Revised Selected and Invited Papers. Lecture Notes in Computer Science. Springer, New York, NY, USA Vol. 7475. pp 1–32. doi:10.1007/978-3-642-35813-5_1. http://dx.doi.org/10.1007/978-3-642-35813-5_1

Dean J, Ghemawat S (2008) MapReduce: simplified data processing on large clusters. Communications of the ACM 51(1):107–113. doi:10.1145/1327452.1327492

Deb K, Kalyanmoy D (2001) Multi-Objective Optimization Using Evolutionary Algorithms. John Wiley & Sons, Inc., New York, NY, USA

Deb K, Pratap A, Agarwal S, Meyarivan T (2002) A fast and elitist multiobjective genetic algorithm: NSGA-II. IEEE Transactions on Evolutionary Computation 6(2):182–197. doi:10.1109/4235.996017

Esfahani N, Elkhodary A, Malek S (2013) A learning-based framework for engineering feature-oriented self-adaptive software systems. IEEE Transactions on Software Engineering 39(11):1467–1493. doi:10.1109/TSE.2013.37

Falessi D, Cantone G, Becker M (2006) Documenting design decision rationale to improve individual and team design decision making: an experimental evaluation. In: Travassos GH, Maldonado JC, Wohlin C (eds). 2006 International Symposium on Empirical Software Engineering (ISESE 2006), September 21-22, 2006, Rio de Janeiro, Brazil. ACM, New York, NY, USA. pp 134–143. doi:10.1145/1159733.1159755. http://doi.acm.org/10.1145/1159733.1159755

Fonseca CM, Fleming PJ (1996) On the performance assessment and comparison of stochastic multiobjective optimizers. In: Voigt H, Ebeling W, Rechenberger I, Schwefel H (eds). Parallel Problem Solving from Nature - PPSN IV, International

Conference on Evolutionary Computation. The 4th International Conference on Parallel Problem Solving from Nature, Berlin, Germany, September 22-26, 1996, Proceedings. Lecture Notes in Computer Science. Springer, New York, NY, USA Vol. 1141. pp 584–593. doi:10.1007/3-540-61723-X_1022. http://dx.doi.org/10.1007/3-540-61723-X_1022

Georgas JC, Taylor RN (2008) Policy-based self-adaptive architectures: a feasibility study in the robotics domain. In: Cheng BHC, de Lemos R, Garlan D, Giese H, Litoiu M, Magee J, Müller HA, Taylor RN (eds). 2008 ICSE Workshop on Software Engineering for Adaptive and Self-Managing Systems, SEAMS 2008, Leipzig, Germany, May 12-13, 2008. ACM, New York, NY, USA. pp 105–112. doi:10.1145/1370018.1370038. http://doi.acm.org/10.1145/1370018.1370038

Georgiadis I, Magee J, Kramer J (2002) Self-organising software architectures for distributed systems. In: Garlan D, Kramer J, Wolf AL (eds). Proceedings of the First Workshop on Self-Healing Systems, WOSS 2002, Charleston, South Carolina, USA, November 18-19, 2002. ACM, New York, NY, USA. pp 33–38. doi:10.1145/582128.582135

Gibbons JD, Chakraborti S (2003) Nonparametric Statistical Inference, Fourth Edition: Revised and Expanded. Statistics: A Series of Textbooks and Monographs. Taylor & Francis, Florence, Kentucky, USA

Golden E, John BE, Bass L (2005) The value of a usability-supporting architectural pattern in software architecture design: a controlled experiment. In: Roman G, Griswold WG, Nuseibeh B (eds). 27th International Conference on Software Engineering (ICSE 2005), 15-21 May 2005, St. Louis, Missouri, USA. ACM, New York, NY, USA. pp 460–469. doi:10.1145/1062455.1062538. http://doi.acm.org/10.1145/1062455.1062538

Good PI (2005) Permutation, Parametric and Bootstrap Tests of Hypotheses, Vol. 3. Springer, New York, NY, USA

Harman M, Mansouri SA, Zhang Y (2012) Search-based software engineering: Trends, techniques and applications. ACM Computing Surveys 45(1):11–11161. doi:10.1145/2379776.2379787

Harman M (2010) Why the virtual nature of software makes it ideal for search based optimization. In: Rosenblum DS, Taentzer G (eds). Fundamental Approaches to Software Engineering, 13th International Conference, FASE 2010, Held as Part of the Joint European Conferences on Theory and Practice of Software, ETAPS 2010, Paphos, Cyprus, March 20-28, 2010. Proceedings. Lecture Notes in Computer Science. Springer, New York, NY, USA Vol. 6013. pp 1–12. doi:10.1007/978-3-642-12029-9_1. http://dx.doi.org/10.1007/978-3-642-12029-9_1

Harman M, Burke EK, Clark JA, Yao X (2012) Dynamic adaptive search based software engineering. In: Runeson P, Höst M, Mendes E, Andrews AA, Harrison R (eds). ACM-IEEE international symposium on Empirical software engineering and measurement. ACM, New York, NY, USA. pp 1–8

Hayes M (2011) Schaums Outline of Digital Signal Processing, 2nd Edition, Schaum's Outline Series. McGraw-Hill Education, New York, NY, USA

Hebig R, Giese H, Becker B (2010) Making control loops explicit when architecting self-adaptive systems. In: SOAR 2010: Proceedings of the Second International Workshop on Self-Organizing Architectures. ACM, Washington, DC, USA. pp 21–28

Huebscher MC, McCann JA (2008) A survey of autonomic computing – degrees, models, and applications. ACM Computing Surveys 40(3):7–1728. doi:10.1145/1380584.1380585

Jiang D, Ooi BC, Shi L, Wu S (2010) The performance of mapreduce: An in-depth study. Proceedings of the VLDB Endowment 3(1):472–483

Kephart JO, Chess DM (2003) The vision of autonomic computing. Computer 36(1):41–50. doi:10.1109/MC.2003.1160055

Křikava F, Collet P, France RB (2012) Actor-based runtime model of adaptable feedback control loops. In: Proceedings of the 7th Workshop on Models@run.time, MRT 2012. ACM, New York, NY, USA. pp 39–44. doi:10.1145/2422518.2422525. http://doi.acm.org/10.1145/2422518.2422525

Landau ID, Lozano R, M'Saad M, Karimi A (2011) Adaptive Control: Algorithms, Analysis and Applications, Communications and Control Engineering. Springer, New York, NY, USA

Malek S, Edwards G, Brun Y, Tajalli H, Garcia J, Krka I, Medvidovic N, Mikic-Rakic M, Sukhatme GS (2010) An architecture-driven software mobility framework. Journal of Systems and Software 83(6):972–989. doi:10.1016/j.jss.2009.11.003

Müller H, Pezzè M, Shaw M (2008) Visibility of control in adaptive systems. In: Proceedings of the 2nd International Workshop on Ultra-large-scale Software-intensive Systems. ULSSIS 2008. ACM, New York, NY, USA. pp 23–26. doi:10.1145/1370700.1370707

Ogel F, Folliot B, Piumarta I (2003) On reflexive and dynamically adaptable environments for distributed computing. In: 23rd International Conference on Distributed Computing Systems Workshops (ICDCS 2003 Workshops), 19-22 May 2003, Providence, RI, USA. IEEE Computer Society, Washington, DC, USA. pp 112–117. doi:10.1109/ICDCSW.2003.1203541

Parunak HVD, Brueckner SA (2011) Software engineering for self-organizing systems. In: Weyns D, Müller JP (eds). 12th International Workshop on Agent-Oriented Software Engineering (AOSE 2011), AAMAS 2011, Taipei, Taiwan

Patikirikorala T, Colman AW, Han J, Wang L (2012) A systematic survey on the design of self-adaptive software systems using control engineering approaches. In: 7th International Symposium on Software Engineering for Adaptive and Self-Managing Systems, SEAMS 2012, Zurich, Switzerland, June 4-5, 2012. IEEE, Washington, DC, USA. pp 33–42. doi:10.1109/SEAMS.2012.6224389

Räihä O (2010) A survey on search-based software design. Computer Science Review 4(4):203–249. doi:10.1016/j.cosrev.2010.06.001

Salehie M, Tahvildari L (2009) Self-adaptive software: landscape and research challenges. ACM Transactions on Autonomous and Adaptive Systems (TAAS) 4(2):14–11442. doi:10.1145/1516533.1516538

Slotine J-JE, Li W (1991) Applied Nonlinear Control. Prentice Hall, Englewood Cliffs (N.J.) http://opac.inria.fr/record=b1132812

Stevens SS (1946) On the Theory of Scales of Measurement. Science 103(2684):677–680. doi:10.2307/1671815

Tilbury DM, Parekh S, Diao Y, Hellerstein JL (2004) Feedback Control of Computing Systems, Wiley interscience publication. Wiley IEEE press, Hoboken, NJ US. http://opac.inria.fr/record=b1119042

van Veldhuizen DA, Lamont GB (1999) Multiobjective evolutionary algorithm test suites. In: SAC. pp 351–357. doi:10.1145/298151.298382

Van Veldhuizen DA, Lamont GB (2000) On measuring multiobjective evolutionary algorithm performance. In: Evolutionary Computation, 2000. Proceedings of the 2000 Congress On. IEEE, Washington, DC, USA Vol. 1. pp 204–211

Vogel T, Giese H (2012) A language for feedback loops in self-adaptive systems: Executable runtime megamodels. In: 7th International Symposium on Software Engineering for Adaptive and Self-Managing Systems, SEAMS 2012, Zurich, Switzerland, June 4-5, 2012. IEEE, Washington, DC, USA. pp 129–138. doi:10.1109/SEAMS.2012.6224399. http://dx.doi.org/10.1109/SEAMS.2012.6224399

Vokác M, Tichy WF, Sjøberg DIK, Arisholm E, Aldrin M (2004) A controlled experiment comparing the maintainability of programs designed with and without design patterns – a replication in a real programming environment. Empirical Software Engineering 9(3):149–195

Wang Q (2005) Handbook of PI and PID controller tuning rules, aidan o'dwyer, imperial college press, London, 375pp, ISBN 1-86094-342-x, 2003. Automatica 41(2):355–356. doi:10.1016/j.automatica.2004.09.012

Weyns D, Iftikhar MU, Söderlund J (2013) Do external feedback loops improve the design of self-adaptive systems? a controlled experiment. In: Litoiu M, Mylopoulos J (eds). Proceedings of the 8th International Symposium on Software Engineering for Adaptive and Self-Managing Systems. SEAMS 2013, San Francisco, CA, USA, May 20-21, 2013. IEEE/ACM, Washington, DC, USA. pp 3–12

Weyns D, Malek S, Andersson J (2012) FORMS: Unifying reference model for formal specification of distributed self-adaptive systems. ACM Transactions on Autonomous and Adaptive Systems (TAAS) 7(1):8

Weyns D, Schmerl BR, Grassi V, Malek S, Mirandola R, Prehofer C, Wuttke J, Andersson J, Giese H, Göschka KM, de Lemos R (2010) On patterns for decentralized control in self-adaptive systems. In: Giese H, Müller HA, Shaw M (eds). Software Engineering for Self-Adaptive Systems II - International Seminar, Dagstuhl Castle, Germany, October 24-29, 2010 Revised Selected and Invited Papers. Lecture Notes in Computer Science. Springer, New York, NY, USA Vol. 7475. pp 76–107. doi:10.1007/978-3-642-35813-5_4

White T (2009) Hadoop: the Definitive Guide: the Definitive Guide. O'Reilly Media, Inc., Sebastopol, CA, USA

Wijayasiriwardhane T, Lai R (2010) Component Point: A system-level size measure for component-based software systems. J Syst Softw 83(12):2456–2470. doi:10.1016/j.jss.2010.07.008

Wohlin C, Runeson P, Höst M, Ohlsson MC, Regnell B (2012) Experimentation in Software Engineering. Springer, New York, NY, USA. doi:10.1007/978-3-642-29044-2

6

Designing fault-tolerant SOA based on design diversity

Amanda S Nascimento[1]*, Cecília MF Rubira[2], Rachel Burrows[3], Fernando Castor[4] and Patrick HS Brito[2,5]

*Correspondence:
anascimento@iceb.ufop.br
[1] Institute of Exact Sciences and
Biology, Federal University of Ouro
Preto, Ouro Preto, MG, Brazil
Full list of author information is
available at the end of the article

Abstract

Background: Over recent years, software developers have been evaluating the benefits of both Service-Oriented Architecture (SOA) and software fault tolerance techniques based on design diversity. This is achieved by creating fault-tolerant composite services that leverage functionally-equivalent services. Three major design issues need to be considered while building software fault-tolerant architectures based on design diversity: (i) selection of variants; (ii) selection of an adjudication algorithm to choose one of the results; and (iii) execution of variants. In addition, applications based on SOA need to function effectively in a dynamic environment where it is necessary to postpone decisions until runtime. In this scenario, control is highly distributed and involves conflicting user requirements. We aim to support the software architect in the design of fault-tolerant compositions.

Methods: Leveraging a taxonomy for fault-tolerant systems, this paper proposes guidelines to aid software architects in making key design decisions. The taxonomy is used as the basis for defining a set of guidelines to support the architect in making decisions related to fault tolerance in SOA. The same taxonomy is used in a systematic literature review of solutions for fault-tolerant composite services.
The review investigates how existing approaches for fault-tolerant composite services address design diversity issues and also specific issues related to SOA.

Results: The contribution of this work is twofold: (i) a set of guidelines for supporting the design of fault-tolerant SOA, based on a taxonomy for fault tolerance techniques; and (ii) a systematic literature review of existing solutions for designing fault-tolerant compositions using design diversity.

Conclusion: Although existing solutions have made significant contributions to the development of fault-tolerant SOAs, there is a lack of approaches for fault-tolerant service composition that support strategies with diverse quality requirements and encompassing sophisticated context-aware capabilities. This paper discusses which design issues have been addressed by existing diversity-based approaches for fault-tolerant composite services. Finally, practical issues and difficulties are summarized and directions for future work are suggested.

Keywords: Software fault tolerance; Design diversity; Service-oriented architecture; Systematic literature review; Fault-tolerant service composition

1 Introduction

Nowadays, society is highly dependent on systems utilizing Service-Oriented Architectures (SOA) for its basic day-to-day functioning (Huhns and Singh 2005; Papazoglou et al. 2007). These systems range from online stores to complex applications, called mashups, that combine their own resources with content retrieved via services from external data sources to create new functionalities (Huhns and Singh 2005; Papazoglou et al. 2007; Zheng and Lyu 2010b). Nevertheless, it is unlikely that services (often controlled by third parties) will ever be completely free of software faults arising from wrong specifications or incorrect coding (Trivedi et al. 2010). Consequently, SOA-based applications should operate according to their specification in spite of faults from reused services. If faults are not tolerated then undesirable consequences could happen, which may range from mildly annoying to great financial losses (Nascimento et al. 2011; Papazoglou et al. 2007; Zheng and Lyu 2010b).

The adoption of software fault tolerance techniques based on design diversity has been advocated as a means of coping with residual software design faults in operational software (Lee and Anderson 1990). Design diversity is the provision of software components called variants, which have the same or an equivalent specification but with different designs and implementations (Gärtner 1999). An assumption of software fault tolerance techniques is that the probability of having the same fault in multiple variant components is lower, meaning that a fault present in a component should be detected and tolerated based on the behaviour of other variants (Lyu 1996). In the nineties, the use of techniques based on design diversity to tolerate software faults was widely criticised since variant software components used to be developed from scratch, which is very expensive (Anderson et al. 1985; Vouk et al. 1993). Therefore these techniques were generally used only in highly critical systems, in which the occurrence of failures would result in large financial losses or even loss of life. Nevertheless, in the context of SOA on the web, there are already many services that provide equivalent functionality, thus making such techniques more practical (Zheng and Lyu 2010b). These variant services might be simply cost-free and open access, or even offered by external organizations to cope with changes to user quality of services (QoS) requirements (Papazoglou et al. 2007). Due to the low cost of reusing existing variant services, several diversity-based approaches have been developed to support reliable SOA-based applications. These approaches operate as mediators between clients and variant services. The latter are structured in fault-tolerant composite web services (Nascimento et al. 2011; Zheng and Lyu 2010b). Hereafter we refer to fault-tolerant composite web services as FT-compositions. From the clients' viewpoint, an FT-composition works as a single, reliable service.

In order to design reliable SOA applications, important design decisions have to be made by the architect. Such decisions are difficult, especially in the context of mashups, since the architect has to consider many aspects related to both fault tolerance and SOA-specific quality requirements. Regarding fault tolerance, the architect has to consider, for example: the availability of variants, the best fault tolerance technique to be used in a certain context, how the system should fail and scenarios involving error detection and handling (failure modes), the categories of faults to be tolerated (fault latency), assumptions about the environment and components (fault assumptions), etc.

The software architect developing a fault-tolerant SOA application should consider three major design issues when using design diversity: (i) selection of variants, since the variants need to be sufficiently diverse and able to tolerate software faults; (ii) selection of an adjudicator to determine the acceptability of the results obtained from the variants (Daniels et al. 1997; Lee and Anderson 1990); and (iii) execution strategy that directs the execution of the variants. For each of these design issues, the architect has to choose the specific fault tolerance technique to be used. Guidelines to support this task should also take into account implementations that realize different sets of quality requirements (e.g. memory consumption, financial cost, response time or reliability). The design decisions are also affected by characteristics of the functionality (e.g., allows re-try, allows undo operation). Variants can be executed either sequentially or in parallel and variant outputs can be adjudicated by adopting different voting and acceptance algorithms (Daniels et al. 1997; Laprie et al. 1990).

When designing a system, the architect may reuse and adapt existing solutions. Nevertheless, existing work regarding fault-tolerant service compositions is written from different viewpoints and relies on different technical backgrounds. As a result, it is hard to compare them and to choose an appropriate solution to be applied. Thus, it is unclear the extent to which existing solutions support the above mentioned design issues related to software fault tolerance based on design diversity. In order to avoid neglecting important design issues related to fault tolerance, architects should use guidelines to support the identification of which design issues and respective solutions should be used depending on the application's requirements.

In this sense, the contribution of this work is twofold: (i) the proposal of guidelines for supporting the design of fault-tolerant SOA based on a taxonomy for fault tolerance techniques and (ii) a systematic review of existing solutions for designing FT-compositions using design diversity. Results from reviewed solutions are presented to support reuse of existing solutions. The central purpose, which unifies the two contributions, is to support the architect in the design of fault-tolerant compositions. The proposed guidelines utilize an existing taxonomy for fault-tolerant systems (Pullum 2001) in order to guide architects in their design decisions. Then, the systematic literature review classifies existing solutions according to the same taxonomy, thus providing a basis for comparison and analysis of the solutions according to the architect's specific needs.

Guidelines support different decisions regarding the design of FT-SOA: first, the guidelines address different failure modes. This enables the architect to plan which faults are to be tolerated. Subsequently, the guidelines support the architect in modelling the faults and the behavioural pattern of how these faults should be tolerated. This decision influences the choice of the adjudicator type. For example, intermittent faults can be detected and tolerated utilizing design diversity and majority election design techniques. Also, the number of variants will be directly affected by the number of concurrent failures to be tolerated. The architect can assess the number of variants that are required to achieve the desired level of reliability. This design decision is also affected by the availability of resources as this will place limits on the number of variants that are feasible.

The systematic review compares characteristics of existing solutions in order to support architectural-level decisions regarding software fault tolerance and SOA quality requirements. We followed the literature review method proposed by Kitchenham (2007). We first investigated design issues related to the selection and the execution of variants, as well as the adjudication of their outputs. Secondly, we investigated which SOA-specific requirements were addressed by the existing solutions. The proposed guidelines address the three major design issues and their different implementation solutions. Finally, we report our main findings and identify gaps in current approaches in order to suggest opportunities for research on reliable SOA-based applications.

The remainder of the paper is structured as follows. Section 2 presents important concepts related to SOA and software fault-tolerance. These concepts are utilized in the taxonomy for fault-tolerant SOA. Section 3 presents the taxonomy combining elements from the fault-tolerance domain with elements from the SOA domain. Section 4 presents the results and discussion. This includes the guidelines for supporting the SOA architect in designing FT-compositions. It also presents results from the systematic literature review.

Section 5 discusses the threats and the validity of the review. Section 6 presents related work, which also considers related literature reviews of software fault tolerance techniques. Finally, Section 7 presents some concluding remarks and directions for continuing work.

2 Background

2.1 Service-Oriented Architecture (SOA)

Many software systems are being implemented following the Service-Oriented Architecture (SOA) approach with the aim of achieving higher levels of interoperability (Huhns and Singh 2005; Papazoglou et al. 2007). SOA is focused on creating a design style, technology, and process framework that allow enterprises to develop, interconnect, and maintain enterprise applications and services efficiently and cost-effectively (Huhns and Singh 2005). A service in SOA is an exposed piece of functionality with three essential properties. Firstly, a service is self-contained in that it maintains its own state. Secondly, a service is platform-independent, implying that the interface contract to the service is limited to platform-independent assertions. Lastly, a service can be dynamically located, invoked and (re)combined (Huhns and Singh 2005; Papazoglou et al. 2007). Therefore, multiple services running over heterogeneous systems may then interact and be used as building blocks for new applications (Papazoglou et al. 2007).

2.2 SOA-specific scenarios

As previously mentioned, software architects can achieve the benefits of both fault-tolerant and service-oriented architectures by structuring variants as FT-compositions. Papazoglou et al. (2006, 2007, 2007) list a set of roles and functionalities that a service composition should encompass for the aggregation of multiple services into a single composite service. We use this list to classify elements of our primary studies as described below:

- *Interoperability Capabilities*: Whenever a service composition provides its functionalities by means of interfaces that are platform-independent, a client from any communication device using any computational platform, operating system, or programming language can reuse the solution. That is, the service composition aggregates services provided by other service providers into a distinct value-added service and may itself act as service provider (Papazoglou et al. 2006).
- *Autonomic composition of services:* service compositions should equip themselves with adaptive service capabilities so that they can continually morph themselves to

respond to environmental demands and changes without compromising operational and financial efficiencies (Papazoglou and Heuvel 2007). Examples of support for autonomic composition of services include automatically discovering new partners to interact with; automatically selecting partners and options that would, for example, maximize benefits and reduce costs (Papazoglou et al. 2006); and automatically detecting that some business composition requirements are no longer satisfied by the current implementation and react to requirement violations (Papazoglou et al. 2006).

- *QoS-aware service compositions:* To be successful service compositions need to be QoS-aware. For example, services should be composed in accordance with an extensible set of Quality-of-Service (QoS) properties and high-level policies (e.g. performance levels, security requirements, SLA stipulations, and so forth). QoS encompasses important non-functional service requirements, such as performance metrics (response time, for instance), security attributes, (transactional) integrity, reliability, scalability, and availability (Papazoglou and Heuvel 2007; Papazoglou et al. 2006).

- *Business-driven automated compositions:* a service composition at the business-level should pose the requirements, possibly from different stakeholders with conflicting needs, and the boundaries for the automatic composition at the system level. While the service composition at the business level should be supported by user-centered and highly interactive techniques, system level service compositions should be fully automated and hidden to the end users. System level compositions should be QoS-aware, should be generated and monitored automatically, and should also be based on autonomic computing principles (Papazoglou and Heuvel 2007; Papazoglou et al. 2006).

2.3   Software fault tolerance and design diversity

A fault is the identified or hypothesized cause of an error (Avizienis et al. 2004; Trivedi et al. 2010). An error is part of the system state that is liable to lead to a failure (Avizienis et al. 2004; Trivedi et al. 2010). A failure, in turn, occurs when the service delivered by the system deviates from the specified service (Avizienis et al. 2004). So, with software fault tolerance, we want to prevent failures by tolerating faults whose occurrences are known when errors are detected (Lee and Anderson 1990). When designing fault tolerance, a first prerequisite is to specify, by means of fault models, the faults that should be tolerated (Gärtner 1999). The next step is to enrich the system under consideration with components or concepts that provide protection against faults from the fault models (Gärtner 1999).

For instance, this work specifically addresses software faults According to Pullum (2001), '*software faults may be traced to incorrect requirements (where the software matches the requirements, but the behaviour specified in the requirements is not appropriate) or to the implementation (software design and coding) not satisfying the requirements*'. Software faults are also called design faults or bugs (Pullum 2001).

Software faults cannot be tolerated by simple replication of identical software components since the same mistake will exist in each copy of the components (Lee and Anderson 1990). A solution to this problem is to introduce diversity into the software replicas (Lee and Anderson 1990; Lyu 1996; Wilfredo 2000). Design diversity is the provision of functionally-equivalent software components, called variants, through different designs and implementations.

Design diversity begins with an initial requirements specification. Each developer or development organization is responsible for a variant and implements the variant according to the specification (Gärtner 1999; Laprie et al. 1990; Pullum 2001). Figure 1 illustrates the basic design diversity concept. Inputs are distributed to variants. The variants execute their operations and produce their results, from which a single correct or acceptable result must be derived, if any (Pullum 2001). The mechanism responsible for this task is called an *adjudicator*.

Adjudicators generally come in two flavours, voters and Acceptance Tests (ATs). A brief description of voter characteristics and differences are presented in Section 3.1, in the context of the proposed taxonomy. We refer to Pullum (2001) for a more detailed description about the various types of adjudicators and their operations (pages 269-324). For example, specific adjudicators covered by Pullum (2001) are exact majority, consensus, formal consensus, formal majority, median, mean, weighted, and dynamic voters; acceptance tests can be based on satisfaction of requirements, accounting tests, computer run-time acceptance tests and reasonableness acceptance tests.

The philosophy behind design diversity is to decrease the probability that variants fail at the same time for the same input value because this usually makes failures of variants detectable (Lyu 1996). To illustrate this point with a hypothetical example, Figure 2 presents a diversity-based solution that leverages three variants and a majority voter to tolerate software faults. For instance, two variants present software faults, however these variants do not fail for the same input cases. Consequently, for the provided input, the

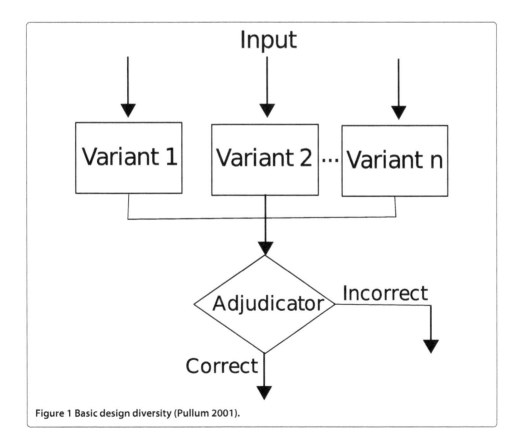

Figure 1 Basic design diversity (Pullum 2001).

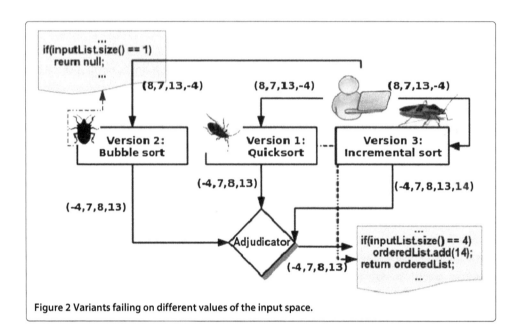

Figure 2 Variants failing on different values of the input space.

majority voter is able to tolerate the software fault whose activation has led to failure of one of the variants. Figure 3 illustrates a diversity-based solution that leverages three variant services such that two of them fail on the same input value, leading to a failure of the majority voter as whole.

2.4   Error recovery

Error recovery is the process in which the erroneous state is substituted with an error-free state (Lee and Anderson 1990). Error recovery is performed using either backward

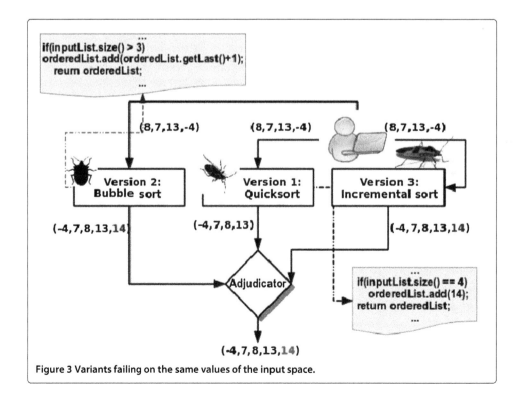

Figure 3 Variants failing on the same values of the input space.

recovery or forward recovery. On the one hand, *backward recovery* attempts to return the system to a correct or error-free state by restoring or rolling back the system to a previously saved state, which is assumed to be error-free. On the other hand, *forward recovery* attempts to return the system to a correct or error-free state by finding a new state from which the system can continue operation. Compared to backward error recovery, forward recovery is usually more efficient in terms of the overhead (*e.g.* time and memory) it imposes (Lee and Anderson 1990). On the other hand, it is usually not possible to design general forward recovery mechanisms.

3   Method

3.1   A taxonomy for software fault tolerance based on design diversity for SOA

We define a taxonomy combining elements from the fault-tolerance domain (Section 2.3) with elements from the SOA domain (Section 2.2).

Figure 4 presents the taxonomy, which considers the common design issues and their different design solutions, as well as the specific roles desirable in SOA-based applications. The proposed taxonomy was adopted to classify our primary studies. Both design issues and decisions were derived from the analysis of fault tolerance techniques based on design diversity (*e.g. Recovery Blocks, N-Version Programming, N-Self Checking Programming, Consensus Recovery Block* and *Acceptance Voting*) and adjudicators (Elmendorf 1972; Horning et al. 1974; Kim 1984; Laprie et al. 1990; Lee and Anderson 1990; Lyu 1996; Pullum 2001; Scott et al. 1987). We also considered the reliable hybrid pattern structure proposed by Kim and Vouk (1997). In comparison with their work, our work *(i)* identifies different types of voters and acceptance tests based on the general taxonomy of adjudicators presented by Pullum (2001); and *(ii)* explicitly distinguishes the different schemes of variant execution (i.e. sequentially or in parallel). Different design decisions employ different measures of quality requirements (Pullum 2001). These differences make each design solution suitable for a particular application. In Section 4.1, we briefly

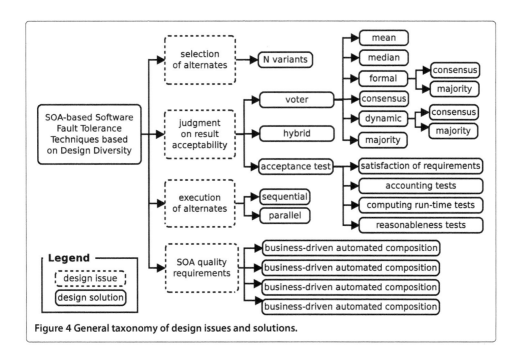

Figure 4 General taxonomy of design issues and solutions.

compare the described design solutions and present some general remarks about their effectiveness.

The elements of the taxonomy are described below.

Design issue I - selection of variants: The number of variant software components (n) must each be provided by components with different software designs and implementations. The main goal of increasing diversity is to detect faults in variant when the variants fail on disjoint subsets of the input space. Even if variants fail on overlapping subsets of the input space, design diversity is still considered a useful measure of reducing the risk from design faults (Laprie et al. 1990; Lyu 1996). If variants have minimal overlaps between their failure regions, a reliable configuration may be formed even when variants individually have modest reliability. Finally, variants might be chosen at different points during the software lifecycle.

Design issue II - judgement on result acceptability: Adjudicators, or decision mechanisms, generally come in two flavours, voters and Acceptance Tests (ATs).

Voters: Voters are based on a relative judgement on result acceptability by comparison of variant results (Pullum 2001). We present an overview of voters that are mostly described in the literature (Lee and Anderson 1990; Pullum 2001). We refer to Pullum (2001) for further details on voter procedures and pseudocode.

- **Exact majority voter:** The exact majority selects the value of the majority of the variants as its presumably the correct result (McAllister and Vouk 1996). This voter is also known as the m-out-of-n voter (Pullum 2001). The agreement number, m, is the number of versions required to match for system success (Eckhardt and Lee 1985). The total number of alternatives, *i.e.* n, is rarely more than 3. Consequently, the majority voter is generally seen as a 2-out-of-3 voter.
- **Consensus voter:** This voter allows the selection of a consensus or set of matching variant results as the adjudicated result if no majority exists (Pullum 2001). That is, this voter is a generalization of the majority voter (Vouk et al. 1993).
- **Formal consensus and Majority voter:** The *Formal Consensus* and *Majority* voters are variations of, respectively, the consensus and the exact majority voters (Pullum 2001). Basically, the formal voter uses a comparison tolerance indicating the maximum distance allowed between two correct output values for the same input. In this way, variant results that are different, but quite close together, are the adjudicated correct answers.
- **Median voter:** The median voter selects the median of the variant output values as its adjudicated result. Variant outputs must be in an ordered space (Pullum 2001).
- **Mean and weighted voter:** The mean and weighted voter select, respectively, the mean or weighted average of the variants' output values, which are in an ordered space, as the adjudicated result (Broen 1975). Additional information related to the trustworthiness of the alternatives might be used to assign weights to the variant outputs, if using the weighted average voter (Pullum 2001).
- **Dynamic majority and Consensus voters:** Unlike the previously described voters, dynamic voters are not defeated when any variant fails to provide a result (Pullum 2001). Dynamic majority and consensus voters operate in a way similar to, respectively, majority and consensus voters, with the exception that dynamic voters can handle a varying number of inputs (Pullum 2001). When the dynamic voter

adjudicates upon two results, a comparison takes place. When comparing, if the results match, the matching value will be output as the correct result. Otherwise, no selected output will be returned.

Acceptance Tests (ATs): ATs rely on an absolute judgement with respect to a specification (Lee and Anderson 1990; Pullum 2001). With ATs, only one variant is executed at a time. The AT is responsible for checking whether the produced result is correct. In case it is not, another variant is executed until a correct result is obtained, if possible.

- **Acceptance tests based on satisfaction of requirements:** ATs are constructed with conditions that must be met at the completion of variant execution (Pullum 2001). These conditions might arise from the problem statement of the software specifications.
- **Accounting tests:** Accounting ATs are suitable for transaction-oriented applications with simple mathematical operations (Pullum 2001). For example, when a large number of records are reordered or transmitted, a tally is made of both the sum over all records and the total number of records of a particular data field. These results can be compared between the source and the destination to implement an accounting check AT (Pullum 2001).
- **Computer run-time tests:** Run-time tests detect anomalous states such as overflow, undefined operation code, underflow, write-protection violations, or end of file (Pullum 2001).
- **Reasonableness tests:** These ATs are used to determine if the state of an object in the system is reasonable, *e.g.*, precomputed ranges or expected sequences of program states (Pullum 2001).
  Hybrid adjudicators: A hybrid adjudicator generally incorporates a combination of AT and voter characteristics. For example, variant results are evaluated by an AT, and only accepted results are sent to the voter (Laprie et al. 1990).

Design issue III - execution of variants: Variants can be executed either sequentially or in parallel. The execution schemes should provide all variants with exactly the same experience of the system state when their respective executions start to ensure consistency of input data (Nascimento et al. 2013), which be can be achieved by employing backward recovery or forward recovery (*Section 2.4*). Sequential execution often requires the use of checkpoints (it usually employs backward recovery), and parallel execution often requires the use of algorithms to ensure consistency of input data (it usually employs forward recovery by invoking all the variants and coordinating their execution through a synchronization regime) (Pullum 2001; Wilfredo 2000).

- **Sequential:** in implementing a sequential execution scheme the variants are executed one at a time. Generally, in the sequential execution scheme, the most efficient variant, *e.g.* in terms of response time or financial cost, is located first in the series, and is termed *primary variant*. The less efficient variants are placed serially after the primary variant and are referred to as (secondary) variants. Thus, the resulting rank of the variants reflects the graceful degradation in the performance of the variants (Pullum 2001).

- **Parallel:** in the parallel execution scheme, variants are executed concurrently. The resulting outputs can be provided to the adjudicator in an *asynchronous* fashion as each version completes, or in a *synchronous* manner (Daniels et al. 1997).

3.2 Systematic literature review method

This review has been conducted as a systematic literature review based on guidelines proposed by Kitchenham and Charters (2007). The guidelines cover three phases of a systematic review: planning, executing and reporting. In our work, the goal of the review is to provide a better understanding of diversity-based approaches for FT-compositions (Kitchenham and Charters 2007), in order to support decisions of the software architect in terms of reuse. In the following, Section 3.3 presents details about the planning of the systematic review, while Section 4.2 presents details about the execution and results.

3.3 Planning

3.3.1 Research questions

This work aims to answer the following research questions.

RQ1 What design issues and respective design solutions related to the fault tolerance taxonomy of Figure 4 are being addressed?

RQ2 What SOA specific requirements are being addressed?

To address RQ1, we classify existing solutions using the proposed taxonomy of design solutions for fault tolerance based on design diversity (Figure 4). To address RQ2, we consider a list of quality requirements that service compositions should address, presented in Section 2.2. Related to RQ1 and RQ2, we also describe some important design issues related to general software fault tolerance techniques, and analyze such solutions in terms of preserving important requirements inherent of SOA.

3.3.2 Search process

Searches for primary studies were performed upon databases of Software Engineering research that met the following criteria (Williams and Carver 2010):

- Contains peer-reviewed software engineering journals articles, conference proceedings, and book chapters.
- Contains multiple journals and conference proceedings, which include volumes that range from 2000 to 2012.
- Used in other software engineering systematic reviews (e.g. (Cardozo et al. 2010; Jorgensen and Shepperd 2007; Kitchenham et al. 2007; Williams and Carver 2010)).

The resulting list of databases was: *(i)* ACM Digital Library; *(ii)* IEEE Electronic Library; *(iii)* SpringerLink; *(iv)* Scopus; and *(v)* Scirus (Elsevier).

3.3.3 Search string

A search string was created to extract data from each database. We adopted various combinations of terms from *(i)* the main purpose of this review; *(ii)* the research question (Kitchenham and Charters 2007; Kitchenham et al. 2009) and *(iii)* meaningful synonyms and variant spellings. Whenever it was necessary, this search string was decomposed into several search terms (*e.g.* Recovery Block AND Service-Oriented Architectures) due to restrictions imposed by some of the search engines. The resulting search string is summarised in following:

(*fault tolerance OR diversity OR fault-tolerant OR redundancy OR Recovery block OR N-Version Programming OR Distributed Recovery Blocks OR N Self-Checking Programming OR Consensus Recovery Block OR Acceptance Voting OR dependability OR dependable OR reliable OR reliability*) < *AND* > (*service-oriented architecture OR SOA OR service computing OR SOC OR web services*)

3.3.4 Study selection

The database searches resulted in a large number of candidate papers. We adopted study selection criteria to identify those studies that provide direct evidence about the research question.

Inclusion criteria:

- Approaches based on software diversity for FT-Compositions that specifically focused on web services. Additionally the solutions that were targeted supported one or more issues identified in the taxonomy (Figure 4), *i.e.*, selection of variant services, execution of variants and judgement on result acceptability.

Exclusion criteria:

- Solutions for reliable SOA-based applications employing solely replicas of identical services - although the adoption of identical replicas can improve system availability, they are not able to tolerate *software* faults (Gärtner 1999; Lee and Anderson 1990).
- Solutions for fault-tolerant SOAs based on data diverse software fault tolerance techniques.
- Solutions for fault-tolerant SOA relying solely on exception handling - variant services are not employed as part of the exception handling mechanism.
- Duplicate reports of the same solution - when several reports of the proposed solution exist in different papers the most complete version of the study was included in the review.
- Short papers, introductions to special issues, tutorials, and mini-tracks.
- Studies presented in languages other than English.
- Papers addressing empirical studies on fault tolerance based on design diversity applied to *SOAs* - not proposing any particular solution to employ FT-compositions.
- Grey literature, that is, informally published written material.

These criteria were applied as performed in (Kitchenham and Charters 2007; Williams and Carver 2010):

1. Reading the title in order to eliminate any irrelevant papers.
2. Reading the abstract and keywords to eliminate additional papers whose title may have fit, but abstract did not relate to the research question.
3. Reading the introduction and, whenever it is necessary, the conclusion to eliminate additional papers whose abstract was not enough to decide whether the inclusion/exclusion criteria are applicable.

4.   Reading the remainder of the paper and including only those that addressed the research question.

3.3.5 Data collection and synthesis

We created a data extraction form to collect all the information needed to address the review question (Kitchenham and Charters 2007). The contents of the designed data form are composed by (Kitchenham and Charters 2007; Kitchenham et al. 2009): the source (*e.g.* journal, conference) and full reference; date of extraction; summary of the proposed solution; supported design issues/solutions (Figure 4); and space for additional notes.

4   Results and discussion

4.1   Design decision guidelines to realize fault tolerance in SOA

The proposed solution encompasses a set of guidelines to support the architect in key decisions relating to fault tolerance. The proposed guidelines address the design decisions of the taxonomy presented in Section 3.1 (Figure 4). Figure 5 presents the activities that are part of the proposed guidelines. First, we show guidelines which advise the architect to specify the failure modes of the system. Then, the guidelines lead the architect to specify the fault latency and the scenarios of fault tolerance. For example, Byzantine faults (intermittent faults) could be acceptable (Lee and Anderson 1990; Randell 1975) whereas other types of faults, such as permanent faults, may be unacceptable. This information may influence the choice of the adjudicator type (e.g., majority election, average value).

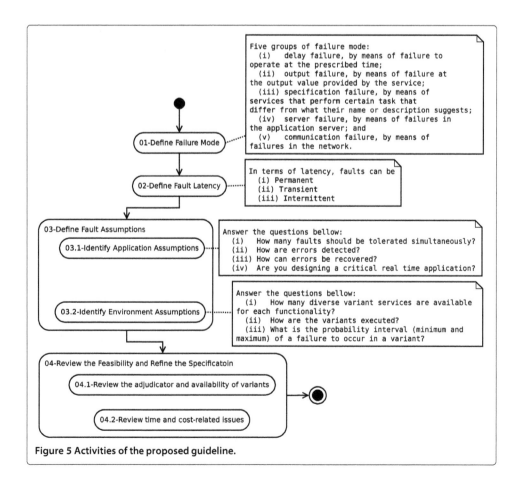

Figure 5 Activities of the proposed guideline.

Finally, the guidelines assist the architect in setting assumptions, in order to outline the scope of fault tolerance. After following the guidelines, the architect will have a classification of the features related to fault tolerance, following the classification of the taxonomy presented.

At the end of the process, the architect can assess whether the projected solution is feasible with respect to the availability of resources: e.g., number of variants. Depending on the number of variants needed to meet the demands of the system, the architect can now assess if it is necessary to reduce the scope of fault tolerance. For example, intermittent faults, also known as Byzantine faults, are usually detected and tolerated utilizing design diversity and majority election techniques. In this case, the number of variants will be directly affected by the number of concurrent faults to be tolerated. Depending on the available variants, the number of concurrent tolerated faults should be decreased.

In the following sections (4.1.1 to 4.1.6) we suggest four steps for designing fault tolerance: (i) define failure mode; (ii) define fault latency; (iii) define fault assumptions; and (iv) review the feasibility and refine the designed solution. After reviewing the solution, the next step is to try to reuse existing solutions. To support the architect, Section 4.2 presents a systematic literature review that classifies existing approaches according to the same taxonomy presented in Section 3.1 that was also used by the guidelines presented here.

4.1.1 Define failure modes

Failure modes can be seen as ways in which a software, equipment, or machine failure can occur. The specification of the failure mode helps the identification of faults in applications, which are the underlying causes of failures or which ones initiate a process which leads to failure.

In terms of SOA-based applications, we consider five groups of failure modes: (i) delay failure, which is a failure to operate at the prescribed time; (ii) output failure, when the output value provided by the service is incorrect; (iii) specification failure, when a service performs a task that differs from what their name or description suggests; (iv) server failure, a failure in the application server; and (v) communication failure, a failure in the network.

The architect must indicate which failure modes need to be addressed within the application model. That is, if its behaviour detection and handling should be part of the application scope. The answer here should be either yes or no. Details about how to consider each group are defined in the next steps: fault latency and fault assumptions.

4.1.2 Define fault latency

Fault latency is defined as the interval between the moments of fault occurrence and error generation (Shin and Lee 1984). This information is extremely important, since it directly affects how to handle the error caused by the fault. In terms of latency, faults can be permanent, transient or intermittent. Permanent faults are continuous and stable. In hardware, permanent faults reflect an irreversible physical change. Permanent faults are also known as "hard" faults. Transient faults result from temporary environmental conditions, and can be fixed by changing the respective conditions that cause the fault. Transient faults are also known as "soft" faults. Intermittent faults are only occasionally present due to unstable hardware or varying hardware or software states. Intermittent and transient faults are the major source of system errors. Even when it is not possible to repair the fault, the use of redundant resources allows the system to tolerate faults (Gärtner 1999; Lee and Anderson 1990). The manifestations of transient and intermittent faults and of incorrect hardware or software design are much more difficult to determine than permanent faults.

Fault latency is part of the fault model. The fault model is a design model that tries to predict what could go wrong, as well as the consequences of particular faults. In order to detail the fault model, the proposed guidelines state that, for each failure mode identified (Section 4.1.1), the architect has to specify how the error caused by the fault is expected to occur: permanently, transiently, or intermittently.

For example, a delay failure (failure mode) is characterised by performance problems, when a service says to execute in a certain period of time, but for some reason it is not able to do so. If the architect is considering this kind of failure in the failure mode, it is necessary to define how these failures can occur: permanently, in a transient way, or in an intermittent way. Considering it as a permanent fault, the error could be detected by time-out and a solution with two variant services would be sufficient to tolerate the error detect the problem by changing the faulty service to another one. If it is a transient fault caused by server overload, the handling could be, for example, to change the server. But assuming a fault model of intermittent faults, in some execution a certain service is faster than another, but in the following execution the scenario can be the opposite. So, redundant services could be executed in parallel and the adjudicator could consider the first reply it receives.

4.1.3   Define fault assumptions

The definition of *fault assumptions* contains information relating to the error detection and error recovery mechanisms. The proposed solution focuses on two types of assumption: (i) application assumptions; and (ii) environmental assumptions. Section 4.1.4 presents the guidelines for identifying assumptions related to the application, while Section 4.1.5 presents the guidelines for identifying assumptions related to the environment.

4.1.4   Identify application assumptions

In order to identify application assumptions, we outline four questions to be answered:

1. *How many faults should be tolerated simultaneously?* The answer to this question should be a number. It will interfere with the number of variants required to tolerate the faults. This also depends on the adopted design solution.
2. *How are errors detected?* The answer to this question can be either *by comparison* or *by checking a single result*. It aims to identify functionalities whose validity can be verified through acceptance tests, with no need of redundancy for error detection. The answer can also affect the number of variants required for fault tolerance.
3. *How can errors be recovered?* The answer to this question can be either *forward* or *backward* error recovery, according to the error recovery strategy of the respective functionalities (see Section 2.4). The answer to this question should support the decision regarding how to execute variants. In some cases, when a forward error recovery strategy is more effective, a sequential execution is recommended. For example, when a billing system is executed in parallel, after

processing redundant bills, some of them should be cancelled, since an undo operation is not applicable in such case.

4. *Are you designing a critical real-time application?* The answer of this yes/no question also supports the decision of which execution strategy to use. In case of a critical real-time system, a parallel execution could be preferable, if redundancy is needed.

4.1.5 *Identify environment assumptions*

Environment assumptions are restrictions related to the services' availability, the diversity amongst the variant services available, as well as existing execution policies. For this, three questions should be answered:

1. *How many diverse variant services are available for each functionality?* The answer to this question should be a number. It also supports the final decision regarding the appropriate design solution. For example, depending on the compatibility between the number of faults to be tolerated and the number of diverse variant services available, the feasibility of a fault-tolerant solution may not be possible.

2. *How are the variants executed?* The answer to this question can be *for free*, *cheap*, or *expensive*. Such answer should support the decision of which execution strategy to use (sequential or in parallel). For example parallelism may have expensive running costs.

3. *What is the probability interval (minimum and maximum) of a failure to occur in a variant?* The answer to this question can guide the architect in choosing and discarding variants based on monitoring data. Besides, this information may also interfere with the choice of the adjudicator, as discussed in Section 4.1.6.

Finally, for each failure mode and fault latency identified by the architect, a proper handling behaviour should be specified. Table 1 illustrates handling behaviour for errors related to faults, according to the failure mode and the assumed fault latency. The example considers scenarios involving the reliability quality attribute. It is important to know that the architect may assume more than one fault latency for the same failure mode. In these cases, the more general solution, which fits all the latencies, should be used.

4.1.6 *Review the feasibility and refine the specification*

After defining the initial specification related to fault tolerance, the last step is to review the feasibility of the designed solution and refine it based on concepts related to classical fault tolerance techniques. In order to make this task easier, in the following we provide a summary comparing classical fault tolerance techniques, which is important for choosing a design solution, giving a special attention to the type of adjudicator. It is important to stress that the design issues presented are compliant with the taxonomy presented in Figure 4. Instead of presenting a full discussion on such techniques, we summarise some of the findings on design diversity, in particular the findings related to non-functional characteristics of the described design solutions, represented by the taxonomy. The analysis of these characteristics provide a good support to define the system fault tolerance (*Section 2.3*). A summary of results and discussion for supporting the SOA architect on choosing fault tolerance techniques is presented in the following. A detailed discussion in the context of a literature review of existing solutions is presented in Section 4.2.

Table 1 Example of fault tolerance specification using the guidelines

Failure mode	Fault latency	Fault assumption	How to tolerate
Delay	Permanent	Inefficient Algorithm	Change the faulty service to another one
		Hardware problem	Change the application server
	Transient	Server overload	Change the application server
	Intermittent	Environmental instability	Execution in parallel to get the fastest reply
Output	Permanent	Software bug	Use variant services to detect and majority election to tolerate
	Transient	Server overload	Use variant services to detect and majority election to tolerate
	Intermittent	Electromagnetic interference	Use variant services to detect and majority election to tolerate
Specification	Permanent	Malicious service	Use variant services to detect and majority election to tolerate
	Transient	DNS mistake due to environmental instability	Use variant services to detect and majority election to tolerate
	Intermittent	Unknown cause	Use variant services to detect and majority election to tolerate
Server	Permanent	Hardware failure	Change the application to a mirror server
	Transient	Memory overload	Change the application to a mirror server
	Intermittent	Environmental instability	Use redundant servers in parallel, and synchronisation algorithms for keeping the consistency among servers
Communication	Permanent	Breaking the optical fibber cable	Change the network link
	Transient	Network overload	Change the network link
	Intermittent	Electromagnetic interference	Use redundant communication channel in parallel

Review the adjudicator and availability of variants Firstly, it is essential to check the availability of variants that are sufficiently diverse in order to decrease the probability of occurrence of coincident failures (Eckhardt et al. 1991; Hilford et al. 1997; Knight and Leveson 1986; Lyu et al. 1994; Nascimento et al. 2012a). Regarding the judgement on the result acceptability, the adjudicator would run its decision-making algorithm on the results and determine which one (if any) to output as the presumably correct result. Just as we can imagine different specific criteria for determining the 'best' item depending on what that item is, so we can use different criteria for selecting the 'correct' or 'most acceptable' result to output. The probabilities of activation of related faults between variants are likely to be greater for voters than for acceptance tests (ATs) (Arlat et al. 1988; McAllister and Vouk 1996). But in general, ATs are more difficult to construct in practice because they are strongly application-dependent and because it is not always possible to determine a criterion to judge variant results (Di Giandomenico and Strigini 1990). As a consequence, voting is a more useful technique in a practical setting, because voting adjudicators are easier to develop (Wilfredo 2000).

The exact majority voter is most appropriately used to examine integer or binary results, but it can be used on any type of input (Saglietti 1992). The majority voter has a high probability of selecting the correct result value when the probability of a variant failure is less than 50% and the number of variants, n, is 'large' (Blough and Sullivan (1990) used $n = 7$ and $n = 15$ in the study). However, when the probability of a variant failure exceeds

50%, then the majority voter performs poorly (Blough and Sullivan 1990). In fact, all voters have a high probability of selecting the correct result value when the probability of variant failures is less than 50% (Blough and Sullivan 1990). A median voter can be defined for variant outputs consisting of a single value in an ordered space (*e.g.* real number). Median voter is a fast algorithm and is likely to select a correct result in the correct range (Blough and Sullivan 1990). If it can be assumed that, for each input value, no incorrect result lies between two correct results, and that a majority of the replicas' outputs are correct, then the median voter produces a correct output (Pullum 2001).

Consensus voting is more stable than majority voting and always offers reliability at least equivalent to majority voting (McAllister and Vouk 1996; Vouk et al. 1993). Nevertheless, in terms of implementation, the consensus voting algorithm is more complex than the majority one, since the consensus voting algorithm requires multiple comparisons (Lee and Anderson 1990). Blough performed a study on the effectiveness of voting algorithms (Blough and Sullivan 1990). He states that the median voter is expected to perform better than the mean voting strategy. He also shows the overall superiority of the median strategy over the majority voting scheme (Blough and Sullivan 1990). Furthermore, under circumstances in which some or all variants might not produce their results (*e.g.* some or all variants not providing their results within the maximum expected time frame; catastrophic failure of some or all of the variants), dynamic voters are the best option since they can process zero to *n* inputs. Finally, acceptance tests, exact majority, consensus and dynamic voters can process any type of variant outputs, while the remaining adjudicators must receive inputs in an ordered space (Pullum 2001).

We summarise some details of the described voters in Table 2, which is based on a summary table by Pullum (2001). We have added the type of variant results in which the voter is able to judge. This table states the corresponding recommended fault tolerance technique, given the type of variant results provided to the voter and the type of voter. To use this table, it is important to consider the primary concerns surrounding the application areas of the software system and details about the output space. For example, if safety is the primary concern, it is recommended to adopt the voter that would rather raise an exception and produce no selected output than present an incorrect output as a presumably correct one (*e.g.* the exact majority or dynamic majority voters) (Pullum 2001). If the primary goal is to avoid cases in which the voter does not reach a decision, i.e., *an* answer is better than no answer, than it is sufficient to adopt the voter that reaches a 'No output' result least often (*e.g.* the median voter) (Pullum 2001). Based on this criterion, exact majority voter, formal majority voter, and dynamic majority voter can be considered the safest voters, because they produce incorrect output 'only' in cases where most or all of the variants produce identical and wrong results.

Review time and cost-related issues With respect to the execution of variants, in the parallel scheme, there is an underlying assumption that sufficient hardware resources are available to enable the execution of variants concurrently. Even with sufficient parallelism, the execution time of this scheme will be constrained by the slowest version - there may be a substantial difference in the execution speeds of the fastest and slowest version because of the need to generate independent designs (Lee and Anderson 1990). When variants are executed in parallel, there is also a synchronisation time overhead. The time required to execute variants in a sequential way will range from the execution time of the primary

Table 2 Voter results given details about variant output space ((Pullum 2001) – page 310)

Variant results	Voter							
	Exact majority	Median	Mean	Weighted average	Consensus	Formal majority	Dynamic majority	Dynamic consensus
All outputs identical and correct	C	C	C	PC	C	C	C	C
Majority Identical and correct	C	C	PC	PC	C	C	C	C
Plurality identical and correct	NO	PC	PC	PC	C	NO	NO	C
Distinct outputs, all correct	NO	C	PC	PC	NO	NO	NO	NO
Distinct outputs, all incorrect	NO	—	PI	PI	NO	NO	NO	NO
Plurality identical and wrong	NO	PI	PI	PI	—	NO	NO	—
Majority identical and wrong	—	—	PI	PI	—	—	—	—
All outputs identical and wrong	—	—	—	—	—	—	—	—
Variant result type	Any type	Ordered space	Ordered space	Ordered space	Any type	Floating-point arithmetic	Any type	Any type

The voter outputs are:
- **C** - Correct: The voter outputs a correct result;
- **PC** - Probably correct: The voter outputs a result that is probably correct, but may be incorrect;
- **PI** - Probably incorrect: The voter outputs a result that is probably incorrect, but may be correct;
- **I** - Incorrect: The voter outputs an incorrect result;
- **NO** - No output: The voter does not output a result; an exception is raised.

variant (if acceptance tests are employed and the primary result is acceptable) to the sum of execution time of all variants, *e.g.* if all variant results are subjected to ATs (Buys et al. 2011). Nevertheless, this time will normally be constrained by the execution time of the primary variant (Lee and Anderson 1990). Furthermore, under some circumstances, a specific execution scheme is not applied, *e.g.*, when there is a processing cost charged for the use of variant services, invoking them in parallel might incur in greater actual cost,*i.e.*, in sequential schemes, not all variants are necessarily executed (Zheng and Lyu 2010a). Moreover, the error recovery strategy defined in the fault assumptions (backward or forward) might also interfere on the way variants should be executed.

In the following we present details about the systematic literature review involving solutions for composing fault-tolerant services. Such a review aims to support the architect in the task of reusing existing solution. The most relevant works are presented and classified in the target taxonomy (Figure 4).

4.2 Systematic literature review results
In this section, we present the results obtained.

4.2.1 Search results
The searches returned thousands of papers that were filtered down to 23, and then to 17 primary studies, three of which are journal articles (Mansour and Dillon 2011; Yuhui and Romanovsky 2008; Zheng and Lyu 2010a), three book chapters (Dillen et al. 2012; Gorbenko et al. 2005; Kotonya and Hall 2010), ten conference papers (Abdeldjelil et al. 2012; Buys et al. 2011; Gonçalves and Rubira 2010; Gotze et al. 2008; Looker et al. 2005; Nascimento et al. 2011, 2012b; Nourani 2011; Santos et al. 2005; Townend et al. 2005), and one workshop paper (Laranjeiro and Vieira 2007).

In the solutions by Dillen et al. (2012), Santos et al. (2005) and Mansour and Dillen (2011), despite each service being named a replica by the authors, these solutions were designed to tolerate different responses by means of adjudicator mechanisms. This suggests these solutions could be also implemented as a diversity-based solution. Therefore, these solutions were included as primary studies.

Regarding the papers excluded from the first filtered 23 publications, the articles (Zheng and Lyu 2008, 2010b) are short versions of another article (Zheng and Lyu 2010a), the article (Abdeldjelil et al. 2012) is also an extended version of the article (Faci et al. 2011). The study presented by Gorbenko et al. in (Gorbenko et al. 2009) and by Nascimento et al. (2012a) are based, respectively, on the solutions proposed in (Gorbenko et al. 2005) and in (Nascimento et al. 2012b) - therefore, we consider the proposed solutions, i.e. (Gorbenko et al. 2005; Nascimento et al. 2012b), as primary studies. Xu (2011) examined challenges in the fields of dependability and security that need to be addressed carefully in order to provide sufficient support to enable service-oriented systems to offer non-trivial Quality of Service guarantees. Then, Xu presents several advanced techniques developed at the University of Leeds to achieve dependability and security in service-oriented systems and applications, including, the solution proposed by Townend et al. (2005). Therefore, only the work by Townend et al. (2005) is included as a primary study. Milanovic and Miroslaw (2007) also highlight the use of techniques to tolerate software faults in SOA, including techniques based on software diversity (e.g. N-Versions); however, no specific solution is proposed in this direction.

4.2.2 Classification of the primary studies

In Additional file 1: Supplementary Table, we present the summary of the design solutions supported by the analysed primary studies. Each primary study was classified as follows:

Y(yes), the design solution is supported by a primary study; **N(no)**, no information at all about the design solution is specified; **U(unknown)** according to the authors the design issue is supported, however, what design solutions are supported cannot be readily inferred.

It is important to emphasise that Additional file 1: Supplementary Table was fashioned to show which design issues have been addressed by existing approaches for FT-compositions. It might be meaningless to rank the primary studies based solely on their 'quantity of *Yes*' since the studies present different purposes (e.g. some solutions are mainly focused on supporting the selection of variant services (Nascimento et al. 2012b; Townend et al. 2005), while other ones are focused on executing variant services (Gonçalves and Rubira 2010; Yuhui and Romanovsky 2008)). Although it's difficult to compare these solutions, Section 4.1 presents non-functional characteristics related to the design solutions supported by the authors - thus supporting researchers' decision making when selecting design solutions more adjusted to different clients requirements.

In the next subsections, we discuss the answers to the two research questions presented in Section 3.3.1 and present the main proposed solutions regarding the design issues (Figure 4). Because of space limitations the summaries of solutions are representative rather than exhaustive.

4.2.3 Selection of variant services

The aims of selecting variants are twofold: *(i)* to increase the probability of selecting variants that are provided by different designs and implementations; *(ii)* to determine an appropriate degree and/or selection of variant services targeting an optimal trade-off between reliability measures as well as performance-related factors such as timeliness, cost and resource consumption. In general, variants have been chosen at different points during the software lifecycle. For instance, they can be chosen at design time by the engineer, configured manually once the software is deployed, or even be discovered and selected at runtime by the software itself.

The solutions by Townend et al. (2005) and by Nascimento et al. (2012b) address the issue of ensuring that variant services are diverse. Townend et al. (2005) aims to detect diverse designs during runtime. This is achieved by monitoring previous results and flow of data from a variant service using interaction provenance in order to reveal evidence that two variants share similar services or workflows. Such evidence may include matching common-mode failures that have propagated back from two variant services. Nascimento et al. (2012b) propose an experimental setup to investigate, from clients' viewpoint and by means of statistical tests, whether variant services present a difference in their outputs and their failure behaviours. Their solution also investigates if and by how much the use of FT-composition improves reliability when compared to a single non-fault-tolerant service (Nascimento et al. 2012b).

Variant services may be chosen using different measurements at different points throughout the execution. Buys et al. (2011) and Dillen et al. (2012) propose a fault tolerance strategy that autonomously changes the amount of redundancy or the selection of variant services. The architecture proposed by Buys et al. (2011) bases this decision upon the current execution context and clients' requirements at the time of request. They propose a measure to infer combinations of variant services that are, in fact, effective. This measure quantifies the historical effectiveness of each variant service by penalising or rewarding it when it disagrees or complies with the majority decision respectively. Differently to this, Gotze et al. (2008) propose a solution where every atomic service provides information about its dependability attributes and every composite service has to provide additional information about their external services that are used to provide the desired functionality. The calculated dependability attributes and probability values of the resulting composite service are then used to manually optimize the composite service towards the user's expectations (Gotze et al. 2008), differing from the solution by Buys (2011) and Dillen et al. (2012) in which variant services are automatically selected.

The solution by Nascimento et al. (2011), Abdeldjelil et al. (2011,2012), Chen and Romanovsky (2008) and Zheng and Lyu (2008,2010b,2010a) allows the dynamic selection of variant services based on a priority schemes where the client defines requirements in terms of QoS. QoS values are updated by monitoring procedures in (Abdeldjelil et al. 2012; Faci et al. 2011; Nascimento et al. 2011; Yuhui and Romanovsky 2008) and by encouraging users to contribute their individually-obtained QoS information of the target Web services in (Zheng and Lyu 2008,2010b,2010a). The solution by Kotonya and Stephen (2010) and by Mansour and Dillon (2011) support a QoS matching scheme that will prioritise services based on reliability and performance metrics. These metrics are not shared with the client, i.e., a client cannot express preference for specific QoS metrics. The solution by Gorbenko (2005) monitors dependability attributes and selects an appropriate service based on them. However, the motivation behind this solution was to manage service upgrades, i.e. switching from an old version to a new version online when the level of dependability of the new service is acceptable.

4.2.4 Execution of variant services

Both parallel and sequential execution schemes have been addressed within existing approaches. The solution by Nascimento et al. (2012b) does not aim to support multiple execution schemes. The solutions by Gotze et al. (2008), Townend et al. (2005) supports execution of variants; however, they do not specify how variants might be executed in parallel, sequentially or both. Most solutions support both execution schemes (Abdeldjelil et al. 2012; Buys et al. 2011; Dillen et al. 2012; Gonçalves and Rubira 2010; Gorbenko et al. 2005; Laranjeiro and Vieira 2007; Mansour and Dillon 2011; Nascimento et al. 2011; Nourani 2011; Yuhui and Romanovsky 2008; Zheng and Lyu 2008,2010b,2010a) the solution by Looker et al. (2005), Santos et al. (2005) and by Kotonya and Stephen (2010) support the parallel execution of variants. An important characteristic of the execution scheme proposed by Laranjeiro and Vieira (2007) is that it can use functionally equivalent web services that have different interfaces, providing developers with more options to build their solutions (*i.e.* input/output adapters). However, their solution operates on a static connectivity mode, requiring static generation of local proxy classes for each variant service (Laranjeiro and Vieira 2007). The solution by Abdeldjelil et al. (2012) allows for the execution of variant services that present diversity also in their interfaces and results by mapping operations and parameters in the domain ontology.

4.2.5 Judgement on result acceptability

A variety of decision mechanisms were found amongst the target papers. The main advantage of diversity-based solutions is that they allow for variant service responses to be compared using a large choice of voter and acceptance test techniques. For instance, majority, consensus, formal and dynamic voters are addressed by some of the existing approaches for FT-compositions. Acceptance tests (ATs) are also supported; however, as they are strongly application-dependent there are fewer approaches supporting ATs.

Majority voters Majority voters are supported by Nourani et al. (2009,2011), Looker et al. (2005), Nascimento et al. (2011) and Zheng and Lyu (2008,2010b,2010a). The solution by Nourani et al. (2009,2011) supports the implementation of FT-compositions by means of the WS-BPEL. In this sense, the authors present details on the prototype implementation by identifying the BPEL structured activities adopted. The adjudication mechanism is also implemented as web service and invoked from a BPEL process. The authors mention the adoption of voters and adjudicators, including majority, dynamic, consensus, acceptance test and hybrid adjudicator. Nevertheless, no details on voting procedures are provided, except for the majority one. Differently from other solutions, they utilise diversity to allow two majority voting mechanisms to be applied to the same input set. In the BPEL process, if for any reason the voter faces faults or if there is an absence of consensus, the second version of voter is invoked using the same inputs. This avoids the voting process to becoming a single point of failure (Nourani 2009; Nourani and Azgomi 2011).

The Web Service-Fault Tolerance Mechanism (WS-FTM) proposed by Looker et al. (2005) supports the majority voter that allows generic result comparison. Nascimento et al. (2011) and Zheng and Lyu (2008,2010b,2010a) do not present additional information on voting procedures. We emphasize, however, that the solution by Zheng and Lyu (2008,2010b,2010a) supports different fault tolerance strategies and the authors describe in detail a dynamic fault tolerance strategy selection algorithm.

Consensus voters A variety of solutions support consensus voters. Nourani et al. (2009,2011) argues that their solution provides support consensus voters. In the solution by Santos et al. (2005), there is a component responsible for arbitrating the adjudicated output based on the output with the highest number of occurrences. Therefore, we inferred that their decision mechanism is based on the consensus voter. The benefits of diverse components is not only limited to the services, in the solution proposed by Laranjeiro and Vieira (2007) the voter protocol supports two voting mechanisms to be utilized at the same time: a unanimous voter and a consensus voter. Their solution also supports an evaluation mechanism that performs a continuous assessment of the quality of services. During the voting process, if an impasse occurs the QoS values of the variants are used to select one response. According to the authors, the impasse occurs whenever different variant results present the same number of occurrences (Laranjeiro and Vieira 2007). However, in their solution, it is not clear how they judge variant result acceptability when variants are executed sequentially.

Formal voters When dealing with greater variability in variant service interfaces, a straightforward consensus voting mechanism may not suffice. Some solutions accept a certain amount of variability and agree that a consensus is formed with multiple equivalent results. The solution by Dillen et al. (2012) supports formal consensus voting, called plurality voting in their paper. For each invocation of the scheme, the variant services will be partitioned based on the equivalence of their results. The result associated to the largest cluster will be accepted as the correct result (Dillen et al. 2012). Abdeldjelil et al. (2011,2012) describe a specific voting algorithm, called equivalence vote, that will decide if multiple concurrent service responses are equivalent or not. This is based on a pre-agreed amount of deviation for answers to be considered equivalent. Their algorithm requires the input to be an ordered set of equivalent results and also for the acceptable functional deviation to be specified.

Dynamic voters Dynamic consensus and dynamic majority voters are supported by a number of solutions (Buys et al. 2011; Gotze et al. 2008; Nourani 2011; Nourani and Azgomi 2009; Townend et al. 2005). This may be more suitable for applications where it is acceptable for some variant services to fail and an answer still be returned from the remaining variant services. Due to the intricacies of dynamic decision mechanisms defined in our taxonomy some classifications in our review have been changed from the classifications used in the target papers. The solution by Gotze et al. (2008) define three FT-protocols, namely, *one*, *any* and *majority*. Only the majority operator allows for the enhancement of reliability and availability. The remaining operators are mainly focused on achieving high levels of availability and are out of the scope of this work. They define the majority as an operation that schedules the same request to all defined services. Afterwards this operation uses the results of all services that did not fail and chooses the most common result. Based on this general definition, we inferred that their solution (according to our taxonomy) in fact supports the dynamic consensus voter instead of the majority one that has been specified by the authors (Gotze et al. 2008).

According to Buys et al. (2011), their solution, called A-NVP composite, supports majority voting. However, for similar reasons to the Gotze et al. classification we decided their solution instead supports a dynamic majority voter. Moreover, the response latency of the A-NVP composite is guaranteed not to exceed a maximum response time defined by the client. If no absolute majority could be established before the maximum response time, an exception will be issued to signal that consensus could not be found (Buys et al. 2011). In addition, according to Townend et al. (2005), their solution supports different types of voting algorithms to choose from. However, we inferred that the dynamic consensus voting is the only decision mechanism supported. The voter is dynamic as it can process 0 to n results, where n is the number of executed variant services. Specifically, the voting discards results of any variant service whose weighting falls below a user-defined value and subsequently performs consensus voting on the remaining results. The weighting is based on the confidence of that service returning a correct result.

Acceptance tests Acceptance tests give the client the freedom to specify accepted values according to pre-defined requirements. Nascimento et al. (2011) propose a solution that supports a mechanism responsible for the error-processing technique, which in turn supports acceptance tests, voters and comparisons. The solution by Dillen et al. (2012) has been designed so that acceptance tests are not hardwired within the FT-composition. Instead, ATs can be configured at runtime through a parameterised assertion holding an

XPath expression that will be used to assess if the variant result is acceptable The solution by Mansour and Dillon (2011) propose a scheme to combine variant web services into parallel and serial configurations with centralized coordination. In this case, the broker has an acceptance testing mechanism that examines the results returned from a particular web service. The acceptance test is conducted using the broker, which might be a single point of failure. To increase the reliability of the broker introduced in their systems and mask out errors at the broker level they suggest a modified general scheme based on triple modular redundancy and N-version programming, which also includes a voting algorithm. The ATs could be specified as examining a post-condition or inalterable association with the service. The solution by Zheng and Lyu (2008,2010b,2010a) and by Chen and Romanovsky (2008) supports recovery block strategy (RB), nevertheless, they do not mention any acceptance tests, the adjudicator employed in RB.

Other quality requirements The solution by Gorbenko et al. (2005) supports an adjudicator, whose type is not explicitly specified, that is also responsible for reconfiguration, recovery of the failed releases and for logging the information which may be needed for further analysis (Gorbenko et al. 2005). Extensibility is an important feature, and is important in SOA architecture when the context and available services are constantly changing. In the solution by Kotonya and Stephen (2010) different adjudicators might be plugged into their solutions. Also, new web services may be discovered and combined with the existing set of services. A particularly robust protocol detailed in this paper, Andros, provides a three-step consensus and authentication solution to tolerate Byzantine faults at a trade-off with system resources.

Chen and Romanovsky (2008) claim that although N-Version programming techniques require voting on results, in a real world application, it is not always possible to vote on results received from different services. In this sense, their solution for fault-tolerant SOAs supports well defined extension-points in which voting implementation might be included. The solution by Gonćalves and Rubira (2010) encapsulates the WS-Mediator proposed by Chen and Romanovsky (2008), therefore, it is possible to include voting implementations at extension-points of the WS-Mediator.

4.2.6   SOA specific requirements

The following discusses evidence that the target solution support specific SOA related quality requirements. The quality requirements selected include (i) interoperability capabilities, (ii) autonomic composition of services, (iii) QoS-aware service compositions and (iv) business-driven automated composition.

Since the studied solutions touch different phases of design, their implementation descriptions are not always available. For instance, some proposed solutions were based on abstract models or early stages of development and therefore it may not be appropriate to judge solutions against each other. Some solutions do not aim to present complete implementations as the contribution of the work is on a specific part of the system design. From the 17 primary studies, 7 showed support for all SOA-specific requirements as displayed in Additional file 1: Supplementary Table, 11 showed support for interoperability within their designs, 8 showed support for within their implementations for autonomic composition of services, 10 showed support for QoS-aware service compositions and 9 showed support for business-driven automated composition.

Solutions supporting all SOA specific requirements Seven solutions support all SOA specific requirements (Buys et al. 2011; Dillen et al. 2012; Gonçalves and Rubira 2010; Kotonya and Hall 2010; Nascimento et al. 2011; Santos et al. 2005; Townend et al. 2005; Zheng and Lyu 2010a).

The solution by Buys et al. (2011) is interoperable since it has been explicitly designed as a generic WSDM-enabled utility WS-Resource so as to support a diversity of applications without the need to generate application-specific proxy classes at design time. WSDM is a standard that defines how networked resources can be managed by exposing their capabilities and properties by means of a web service interface. This solution also supports an adaptive fault-tolerant strategy that autonomously tunes the amount of redundancy or dynamically alters the selection of variant services currently employed in the redundancy scheme. That is, their solution supports autonomic composition of services. Moreover, the proposed solution aims to achieve an optimal trade-off between dependability as well as performance-related objectives such as load balancing and timeliness.

Also, application-specific intricacies are taken into account, in that the redundancy dimensioning and variant selection models can be configured by means of a set of user-defined parameters. Therefore, the solutions supports both QoS-aware and business-driven automated compositions.

The FT-composition proposed by Townend et al. (2005) invokes variant services, and results are weighted based on a confidence metric for each service. The weighting algorithms, which are performed dynamically, take into account whether variant services are composed by common shared services and historic data of how often variant outputs agrees with the consensus. Services whose weighting is lower than a user-defined level are eliminated from the voting procedure for the remaining variants. Variant service endpoints are specified by the client. This means the solution is not able to dynamically bind new variants. Moreover, the functionalities of the proposed FT-compositions are exposed as web services operations. Therefore, we infer that this solution supports interoperable, QoS-aware, business-driven automated and autonomic compositions.

The solution proposed by Dillen et al (2012) dynamically manages the degree of redundancy of multi-version fault-tolerance mechanisms. The client specifies the parameters of the dependability requirements and its available budget at request level. The system will autonomously select an appropriate degree and selection of variants and integrate them within an appropriate fault-tolerant redundancy scheme. Their solution is also responsible for maintaining a pool of variants of a specific web service and is capable of autonomously deploying additional variants, or removing poorly performing variants.

Therefore, their solution supports all described SOA specific requirements.

Nascimento et al. (2011) proposes a feature model that captures the variabilities and commonalities among software fault tolerance strategies (for instance, recovery blocks, N-version programming and N-self-checking programming). The identified variability is mapped into design decisions represented as variation points into a Product Line Architecture. The authors propose an infrastructure that encompasses both the feature model and PLA and relies on key activities of the autonomic control loop (i.e. collect, analyze, plan and execute) to support dynamic management of software variability. Based on changes of (i) user requirements and (ii) QoS level, and high-level policies, which are represented as adaptation rules, the control loop decides an appropriate fault tolerance strategy to be executed. Consequently, this infrastructure is responsible for the dependable mediation logic between service clients and redundant services. Moreover, since functionally equivalent services may appear with completely different function names, input parameters and return types, hence complicating the dynamic discovery of redundant services. To alleviate this difficulty, their solution relies on the Semantic Web (SW) in order to support dynamic provision of redundant services by describing them in terms of semantics. Also the infrastructure itself may be deployed to be remotely accessible via web technology. Therefore, their solution supports all the described SOA specific requirements.

The FT-composition proposed by Santos et al (2005) relies on a set of components and services, some based on OMG's FT-CORBA standard's models and concepts. In order to create the groups of variant services, Santos et al (2005) adopts the service domain concept. A service domain allows aggregation and sharing of multiple web service descriptions (WSDL). The binding information refers to the group, allowing several services to be virtualized as a single service. Their solution is able to dynamically add new variant services and the remove faulty variant services according to predefined rules. In particular, if a variant service presents a fault at the moment of its execution or does not respond within the time limit established in the service configuration, the faulty variant is removed from the service group. In this case, the faulty variant service stays out of the group until its state has been reestablished through the recovery mechanisms. In order to carry out the monitoring and recovery process, variant services must implement predefined interfaces. Therefore, their solution supports all the described SOA specific requirements.

Zheng and Lyu. (2010a) propose an adaptive fault tolerance strategy for automatic system reconfiguration at runtime based on the subjective user requirements and objective QoS information of the target Web services. Users are encouraged to contribute their individually-obtained QoS information of the target Web services by employing user-participation and collaboration. In this way, this solution is able to collect a large quantity of QoS data from the users located in different geographical locations under various network conditions. This data is used to objectively evaluate the target Web services. This solution supports various software fault tolerance techniques and adjusts the optimal fault tolerance strategy based on the overall QoS information and the individually recorded QoS information of the variant services.

The framework by Kotonya and Stephen (2010) supports interoperability capabilities, autonomic composition of services, QoS-aware service composition and and business-driven automated composition. Their framework implements fault tolerance protocols as process models and exposes them as discoverable services. At runtime, the framework provides a service differentiation mechanism based on quality of services. In this way, their solution is able to dynamically instantiate fault tolerance techniques tailored to the specific needs of different clients and contexts (e.g. requirements in terms of QoS).

Solutions supporting partial SOA specific requirements The solution by Nourani et al. (2009, 2011) supports interoperability. Its variant execution scheme and adjudicators are offered as web services, and, in the prototype implementation, invoked in a fault-tolerant BPEL process that leverages variant web services.

The solution by Laranjeiro and Vieira (2007) support QoS-aware and business-driven automated service compositions as in their solution the web services execution sequence is defined based on the information available for each variant. The variant services are ranked based on evaluation metrics (for instance, response time, availability and correctness of variants) as selected by the programmer. The evaluation metrics might be collected offline (before deployment of variants) and online (during utilization of variants). However, the QoS values are not used to select variant services, since service endpoints are hard-coded. Their solution for fault-tolerant SOAs also supports interoperability capabilities by exposing their main functionalities by means of a proxy web service.

The solution by Chen and Romanovsky (2008), called WS-Mediator, supports Web service resilience-explicit dynamic reconfiguration in order to adapt fault-tolerance techniques and use the available service redundancy. Their solution monitors web services and generates resilience metadata representing dependability attributes, such as response time, failure rate, failure types and so on (Yuhui and Romanovsky 2008). This metadata's structure can be designed for particular application scenarios and the resilience-explicit decision-making mechanism uses it to dynamically select the most dependable web service according to the client's preference. Nevertheless, the solution by Chen and Romanovsky (2008) cannot be directly accessible via web services technology because it is a Java stand-alone package. The solution by Gonćalves and Rubira (2010) extends WS-Mediator (Yuhui and Romanovsky 2008) in order to make it interoperable. Therefore, the solution by Chen and Romanovsky (2008) supports autonomic composition of services, QoS-aware service composition and business-driven automated composition, while the solution by Gonćalves and Rubira (2010) supports these quality requirements and also interoperability capabilities.

The solution by Mansour and Dillon (2011) supports both autonomic composition of services and QoS-aware service composition. The solution develops a model used to improve the reliability of the composite service based on the prediction of the failure rates of individual services. For instance, it allows for execution schemes to be optimized by choosing effective rollback schemes. The focus of the solution is therefore to support self-optimizing autonomic composition of services. The approach subsequently allows for both the increased dependability of the composite service and increase trust from the end-user.

4.3 Discussion

4.3.1 *Guidelines for designing fault-tolerant service applications*
In order to evaluate the guidelines presented in Section 4.1 we gathered qualitative feedback using a questionnaire. Five graduate developers of service-based applications were given the questionnaire with questions about certain qualitative aspects of the guidelines. Two of the volunteers had experience on software fault tolerance techniques while three had no previous experience on designing fault-tolerant software. The questionnaire had a total of nine questions: (i) one to collect information about the previous experience of the volunteers when developing service-based applications; (ii) one to collect information about the previous experience of the volunteers when developing fault-tolerant software; and (iii) seven questions to collect information about qualitative aspects of the guidelines.

The seven qualitative questions were: (1) *What are the positive aspects of the guidelines?*; (2) *What are the negative aspects of the guidelines?* (3) *Would you use it to develop your next fault-tolerant web service?* (4) *Why?* (5) *Would you recommend the use of the presented guidelines to develop fault-tolerant web service?* (6) *Why?* (7) *Suggestions.* Except for Questions 3 and 5, which are yes/no questions, the other five qualitative questions had free answers.

All the volunteers agreed that the proposed guidelines make the design process more predictive and systematic. Moreover, according to the two volunteers that already had experience in designing fault-tolerant systems, the activities of the guidelines prevents important aspects of the software fault tolerance be neglected by the software designer. One of the volunteers suggested that the guidelines could be incorporated into a wizard tool to assist the designer in a more effective and easy to follow fashion.

Although the qualitative results are preliminary, they are important as a feedback and show a positive first impression that provides evidence that these guidelines are a potential help for less-experienced developers of fault-tolerant applications.

4.3.2 Systematic literature review

Related to the selection of variant services, we have considered two main issues, to select diverse variants and to determine an appropriate degree and/or selection of variant services. We should emphasize that these two different purposes are complementary. This is because the reliability of fault-tolerant compositions depends upon design diversity of their variant services to increase the probability that they fail on disjoint input spaces. For most of the proposed approaches for FT-compositions there is an underlying assumption that variant services can always be efficiently employed by means of diversity-based techniques (Gotze et al. 2008; Kotonya and Hall 2010; Zheng and Lyu 2008,2010b,2010a). However, Nascimento et al. (2012a) presents an empirical study to investigate whether variant services are able to tolerate software faults. They concluded that the benefits of diversity-based solutions applied to SOAs are not straightforward. Even when variants seem to present design diversity, this diversity might not be sufficient to improve system reliability in case the chosen variants have coincident faults activated on important execution scenarios. That is, the chosen set of variants will impact on the success of the FT-strategy used.

Runtime decisions regarding which variant services are used require trade-offs according to which specific QoS attributes to use, and their feasibility of obtaining them. There are important considerations for delegating QoS responsibility to different components of the architecture. It may be less process intensive to require each atomic service to provide quality measurements of themselves; however, lack of trust or need to ensure data integrity may mean that QoS is monitored from the client. For instance, many approaches measure availability by monitoring the variant service 'heartbeat' - this is certainly feasible with most available services. However, a particular challenge for fault tolerance is to find a feasible way of measuring other QoS attributes, for example, the security of potential services, an issue tackled by Gotze et al. (2008) where various levels of service transparency are taken into account. Moreover, while many solutions provide means of optimizing service selection once the variant services have been chosen, we see there is a growing need to integrate test activities to ensure a specific service as being suitable as a candidate variant service. This is particularly needed with growing capabilities of fault-tolerant SOA in terms of autonomic searching, discovering and selection of variant services.

With respect to the execution scheme, both parallel and sequential execution schemes have been addressed. This is particularly important, as the type of execution scheme will affect important QoS attributes such as execution time and resource consumption (*Section 4.1*). Related to the decision mechanisms, it is important to notice that the expected behaviour of variant services is likely to affect the complexity of the chosen decision mechanism. For example, to choose among voting algorithms presented in the proposed taxonomy (Figure 4), we should consider the primary concerns surrounding the software's application and details about the output space (*Section 4.1*). As we can observe in the proposed classification (Additional file 1: Supplementary Table) there are still some adjudicators not addressed by current approaches for FT-compositions, e.g., median, mean voters and acceptance tests. One can claim that existing solutions might be easily extended.

On one hand, when looking beyond the implementation of solely the decision mechanism, we can also find interesting architectural solutions that provide additional functionality at the same point. For instance, by defining key extension points or ability for pluggable FT strategies enhances the flexibility and interoperability of fault-tolerant SOA design. Many publications that discuss this do not explicitly describe how to extend their solutions, therefore, the reader is unable to determine what interfaces must be implemented when inserting a custom adjudicator (Kotonya and Hall 2010; Laranjeiro and Vieira 2007; Nascimento et al. 2011; Yuhui and Romanovsky 2008). In fact adjudication procedures are marginally described. For example authors do not specify which type of variant outputs their solutions are able to process. Also, they don't specify how to navigate through elements and attributes in messages returned by the variant services in order to adjudicate the acceptability of specific fragments from these messages (Dillen et al. 2012; Kotonya and Hall 2010; Nascimento et al. 2011; Santos et al. 2005). In other words, most of the authors do not specify clear guidelines on the reuse and, in particular, customization of their decision mechanisms in practical settings.

In addition, related to the decision mechanism, many FT-protocols within diversity-based fault tolerance solutions frequently selected results based on properties other than the actual response values, such as response time or likelihood of failure. This perhaps reflects the reality that even when reliability of results is uncertain, the fastest response time remains one of the main sought-after service qualities. Alternatively, it highlights the need for future research to address these challenging issues. Finally, it is interesting to observe that although various design issues and respective design solutions related to software fault tolerance techniques have been supported, they are spread among existing approaches for FT-compositions. That is, there is no a single solution able to cope with conflicting client requirements by employing at the same time a wide variety of schemes to select and execute variant services and to determine the adjudicated result from the variant services. There is a lack of solutions able to bring out a set of closely related fault tolerance techniques based on design diversity in close accordance with customers' requirements and high-level policies (e.g. to adopt a fault tolerance technique based on parallel execution scheme for better response time).

The classification of the primary studies according to SOA-specific requirements in Additional file 1: Supplementary Table provides a useful starting point to understanding the capabilities of specific solutions. From the 17 primary studies, 7 showed support for all SOA-specific requirements. In fact, design decisions chosen to support one SOA-specific requirement often addressed the others at the same time. For instance, mechanisms that gather QoS data can be utilised to select appropriate services. Consequently, the mechanisms to collect this information are often utilized to satisfy all requirements relating to the composition of services.

Many solutions provided QoS-aware service compositions. However, the way in which quality of service was measured may have been based on multiple properties such as response time, availability and correctness of variants or alternatively solely by monitoring the availability of a variant. As mentioned previously, these differences between solutions with respect to their underlying mechanisms for SOA-specific features impact on the capabilities of the SOA to satisfy the remaining design issues such as how to select, execute and judge variants.

Finally, we noticed that the field of defining fault-tolerant service compositions is relatively recent, since the analyzed solutions present illustrative examples to evaluate their feasibility. To the best of our knowledge there are no commercial or open source solutions for implementing fault-tolerant service composition based on design diversity.

5   Threats to validity

We identified some possible threats to validity (Wohlin et al. 2000) and the measures we took to reduce the risks.

5.1   Internal validity

In terms of internal validity, our study is based on 17 papers that matched our criteria (*Section 3.3.2*). This number is not high, nevertheless, it is representative of this area of research (Burrows et al. 2010; Kitchenham et al. 2009). To mitigate this risk, we adopted a search strategy that aims to detect as much of the relevant literature as possible (Kitchenham and Charters 2007). Despite this, the size of the sample should be kept in mind when assessing the generality of our results.

5.2   Construct validity

We identified two threats to construct validity: the study selection and data extraction are error-prone activities. Related to the study selection, this activity was performed by one of the researches at two different points in time, thus reducing the risk of having the inclusion/exclusion criteria applied inconsistently. Related to the data extraction, data might have been extracted in an inconsistent manner and to reduce this risk, as suggested by Kitchenham and Charters (2007), all primary studies were assigned to one of the researchers, responsible for extracting the data (Kitchenham and Charters 2007). Another researcher was asked to perform data extraction on a subset of primary studies chosen at random (for instance, on 6 studies). Data from the researches were compared and disagreements were resolved by consensus among researchers.

5.3   Conclusion validity

We identified one threat to conclusion validity, which is the reliability of the taxonomy itself used to classify the primary studies. To mitigate the risks of employing an inadequate taxonomy, before it was built, we had analysed the domain knowledge of software fault tolerance techniques based on design diversity in depth (e.g. (Elmendorf 1972; Horning et al. 1974; Kim 1984; Laprie et al. 1990; Lee and Anderson 1990; Lyu 1996; Pullum 2001; Scott et al. 1987)).

6 Related work

We are not familiar with any work that surveys diverse fault-tolerant SOAs. As a consequence, we address, in turn, work related to literature review of fault tolerance techniques in general.

Garcia et al. (2001) present a comparative study of exception handling mechanisms for building dependable object-oriented software. The authors define a taxonomy to help address main basic technical aspects for a given exception handling proposal. By means of the proposed taxonomy, the authors survey various exception mechanisms implemented in different object-oriented languages, evaluates and compares different designs. Our classification of software fault tolerance solutions is also based on a general taxonomy of design issues. However, compared to their work, we do not provide a rating of the primary studies according to a quality assessment.

Carzaniga et al (2008) identify some key dimensions upon which they define a taxonomy of fault tolerance and self-healing techniques in order to survey and compare the different ways redundancy has been exploited in the software domain. These are the intention of redundancy (deliberate or opportunistic), the type of redundancy (code, data, environment), the nature of triggers and adjudicators that can activate redundant mechanisms and use their results (preventive - implicit adjudicator or reactive or-implicit/explicit adjudicator), and lastly the class of faults addressed by the redundancy mechanisms (Bohrbugs or Heisenbugs). The proposed taxonomy is used to classify well known techniques, for example, N-version programming, exception handling and data diversity. The concepts presented in their taxonomy and the ones presented in the taxonomy we employed are orthogonal. In fact, our classification is performed in lower level of abstraction.

Ammar et al. (2000) propose a survey of the different aspects of system fault tolerance and discuss some issues that arise in hardware fault tolerance and software fault tolerance. In this context, the authors distinguish information, spatial and temporal redundancy; present the three fundamental concepts of fault tolerance (i.e. failure, error, fault); describe the four steps of fault tolerance (i.e. error detection, damage assessment, error recovery, and fault removal) and relate these to the differences of redundant techniques for handling hardware as well as software faults. According to the authors, since redundancy may be used under a variety of forms to achieve fault tolerance, the design of a fault-tolerant system involves a set of trade-offs between redundancy requirements (imposed by the need for fault tolerance) and requirements of economy (economy of the process, and the product) (Ammar et al. 2000). The authors also emphasize that program fault tolerance is no panacea, like almost everything in software engineering. We refer to their work for an interesting discussion on reasons to support this claim.

Florio and Blonda (2008) present a survey of linguistic structures for application-level fault tolerance (ALFT). The authors emphasize the importance of employing appropriate structuring techniques to support an adequate separation between the functional and fault tolerance concerns. They claim the design choice of which fault tolerance provisions to support can be conditioned by the adequacy of the syntactical structure at 'hosting' the various provisions, called *syntactical adequacy*. Moreover, offline and online (dynamic) management of fault tolerance provisions and their parameters may be an important requirement for managing the fault-tolerant code in an ALFT, called *adaptability*. These three properties, separation of concerns, adaptability and syntactical adequacy are referred as the *structural attributes* of ALFT. The structural attributes are adopted to classify and analyse a number of ALFTs, including, recovery blocks and n-version programming. This classification is also orthogonal to the classification we have provided.

7 Conclusion

Due to the low cost of reusing existing functionally equivalent services, called variant services, several approaches based on design diversity exist to support fault-tolerant Service-Oriented Architecture (SOA). These solutions operate in the communication between clients and variant services, which are structured in fault-tolerant compositions. Regarding fault tolerance based on software diversity, three major design issues need to be considered, namely, selection of variants; variant execution schemes; and judgement on results acceptability. These design issues may be realised by different design solutions. Different design decisions involve different measures of quality requirements (e.g. memory utilisation, execution time, reliability, financial costs and availability). With respect to service-oriented computing, it is well known that SOA systems *(i)* exhibit highly dynamic characteristics, and changes in the quality of services are likely to occur frequently and *(ii)* should support conflicting user requirements. Therefore, effective SOA solutions should address these design challenges.

In this paper we define a general taxonomy for these design challenges, their solutions, and functionalities required for the aggregation of multiple services into a single composite service. We also compare current design solutions and give an overview of their effectiveness. Based on this information and by means of systematic literature review method, we present a comprehensive survey of existing solutions for fault-tolerant service composition. The solutions were classified according to the elements of the proposed taxonomy and the checklist they support, thus facilitating the process of choosing from existing solutions by a SOA architect, according to specific needs of each SOA-application and execution environment. The classification guidelines support decisions related to four important aspects of fault-tolerant SOA-based applications: *(i)* failure mode, by defining the ways a failure can occur; *(ii)* fault latency, by defining details related to the failure behaviour, such as the interval between the moments of fault occurrences; *(iii)* fault assumptions, guiding the architect on the analysis of error detection and recovery mechanisms and the identification of restrictions related to the services available; and *(iv)* comparison amongst existing design solutions, by means of a systematic literature review which provides valuable information about the characteristics of classical software fault tolerance techniques.

Additional file

Additional file 1: Supplementary Table S1. Classification of the Primary Studies.

Competing interests
The authors declare that they have no competing interests.

Authors' contributions
ASN and RB planned the systematic review, carried it out and analyzed its results. ASN, RB and FC analyzed threats to the validity of the performed systematic review and the measures we took to reduce the risks. PHSB and ASN specified the design decision guidelines to realize fault tolerance in Service-Oriented Architecture (SOA). The format of the manuscript

was decided by PHSB, ASN and RB. The manuscript was prepared by PHSB, corrections and reviews are made by RB, FC and CMFR. All authors read and approved the final manuscript.

Acknowledgements

We would like to thank the anonymous referees, who helped to improve this paper. This research was partially supported by UOL (www.uol.com.br), through its UOL Bolsa Pesquisa program, process number 20120217172801. Cecília is supported by CNPq (305331/2009-4) and FAPESP (2010/00628-1). Fernando is supported by CNPq/Brazil (306619/2011-3), FACEPE/Brazil (APQ-0395-1.03/10 and APQ-1359-1.03/12), and by INES (CNPq 573964/2008-4 and FACEPE APQ-1037-1.03/08). Rachel is supported by EPSRC grant reference EP/K002465/1.

Author details

[1] Institute of Exact Sciences and Biology, Federal University of Ouro Preto, Ouro Preto, MG, Brazil. [2] Institute of Computing, University of Campinas, Campinas, SP, Brazil. [3] Department of Computer Science, University of Bath, Bath, UK. [4] Informatics Center, Federal University of Pernambuco, Recife, PE, Brazil. [5] Institute of Computing, Federal University of Alagoas, Maceió, AL, Brazil.

References

Abdeldjelil H, Faci N, Maamar Z, Benslimane D (2012) A diversity-based approach for managing faults in web services. In: Proceedings of the IEEE 26th International Conference on Advanced Information Networking and Applications. IEEE Computer Society, Los Alamitos, CA, USA. pp 81–88

Ammar HH, Cukic B, Mili A, Fuhrman C (2000) A comparative analysis of hardware and software fault tolerance: impact on software reliability engineering. Ann Software Eng 10(1–4):103–150

Anderson T, Barrett PA, Halliwell DN, Moulding MR (1985) Software fault tolerance: An evaluation. IEEE Trans Software Eng SE-11(12):1502–1510

Arlat J, Kanoun K, Laprie JC (1988) Dependability evaluation of software fault-tolerance. In: Digest of Papers of the 18th International Symposium on Fault-Tolerant Computing (FTCS'18). Society, Washington, DC, USA. pp 142–177

Avizienis A, Laprie JC, Randell B, Landwehr C (2004) Basic concepts and taxonomy of dependable and secure computing. IEEE Trans Dependable Secure Comput 1(1):11–33

Blough DM, Sullivan GF (1990) A comparison of voting strategies for fault-tolerant distributed systems. In: Proceedings of the 9th Symposium Reliable Distributed Systems (SRDS'09). IEEE Computer Society, Washington, DC, USA. pp 136–145

Broen RB (1975) New voters for redundant systems. J Dyn Syst Meas Contr 97(1):41–45

Burrows R, Garcia A, Taiani F (2010) Coupling metrics for aspect-oriented programming: A systematic review of maintainability studies. In: Maciaszek L, Gonzalez-Perez C, Jablonski S (eds). Evaluation of Novel Approaches to Software Engineering. Springer, Berlin. pp 277–290

Buys J, De Florio V, Blondia C (2011) Towards context-aware adaptive fault tolerance in soa applications. In: Proceedings of the 5th ACM International Conference on Distributed Event-Based System (DEBS'11). ACM, New York, NY, USA. pp 63–74

Cardozo ESF, Araújo Neto JBF, Barza A, França ACC, da Silva FQB (2010) Scrum and productivity in software projects: a systematic literature review. In: Proceedings of the 14th International Conference on Evaluation and Assessment in Software Engineering (EASE'10). British Computer Society, Swinton, UK, UK. pp 131–134

Carzaniga A, Gorla A, Pezzè M (2008) Handling software faults with redundancy. In: de Lemos R, Fabre JC, Gacek C, Gadducci F, ter Beek MH (eds). WADS, Lecture Notes in Computer Science, vol. 583. Springer, Berlin. pp 148–171

Daniels F, Kim K, Vouk MA (1997) The reliable hybrid pattern: a generalized software fault tolerant design pattern. In: Proceedings of the 4th Conference of Patter Languages of Programming Conference (PloP'97). Washington University, St. Louis, MO, USA. pp 1–9

Di Giandomenico F, Strigini L (1990) Adjudicators for diverse-redundant components. In: Proceedings of the 9th Symposium on Reliability in Distributed Software and Database Systems (SRDS'90). IEEE Computer Society, Washington, DC, USA. pp 114–123

Dillen R, Buys J, Florio V, Blondia C (2012) Wsdm-enabled autonomic augmentation of classical multi-version software fault-tolerance mechanisms. In: Ortmeier F, Daniel P (eds). Computer Safety, Reliability, and Security. Springer, Berlin. pp 294–306

Eckhardt DE, Lee LD (1985) A theoretical basis for the analysis of multiversion software subject to coincident errors. IEEE Trans Software Eng SE-11(12):1511–1517

Eckhardt DE, Caglayan AK, Knight JC, Lee LD, McAllister DF, Vouk MA, Kelly JPJ (1991) An experimental evaluation of software redundancy as a strategy for improving reliability. IEEE Trans Software Eng 17(7):692–702

Elmendorf WR (1972) Fault-tolerant programming. In: Proceedings of the 2nd IEEE International Symposium on Fault Tolerant Computing (FTCS'2). pp 79–83

Faci N, Abdeldjelil H, Maamar Z, Benslimane D (2011) Using diversity to design and deploy fault tolerant web services. In: Proceedings of the 20th IEEE International Workshop on Enabling Technologies: Infrastructure for Collaborative Enterprises (WETICE'11). IEEE Computer Society, Washington, DC, USA. pp 73–78

Florio VD, Blondia C (2008) A survey of linguistic structures for application-level fault tolerance. ACM Comput Surv 40(2):6:1–6:37

Garcia AF, Rubira CMF, Romanovsky AB, Xu J (2001) A comparative study of exception handling mechanisms for building dependable object-oriented software. J Syst Software 59(2):197–222

Gärtner FC (1999) Fundamentals of fault-tolerant distributed computing in asynchronous environments. ACM Comput Surv 31(1):1–26

Gonçalves EM, Rubira CMF (2010) Archmeds: an infrastructure for dependable service-oriented architectures. In: Proceedings of the 17th IEEE International Conference and Workshops on the Engineering of Computer-Based Systems (ECBS'10). IEEE Computer Society, Washington, DC, USA. pp 371–378

Gorbenko A, Kharchenko V, Popov P, Romanovsky A (2005) Dependable composite web services with components upgraded online. In: Lemos R, Gacek C, Romanovsky A (eds). Architecting Dependable Systems III. Springer-Verlag, Berlin. pp 92–121

Gorbenko A, Kharchenko V, Romanovsky A (2009) Using inherent service redundancy and diversity to ensure web services dependability. In: Butle M, Jones C, Romanovsky A, Troubitsyna E (eds). Methods, Models and Tools for Fault Tolerance. Springer, Berlin. pp 324–341

Gorbenko A, Romanovsky A, Kharchenko V, Tarasyuk O (2012) Dependability of service-oriented computing: time-probabilistic failure modelling. In: Avgeriou P (ed). Software Engineering for Resilient Systems. Springer, Berlin. pp 121–133

Gotze J, Muller J, Muller P (2008) Iterative service orchestration based on dependability attributes. In: Proceedings of the 34th Euromicro Conference on Software Engineering and Advanced Applications (SEAA'08). IEEE Computer Society, Washington, DC, USA. pp 353–360

Hilford V, Lyu MR, Cukic B, Jamoussi A, Bastani FB (1997) Diversity in the software development process. In: Proceedings of the 3rd Workshop on Object-Oriented Real-Time Dependable Systems (WORDS,97). IEEE Computer Society, Washington, DC, USA. pp 129–136

Horning JJ, Lauer HC, Melliar-Smith PM, Randell B (1974) A program structure for error detection and recovery. In: Proceedings of an International Symposium on Operating Systems: Theoretical and Practical Aspects. Springer, London, UK. pp 171–187

Huhns MN, Singh MP (2005) Service-oriented computing: key concepts and principles. IEEE Internet Comput 9(1):75–81

Jorgensen M, Shepperd M (2007) A systematic review of software development cost estimation studies. IEEE Trans Software Eng 33(1):33–53

Kim KH (1984) Distributed execution of recovery blocks: An approach to uniform treatment of hardware and software faults. In: Proceedings of 4th the International Conference on Distributed Computing Systems (ICDSC'84). IEEE Computer Society, Washington, DC, USA. pp 526–532

Kitchenham B, Charters S (2007) Guidelines for performing systematic literature reviews in software engineering. Tech. Rep. Technical Report EBSE 2007-001. Department of Computer Science, University of Durham

Kitchenham BA, Mendes E, Travassos GH (2007) Cross versus within-company cost estimation studies: a systematic review. IEEE Trans Software Eng 33(5):316–329

Kitchenham BA, Pearl Brereton O, Budgen D, Turner M, Bailey J, Linkman S (2009) Systematic literature reviews in software engineering - a systematic literature review. Inform Software Tech 51(1):7–15

Knight JC, Leveson NG (1986) An experimental evaluation of the assumption of independence in multiversion programming. IEEE Trans Software Eng 12(1):96–109

Kotonya G, Hall S (2010) A differentiation-aware fault-tolerant framework for web services. In: Maglio PP, Weske M, Yang J, Fantinato M (eds). Service-Oriented Computing. Springer, Berlin. pp 137–151

Laprie JC, Béounes C, Kanoun K (1990) Definition and analysis of hardware and software-fault-tolerant architectures. Computer 23(7):39–51

Laranjeiro N, Vieira M (2007) Towards fault tolerance in web services compositions. In: Proceedings of the 2nd International Workshop on Engineering Fault Tolerant Systems (EFTS'07). ACM, New York, NY, USA

Lee PA, Anderson T (1990) Fault tolerance: principles and practice. 2nd edn. Springer-Verlag New York, Inc., Secaucus

Looker N, Munro M, Xu J (2005) Increasing web service dependability through consensus voting. In: Proceedings of the 29th annual International Conference on Computer Software and Applications (COMPSAC-W'05). IEEE Computer Society, Washington, DC, USA. pp 66–69

Lyu MR (1996) Handbook of Software Reliability Engineering. Inc., Hightstown

Lyu MR, Chen JH, Avizienis A (1994) Experience in metrics and measurements of n-version programming. Int J Reliab Qual Saf Eng 1(1):41–62

Mansour H, Dillon T (2011) Dependability and rollback recovery for composite web services. IEEE Trans Serv Comput 4(4):328–339

McAllister DF, Vouk MA (1996) Handbook of software reliability engineering. McGraw-Hill, Inc., Hightstown. pp 567–614. chap Fault-tolerant Software Reliability Engineering, http://dl.acm.org/citation.cfm?id=.239425239466

Milanovic N, Malek M (2007) Service-oriented operating system: A key element in improving service availability. In: Proceedings of the 4th International Symposium on Service Availability (ISAS '07). Springer, Berlin. pp 31–42

Nascimento AS, Rubira CMF, Lee J (2011) An spl approach for adaptive fault tolerance in soa. In: Proceedings of the 15th International Software Product Line Conference (SPLC'11). pp 1–8

Nascimento AS, Castor F, Rubira CMF, Burrows R (2012a) An empirical study on design diversity of functionally equivalent web services. In: Proceedings of the 7th International Conference on Availability, Reliability and Security (ARES'12). ACM, New York, NY, USA. pp 236–241

Nascimento AS, Castor F, Rubira CMF, Burrows R (2012b) An experimental setup to assess design diversity of functionally equivalent services. In: Proceedings of the 16th International Conference on Evaluation and Assessment in Software Engineering (EASE'12). IET, Herts, UK. pp 177–186

Nascimento AS, Rubira CMF, Burrows R, Castor F (2013) A model-driven infrastructure for developing product line architectures using cvl. In: Proceedings of the 7th International Conferences on Self-Adaptive and Self-Organizing Systems (SBCARS'13). IEEE Computer Society, Washington, DC, USA

Nourani E (2011) A new architecture for dependable web services using n-version programming. In: Proceedings of 3rd International Conference on Computer Research and Development (ICCRD'11). IEEE Computer Society, Washington, DC, USA. pp 333–336

Nourani E, Azgomi MA (2009) A design pattern for dependable web services using design diversity techniques and ws-bpel. In: Proceedings of the 6th International Conference on Innovations in Information Technology (IIT'09). pp 290–294

Papazoglou MP, Heuvel WJ (2007) Service oriented architectures: approaches, technologies and research issues. Int J Very Large Data Bases 16(3):389–415

Papazoglou MP, Traverso P, Dustdar S, Leymann F (2006) Service-oriented computing research roadmap. In: Dagstuhl Seminar Proceedings 05462. Universidad de Talca, Talca. pp 1–29

Papazoglou MP, Traverso P, Dustdar S, Leymann F (2007) Service-oriented computing: state of the art and research challenges. Computer 40(11):38–45

Pullum LL (2001) Software fault tolerance techniques and implementation. Artech House, Inc., Norwood

Randell B (1975) System structure for software fault tolerance. In: Proceedings of the 1st International Conference on Reliable Software. pp 437–449

Saglietti F (1992) The impact of voter granularity in fault-tolerant software on system reliability and availability. In: Kersken M, Saglietti F (eds). Software Fault Tolerance. Springer-Verlag, Berlin. pp 199–212

Santos GT, Lung LC, Montez C (2005) Ftweb: a fault tolerant infrastructure for web services. In: Proceedings of the 9th IEEE International EDOC Enterprise Computing Conference (EDOC '05). IEEE Computer Society, Washington, DC, USA. pp 95–105

Scott RK, Gault JW, Mcallister DF (1987) Fault-tolerant software reliability modeling. IEEE Trans Software Eng SE 13(5):582–592

Shin K, Lee YH (1984) Error detection process: model, design, and its impact on computer performance. IEEE Trans Comput 33(6):529–540

Townend P, Groth P, Xu J (2005) A provenance-aware weighted fault tolerance scheme for service-based applications. In: Proceedings of the 8th IEEE International Symposium on Object-Oriented Real-Time Distributed Computing (ISORC'05). IEEE Computer Society, Washington, DC, USA. pp 258–266

Trivedi KS, Grottke M, Andrade E (2010) Software fault mitigation and availability assurance techniques. Int J Syst Assur Eng Manage 1(4):340–350

Vouk MA, Mcallister DF, Eckhardt DE, Kim K (1993) An empirical evaluation of consensus voting and consensus recovery block reliability in the presence of failure correlation. J Comput Software Eng 1(10):364–388

Wilfredo T (2000) Software fault tolerance: a tutorial. Tech. Rep. Technical Report NASA/TM-2000-210616, National Aeronautics and Space Administration (NASA)

Williams BJ, Carver JC (2010) Characterizing software architecture changes: A systematic review. Inform Software Tech 52(1):31–51

Wohlin C, Runeson P, Höst M, Ohlsson MC, Regnell B, Wesslén A (2000) Experimentation in Software Engineering: An Introduction. Kluwer Academic Publishers, Norwell

Xu J (2011) Achieving dependability in service-oriented systems. In: Jones CB, Lloyd JL (eds). Dependable and Historic Computing. Springer, Berlin. pp 504–522

Yuhui C, Romanovsky A (2008) Improving the dependability of web services integration. IT Professional 10(3):29–35

Zheng Z, Lyu MR (2008) Ws-dream: a distributed reliability assessment mechanism for web services. In: Proceedings of the International Conference on Dependable Systems and Networks. IEEE Computer Society, Washington, DC, USA. pp 392–397

Zheng Z, Lyu MR (2010a) An adaptive qos-aware fault tolerance strategy for web services. Empir Software Eng 15(4):323–345

Zheng Z, Lyu MR (2010b) Collaborative reliability prediction of service-oriented systems. In: Proceedings of the 32nd ACM/IEEE International Conference on Software Engineering (ICSE'10). pp 35–44

7

Model-based reuse for crosscutting frameworks: assessing reuse and maintenance effort

Thiago Gottardi[1]*, Rafael Serapilha Durelli[2], Óscar Pastor López[3] and Valter Vieira de Camargo[1]

*Correspondence:
thiago_gottardi@dc.ufscar.br
[1] Departmento de Computação, Universidade Federal de São Carlos, Caixa Postal 676, 13.565-905, São Carlos, São Paulo, Brazil
Full list of author information is available at the end of the article

Abstract

Background: Over the last years, a number of researchers have investigated how to improve the reuse of crosscutting concerns. New possibilities have emerged with the advent of aspect-oriented programming, and many frameworks were designed considering the abstractions provided by this new paradigm. We call this type of framework Crosscutting Frameworks (CF), as it usually encapsulates a generic and abstract design of one crosscutting concern. However, most of the proposed CFs employ white-box strategies in their reuse process, requiring two mainly technical skills: (i) knowing syntax details of the programming language employed to build the framework and (ii) being aware of the architectural details of the CF and its internal nomenclature. Also, another problem is that the reuse process can only be initiated as soon as the development process reaches the implementation phase, preventing it from starting earlier.

Method: In order to solve these problems, we present in this paper a model-based approach for reusing CFs which shields application engineers from technical details, letting him/her concentrate on what the framework really needs from the application under development. To support our approach, two models are proposed: the Reuse Requirements Model (RRM) and the Reuse Model (RM). The former must be used to describe the framework structure and the later is in charge of supporting the reuse process. As soon as the application engineer has filled in the RM, the reuse code can be automatically generated.

Results: We also present here the result of two comparative experiments using two versions of a Persistence CF: the original one, whose reuse process is based on writing code, and the new one, which is model-based. The first experiment evaluated the productivity during the reuse process, and the second one evaluated the effort of maintaining applications developed with both CF versions. The results show the improvement of 97% in the productivity; however little difference was perceived regarding the effort for maintaining the required application.

Conclusion: By using the approach herein presented, it was possible to conclude the following: (i) it is possible to automate the instantiation of CFs, and (ii) the productivity of developers are improved as long as they use a model-based instantiation approach.

1 Content

This article is organized as follows: In Section 2 is presented the introduction of this article. Section 3 presents the necessary background to understand this article. More specifically, it is split into three sections, they are: Section 3.1 presents the concepts of Model-Driven Development, Section 3.2 showns the general notion of Aspect oriented programming and in Section 3.3 is presented the concepts of Crosscutting frameworks. In Section 4 is presented the proposed approach. In Section 5 is presented the evaluation of our approach. In Section 7 is presented some related works. Finally, in Section 8 we present the conclusion of this article.

2 Introduction

Aspect-Oriented Programming (AOP) is a programming paradigm that overcomes the limitations of Object- Orientation (Programming) providing more suitable abstractions for modularizing crosscutting concerns (CC) such as persistence, security, and distribution. AspectJ is one of the programming languages that implements these abstractions (AspectJ Team 2003). Since the advent of AOP in 1997, a substantial effort has been invested in discovering how such abstractions can enhance reuse methodologies such as frameworks (Fayad and Schmidt 1997) and product lines (Clements and Northrop 2002). One example is the research that aims to design a CC in a generic way so that it can be reused in other applications (Bynens et al. 2010; Camargo and Masiero 2005; Cunha et al. 2006; Huang et al. 2004; Kulesza et al. 2006; Mortensen and Ghosh 2006; Sakenou et al. 2006; Shah and Hill 2004; Soares et al. 2006; Soudarajan and Khatchadourian 2009; Zanon et al. 2010). Because of the absence of a representative taxonomy for this kind of design, in our previous work we have proposed the term "Crosscutting Framework" (CF) to represent a generic and abstract design and implementation of a single crosscutting concern (Camargo and Masiero 2005).

Most of the CFs which are found in the literature adopt white-box reuse strategies in their reuse process, relying on writing source code to reuse the framework (Bynens et al. 2010; Camargo and Masiero 2005; Cunha et al. 2006; Huang et al. 2004; Kulesza et al. 2006; Mortensen and Ghosh 2006; Sakenou et al. 2006; Shah and Hill 2004; Soares et al. 2006; Soudarajan and Khatchadourian 2009; Zanon et al. 2010). This strategy is flexible in terms of framework evolution; however, application engineers need to cope with details not directly related to the requirements of the application under development. Therefore, the following problems exist when using such strategies: (i) the learning curve is steep because application engineers need to learn the programming paradigm employed in the framework design; (ii) a number of errors can be inserted because of the manual creation of the source code.; (iii) the development productivity is negatively affected as several lines of code must be written to define a small number of hooks, and (iv) the reuse processes can only be initiated during the implementation phase as there is no source code available in earlier phases.

To overcome these problems, we present a new approach for supporting the reuse of CFs using a Model-Driven Development (MDD) strategy. MDD consists of a combination of generative programming, domain-specific languages and model transformations. MDD aims at reducing the semantic gap between the program domain and its implementation, using high-level models that screen software developers from complexities of the underlying implementation platform (France and Rumpe 2007). Our approach is based on two models: the Reuse Requirements Model (RRM) and the Reuse Model (RM). Built by a framework engineer, RRM documents all the features and variabilities of a CF. Application engineers can then select just the desired features from the RRM and generate a more specific model, referred to as the RM. Later, the application engineer can conduct the reuse process by completing the RM fields with information from the application and automatically generate the reuse code.

Furthermore, we present the results of two comparative experiments which used the same Persistence CF (Camargo and Masiero 2005). The first experiment aimed to compare the productivity of conducting a reuse process when using our model-based approach versus the ad-hoc approach, i.e., writing the source code manually. The purpose of the second experiment was to compare the effort of maintaining applications developed with both our model-based approach versus the ad-hoc way. Our approach presented clear benefits for the instantiation time (productivity); however, no differences were identified regarding the maintenance effort. Therefore, the main contribution of this paper is twofold: (*i*) introduction of a model-based approach for supporting application engineers during the reuse process of CFs and (*ii*) presentation of the results of two experiments.

3   Background

This section describes the background necessary to understand our proposed models. It is split into three subsections: the first one contains the concepts of Model-Driven Development, the second subsection has a basic description of aspect-oriented programming and the third one exposes the general notion of Crosscutting Frameworks.

3.1   Model-driven development

Software systems are becoming increasingly complex as customers demand richer functionality be delivered in shorter timescales (Clark et al. 2004). In this context, Model-Driven Development (MDD) can be used to speed up the software development and to manage its complexity in a better way by shifting the focus from the programming level to the solution-space.

MDD is an approach for software development that puts a particular emphasis upon making models the primary development artifacts and upon subjecting such models to a refinement process by using automatic transformations until a running system is obtained. Therefore, MDD aims to provide a higher abstraction level in the system development which further results in the improved understanding of complex systems (Pastor and Molina 2007).

Furthermore, MDD can be employed to handle software development problems that originate from the existence of heterogeneous platforms. This can be achieved by keeping different levels of model abstractions and by transforming models from Platform Independent Models (PIMs) to Platform Specific Models (PSMs) (Pastor and Molina 2007). Therefore, the automatic generation of application specific code offers many advantages such as: a rapid development of high quality code; a reduced number of accidental programming errors and the enhanced consistency between the design and the code (Schmidt 2006).

It is worth highlighting that models in MDD are usually represented by a domain-specific language (Fowler 2010), i.e., a language that adequately represents the information of a given domain. Instead of representing elements using a general purpose language

(GPL), the knowledge is described in the language which domain experts understand. Besides, as the experts use a suitable language to describe the system at hand, the accidental complexity that one would insert into the system to describe a given domain is reduced, leaving just the essential complexity of the problem.

3.2 Aspect-Oriented Programming

Aspect-Oriented Programming (AOP) aims at improving the modularization of a system by providing language abstractions that are dedicated to modularize crosscutting concerns (CCs). CCs are concerns which cannot be accurately modularized by using conventional paradigms (Kiczales et al. 1997). Without proper language abstractions, crosscutting concerns become scattered and tangled with other concerns of the software, affecting maintainability and reusability. In AOP, there is usually a distinction between base concerns and crosscutting concerns. The base concerns (or Core-concerns) are those which the system was originally designed to deal with. The crosscutting concerns are the concerns which affect on other concerns. Examples of crosscutting concerns include global restrictions, data persistence, authentication, access control, concurrency and cryptography (Kiczales et al. 1997).

Aspect-Oriented Programming languages allow programmers to design and implement crosscutting concern decoupled from the base concerns. The AOP compiler has the ability to weave the decoupled concerns together in order to attain a correct software system. Therefore, on the source-code level, there is a complete separation of concerns and the final release delivers the functionality expected by the users.

In this work we have employed the AspectJ language (Kiczales et al. 2001), which is an aspect-oriented extension for Java, allowing the Java code to be compiled seamlessly by the AspectJ compiler. The main constructs in this language are: aspect - a structure to represent a crosscutting concern; pointcut - a rule used to capture join points of other concerns; advices - types of behavior to be executed when a join point is captured; and intertype declarations - the ability to add static declarations from the outside of the affected code. In our work, intertype declarations are used to insert more interface realizations into classes of the base concern.

3.3 Crosscutting frameworks

Crosscutting Frameworks (CF) are aspect-oriented frameworks which encapsulate the generic behavior of a single crosscutting concern (Camargo and Masiero 2005; Cunha et al. 2006; Sakenou et al. 2006; Soudarajan and Khatchadourian 2009). It is possible to find CFs to support the implementation of persistence (Camargo and Masiero 2005; Soares et al. 2006), security (Shah and Hill 2004), cryptography (Huang et al. 2004), distribution (Soares et al. 2006) and other concerns (Mortensen and Ghosh 2006). The main objective of CFs is to make the reuse of crosscutting concerns a reality and a more productive task during the development of an application.

As well as other types of frameworks, CFs also need specific pieces of information regarding the base application to be reused correctly and to work properly. We name this kind of information "Reuse Requirements" (RR). For instance, the RR for an Access Control CF includes: 1) the application methods that need to have their access controlled; 2) the roles played by users; 3) the number of times a user is allowed get an incorrect password. This information is commonly documented in manuals known as "Cookbooks".

Unlike application frameworks, which are used to generate a whole new application, a CF needs to be coupled to a base application to become operational. The conventional process to reuse a CF is composed by two activities: instantiation and composition. During the instantiation, an application engineer chooses variabilities and implements hooks, while during the composition, he/she provides composition rules to couple the chosen variabilities to a base code.

CF-based applications, i.e, applications which were developed with the support of CFs, are composed by three types of modules: a base code module, a reuse code module and framework itself. The "base code" represents the source code of the base application and the "framework code" is the CF source code, which is untouched during the reuse process. The "reuse module" is the connection between the base application and the framework and it is developed/written by the application engineer. Applications can be composed by several CFs, each one coupled by one reuse module. The source code created specifically to reuse a CF, is referred here as "reuse code".

In our previous work we have developed a Persistence CF (Camargo et al. 2004) which is used here as a case study. This CF was designed like a product-line, so it has certain mandatory features, for instance, "Persistence" and "Connection". The first one aims to introduce a set of persistence operations (e.g., store, remove, update, etc) into application persistence classes. The second feature is related to the database connection and identifies points in the application code where a connection needs to be established or closed. This feature has variabilities as the Database Management System (e.g., MySQL, SyBase, Native and Interbase). This CF also has a set of optional features such as "Caching", which is used to improve the performance by keeping copies of data in the local memory, and "Pooling", which represents a number of active database connections.

4   Model-based reuse approach

In this section we present our approach and the models that support during the instantiation and composition of CFs: Reuse Requirements Model (RRM) and Reuse Model (RM). These models have been formulated on top of Eclipse Modeling Framework and Graphical Modeling Framework (Eclipse Consortium 2011). The formal definition of both models is specified by the metamodel shown in Figure 1. It is comprised of a set of enumerations, abstract and concrete metaclasses.

The metamodel was built based on the vocabulary commonly used in the context of CFs, for example: pointcuts, classifier extensions, method overriding, and variability selection. These concepts were mapped into concrete metaclasses, which are visible under the dashed line of Figure 1.

Above the dashed line, there are also the following enumerations: "Visibility", "SuperType" and "CompositionType", which are sets of literals used as metaclass properties. The other elements above the line are abstract metaclasses, which were created after generalizing the properties of the concrete metaclasses. These abstract metaclasses can be applied in similar approaches and are also important to improve modularity and to avoid code replication of the reuse code generator.

Both of our proposed models are identical, however they are employed in different moments of the process. The first proposed model, the RRM, is a graphical documentation for Reuse Requirements, i.e., it graphically documents all the information needed to couple a CF to a base application. Conventionally, this is known as "cookbooks". This

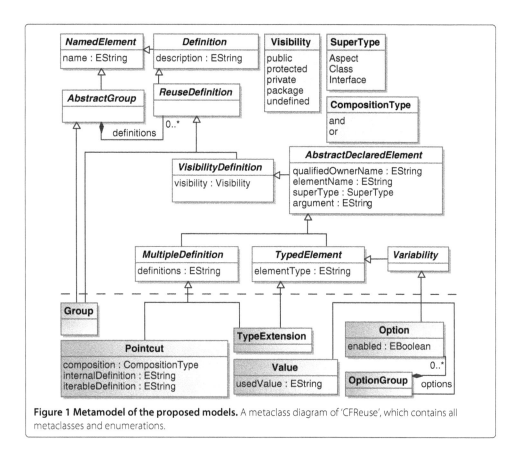

Figure 1 Metamodel of the proposed models. A metaclass diagram of 'CFReuse', which contains all metaclasses and enumerations.

model involves information regarding all CF features and must be developed/provided by a framework engineer. The second model, the RM, is a subset of the RRM and contains only the selected features for conducting a reuse process. Since both models share the same metamodel, it is possible to employ a direct model transformation to instantiate a RM from a RRM by selecting a valid set of features. Both of our models are represented as forms containing boxes, as seen in Figure 2. Each box is an instance of a concrete meta-class element and represents a reuse requirement. Each box contains three lines. The first one contains both an icon representing the type of the element, (which is the same type visible in the "Palette") and the name of the reuse requirement. The second line shows a description and the last line must be filled by the application engineer to provide the necessary information regarding the base application. Notice that the last line is used only in RMs.

By analyzing a RRM, the application engineer can identify all the information required by the framework to conduct the reuse process. For example, this model represents the variabilities that must be chosen by the application engineer and also indicates join-points of the base code where crosscutting behavior must be applied to, as well as classes, interfaces, or aspect names that must be affected.

Framework variabilities that must be chosen during reuse process are also visible. For example, to instantiate a persistence CF, several activities must be done, among them: i) informing points of the base application in which the connection must be open and closed; ii) informing methods that represent data base transactions and iii) choosing variabilities, e.g., the driver that should be used to connect to the database.

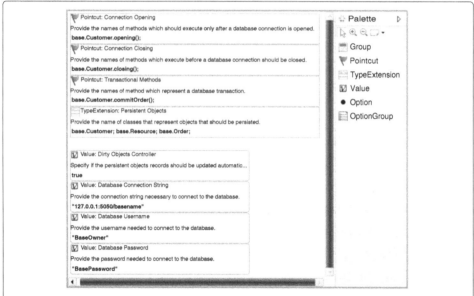

Figure 2 Reuse requirements models and a reuse models editor. A graphical user interface of the model editor. The editor is capable of editing Reuse Requirement Models and Reuse Models. The pallete on the right of the figure lists every concrete metaclass, which can be modelled on model level by dragging and dropping.

The another model, the RM, is shown in Figure 2. It supports the reuse process of a crosscutting framework by filling in the third line of the boxes. Therefore, RM must be used by the application engineer to reuse a framework. For instance, the value "*base.Customer.opening()*" is a method of the base application that was inserted by the application engineer into the third line of the "Connection Opening" box to inform that the DB connection must be established before this method runs.

The code generator transforms the Reuse Model into the Reuse Code, which consists of pieces of AspectJ code used to couple the base application to the crosscutting framework. This transformation is not a one to one conversion, i.e., every element in the model not always generates the same number of code elements. This was a special underlying challenge we have experienced when implementing this approach. The code generator needs to read the RM completely and to aggregate all data to identify how many files need to be generated.

The reuse model elements contain attributes to define the super classes to be extended; several elements may identify the same superclass. Therefore, the code generator must identify every superclass in order to create a single subclass per superclass when generating "Pointcuts", "Options" and "Value Definitions".

The generation of "Type Extensions" is slightly different. Whenever there is a single type extension, the code generator creates a single aspect that aggregates every type extension using "declare parents"; a specific type of intertype declaration.

The architecture of the generator is represented in Figure 3. Initially, the XTend (Efftinge 2006) library is used as a front end of the compiler, loading the data of the model into a hierarchical structure in memory, similar to a Domain Object Model. After the structure is loaded, it is processed in order to identify the units that must be generated. This process creates another structure that represents the resulting code, which is similar to an abstract syntax tree. The "AJGenerator" is a back end of the generator that we have also created; it is capable of transforming this tree into actual files of valid AspectJ code.

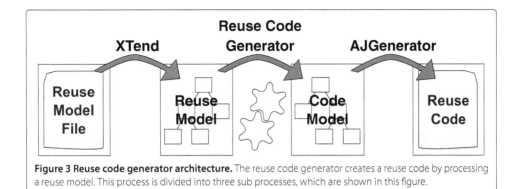

Figure 3 Reuse code generator architecture. The reuse code generator creates a reuse code by processing a reuse model. This process is divided into three sub processes, which are shown in this figure.

4.1 Reuse process

This subsection explains the reuse process that is defined when using the new proposed models (RRM and RM). From this point it is important to clarify the distinction between the terms *model* and *diagram*. Model is a more generic term and it is physically represented by XML files, while a diagram is a visual representation of a model. So, in our case, the Reuse Requirements Diagram (RRD) is a diagram that represents the Reuse Requirements Model and the Reuse Diagram (RD) is a diagram that represents the Reuse Model. It is also worth mentioning that these diagrams are similar to forms, in which they must be filled in. In order to explain the new process, there is an activity diagram in Figure 4 illustrating the perspective of both developers: framework engineers and application engineers.

Since the CF must be completely defined before its reuse process is started, this explanation begins from the framework engineer's point of view. At the right side of the Figure 4, the framework engineer starts developing a new CF for a specific crosscutting concern. The first activity is to develop the framework itself (marked with 'A'). Then, the engineer should make the CF code available for reuse ('B') and should create the RRD ('C'), graphically indicating the information required to couple his CF to a base application. This diagram ('D') will be available for the application engineer. Upon finishing this process, the framework engineer has two artifacts that will be used by the application engineer: the Reuse Requirements Diagram ('D') and the Framework code ('B').

The reuse process starts on the left side of the figure, where the perspective of application engineers is considered. This engineer is responsible for developing the application, which is composed by both the "Base" and "Reuse" modules. By analyzing the application being developed ('a'), the application engineer must identify the concerns that would affect the software, possibly by using an analysis diagram ('b'). By having these concerns identified, the application engineer is able to select the necessary frameworks and to start the reuse process since the earlier development phases. After selecting and analyzing the RRD of the selected frameworks ('c'), it is necessary to select a subset of the optional variabilities ('d') because some elements may not be necessary (since the framework may be supplied with default values), or to select mutually exclusive features. The selected elements will be carried to a new "Reuse" diagram ('e'). If there are more than one CF being reused, then there should be a "Reuse" diagram for each one of them. The application engineer should then design the base application ('g') documenting the name of the units,

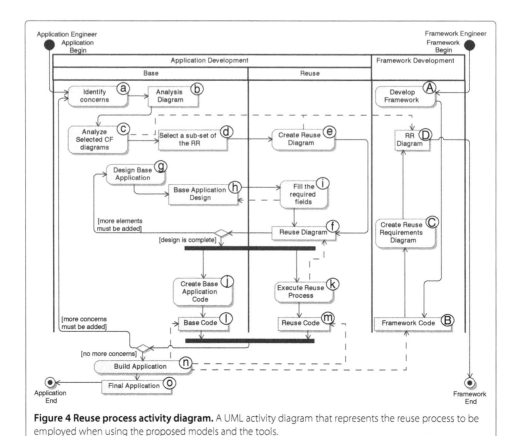

Figure 4 Reuse process activity diagram. A UML activity diagram that represents the reuse process to be employed when using the proposed models and the tools.

methods and attributes found on the base application ('h'). By designing the names of elements needed by the framework, they will become available, meaning that it is already possible to enter these names in the RD. This should be done before all required elements of the iteration are designed. After defining these names, which are the values needed by the reuse portion, they must be filled ('i') in the reuse diagram ('f') to enable the coupling among the modules.

The base application can be developed ('j') in parallel with the reuse process execution ('k'), which is a model transformation to generate the "Reuse Code" ('m') from the "Reuse Diagram" ('f'). After completing the "Base Code" ('l') and the "Reuse Code" ('m'), the application engineer may choose between adding a new concern (and extending the base application) or finishing the process. At that moment, the following pieces of code are available: the "Base Code" ('l'), the "Reuse Codes" ('m') and the selected "Framework Codes" ('B'). All of these codes are processed to build ('n') the "Final Application" ('o') and to conclude the process.

The transformation employed to create the RD avoids manual creation of this model. This is possible by identifying the selected framework and by processing its RRD. Besides accelerating the creation of this model, this also allows the RD to take all the needed elements from the earlier diagram to the code generation. However, the values regarding the base application are still needed and must be informed by the application engineer. The RRD contains information needed by the framework being reused. By identifying that information during earlier development phases it is easier to define it correctly. Consequently, the base application is not oblivious of the framework and its behaviors, however, the modules are completely isolated and have no code dependency among them. It is important to point out that the Reuse Code itself depends on the Base Code during the creation process, however, its definition can be made as soon as the base application design is complete.

4.2 Approach usage example

An usage example of our approach is described in this section. Firstly, we briefly describe the domain engineering which contains the creation of the framework reuse model. Finally, the application engineering is described, which consists of reuse model completion and reuse code generation, thus completing the process.

4.3 Domain engineering

The domain engineer must create a reuse model which contains the information necessary to reuse a crosscutting framework. In the example provided herein, every information needed to create a reuse model for a persistence framework. After the model creation, its completion is shown during application engineering to reuse the framework and couple it to an example application.

The reuse model template for the crosscutting framework in Figure 5, which was derived from a reuse requirements model by describing the framework hotspots. In Figure 6, the reuse model is shown after its completion.

The model elements are defined as follows: there are four value objects, two pointcut objects, and one type extension object. The value objects are used to define strings needed

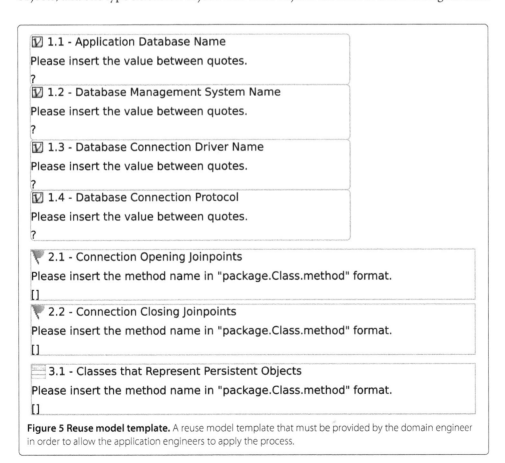

Figure 5 Reuse model template. A reuse model template that must be provided by the domain engineer in order to allow the application engineers to apply the process.

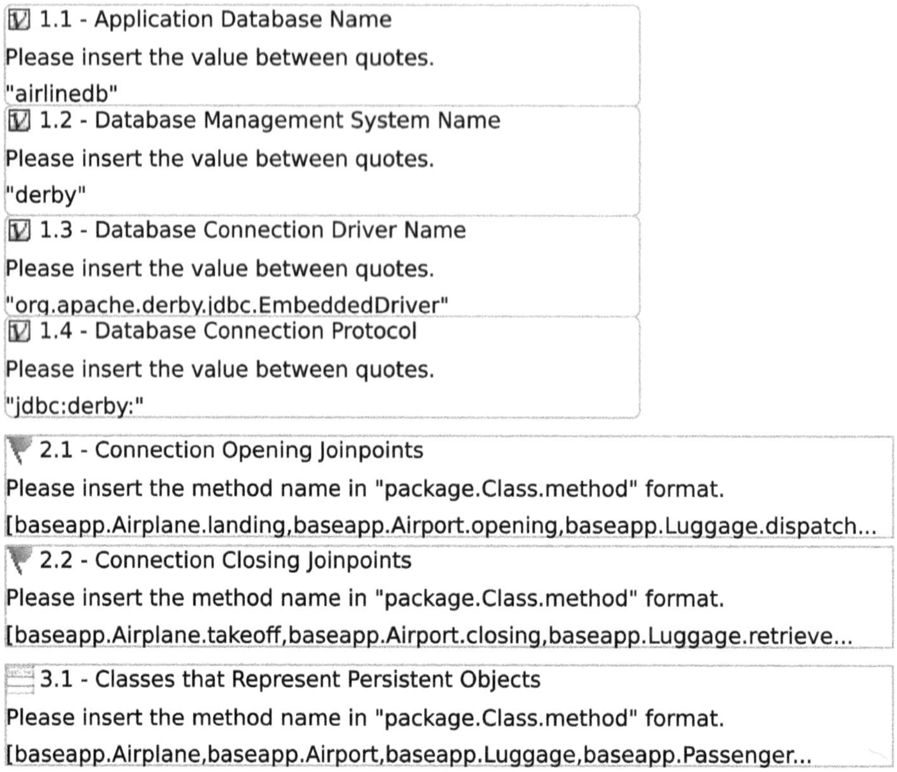

☑ 1.1 - Application Database Name

Please insert the value between quotes.

"airlinedb"

☑ 1.2 - Database Management System Name

Please insert the value between quotes.

"derby"

☑ 1.3 - Database Connection Driver Name

Please insert the value between quotes.

"org.apache.derby.jdbc.EmbeddedDriver"

☑ 1.4 - Database Connection Protocol

Please insert the value between quotes.

"jdbc:derby:"

▼ 2.1 - Connection Opening Joinpoints

Please insert the method name in "package.Class.method" format.

[baseapp.Airplane.landing,baseapp.Airport.opening,baseapp.Luggage.dispatch...

▼ 2.2 - Connection Closing Joinpoints

Please insert the method name in "package.Class.method" format.

[baseapp.Airplane.takeoff,baseapp.Airport.closing,baseapp.Luggage.retrieve...

▦ 3.1 - Classes that Represent Persistent Objects

Please insert the method name in "package.Class.method" format.

[baseapp.Airplane,baseapp.Airport,baseapp.Luggage,baseapp.Passenger...

Figure 6 Complete reuse model. A complete reuse model after the application engineer provides the information regarding the base application, which will allow framework reuse by code generation.

---

by the framework in order to connect it to the database. They are used to define the database name, the name of the database management system, the database connection driver, and the database connection protocol. Every property of these items are then represented on Tables 1, 2, 3 and 4.

The pointcut objects are used to define joinpoints of the base application. The first pointcut object is represented on Table 5 and it must be used to inform where DB connections must be established. To do that, the application engineer needs to inform which methods execute right after a DB connection is established, i.e., methods that operate properly only if there is a connection open. The second point cut object is represented on Table 6 and it is used to inform methods that execute right before the connection is closed, therefore, the last method that needs an open connection.

The last object is represented on Table 7, which is used to define the classes found in the base application. These base application define object types that must be persisted on the database.

This reuse model is provided along with the crosscutting framework to be used by the application engineer in order to instantiate the framework, which is described in Section 4.3.

4.4 Application engineering

An example of an application development is given in this subsection. This application is referred to as Airline Ticket Management and must be coupled to the persistence CF

Table 1 Application database name

Value object: application database name	
Name	*Name*
"1.1 - Application database name"	
Description	*Description*
"Please insert the value between quotes."	
Qualified name of the owner	*QualifiedOwnerName*
"persistence.instantiation.helper.ExtendedConnectionVariabilities"	
Method to be overridden	*ElementName*
"ExtendedConnectionVariabilities.setDatabaseName"	
Value data type	*ElementType*
"String"	
Select supertype (aspect, class or interface)	*SuperType*
"Class"	

A string needed by the database connection API in order to connect to a specific database managed by the database system.

previously mentioned. This application uses the Apache Derby Database Management System (Apache Software Foundation 2012). The design of this application is shown on Table 8.

Upon the reuse model completion, the resulting reuse model is similar to that shown in Figure 7. Despite not being shown in the application details, every base application class was created inside the package "baseapp". After validating the model, the reuse code is generated; it is divided into three units.

The first generated unit is an aspect that extends a framework class. The overridden methods are used to return constant values that are necessary for the framework to successfully get connected to the database. It is important to emphasize that the four values have been defined in the same unit because they are owned by the same superclass. This would not happen if their superclasses were different.

The second unit is shown in Figure 8, which is an aspect that overrides point-cuts *openConnection* and *closeConnection*. These pointcuts are used to capture base

Table 2 Database management system name

Value object: database management system name	
Name	*Name*
"1.2 - Database management system name"	
Description	*Description*
"Please insert the value between quotes."	
Qualified name of the owner	*QualifiedOwnerName*
"persistence.instantiation.helper.ExtendedConnectionVariabilities"	
Method to be overridden	*ElementName*
"ExtendedConnectionVariabilities.setSpecificDatabase"	
Value data type	*ElementType*
"String"	
Select supertype (aspect, class or interface)	*SuperType*
"Class"	

A string needed by the database connection API in order to select the database connection driver.

Table 3 Connection driver protocol

Value object: database connection driver name	
Name	*Name*
"1.3 - Database connection driver name"	
Description	*Description*
"Please insert the value between quotes."	
Qualified name of the owner	*QualifiedOwnerName*
"persistence.instantiation.helper.ExtendedConnectionVariabilities"	
Method to be overridden	*ElementName*
"ExtendedConnectionVariabilities.getDriver"	
Value data type	*ElementType*
"String"	
Select supertype (aspect, class or interface)	*SuperType*
"Class"	

A string needed by the database connection API in order to select the database connection driver.

application joinpoints that trigger the database connections and disconnections. They are defined in a single aspect because they also share the same superclass.

Figure 9 shows another aspect, which uses static crosscutting features to define classes that extend the interface specified by domain engineer by using the "Declare Parents" syntax.

Our model generator is also capable of generating a validation code, which checks if the base element names inserted into the reuse model are valid.

5   Methods

Two experiments have been conducted to compare our model-based reuse approach with the conventional way of reusing CFs, i.e., manually creating the reuse code. The first experiment is called Reuse Study and was planned to identify the gains in productivity when reusing a framework. The second experiment is denominated "Maintenance Study" and was designed to identify whether the our models help or not in the maintenance of

Table 4 Connection driver protocol

Value object: database connection protocol	
Name	*Name*
"1.4 - Database connection protocol name"	
Description	*Description*
"Please insert the value between quotes."	
Qualified name of the owner	*QualifiedOwnerName*
"persistence.instantiation.helper.ExtendedConnectionVariabilities"	
Method to be overridden	*ElementName*
"ExtendedConnectionVariabilities.getJDBC"	
Value data type	*ElementType*
"String"	
Select supertype (aspect, class or interface)	*SuperType*
"Class"	

A string needed by the database connection API in order to connect to the database system.

Table 5 Connection opening joinpoint definition

Pointcut Object: connection opening joinpoints	
Name	**Name**
"2.1 - Connection opening joinpoints"	
Description	**Description**
"Please insert the method name in "package.Class.method" format."	
Qualified name of the owner	**QualifiedOwnerName**
"persistence.instantiation.helper.ExtendedConnectionCompositionRules"	
Pointcut to be overridden	**ElementName**
"openConnection"	
Composition operator	**Composition**
"or"	
Internal pointcut definition	**InternalDefinition**
""	
Iterable pointcut definition	**IterableDefinition**
"execution (* %s(..))"	
Select supertype (aspect, class or interface)	**SuperType**
"Class"	

The second pointcut object is used to define methods that run right after the database connection must be open.

a CF-based application. This second study is important because maintenance activities are usually performed more often than the reuse process. Each experiment has been performed twice. In this paper, the first execution is referred to as "First" and the second execution is referred to as "Replication". Since there have been only two executions for each experiment, we present four study executions in this section. The structure of the studies has been defined according to the recommendations of Wohlin et al. (2000).

Table 6 Connection closing joinpoint definition

Pointcut object: connection closing joinpoints	
Name	**Name**
"2.2 - Connection closing joinpoints"	
Description	**Description**
"Please insert the method name in "package.Class.method" format."	
Qualified name of the owner	**QualifiedOwnerName**
"persistence.instantiation.helper.ExtendedConnectionCompositionRules"	
Pointcut to be overridden	**ElementName**
"closeConnection"	
Composition operator	**Composition**
"or"	
Internal pointcut definition	**InternalDefinition**
""	
Iterable pointcut definition	**IterableDefinition**
"execution (* %s(..))"	
Select supertype (aspect, class or interface)	**SuperType**
"Class"	

The second pointcut object is used to define methods that run right before the database connection must be closed.

Table 7 Persistent objects definition

Type extension object: persistent objects	
Name	*Name*
"3.1 - Classes that represent persistent objects"	
Description	*Description*
"Please insert the class name in "package.Class" format."	
Qualified name of the owner	*QualifiedOwnerName*
"persistence.PersistentRoot"	
Select supertype (aspect, class or interface)	*SuperType*
"Interface"	

The last object from the example that is used to define the persistent objects of the application.

5.1 Reuse study definition

The objective was to compare the effort of reusing frameworks by using a conventional technique with the effort of using a model-based technique. The Persistence CF, briefly presented in Subsection 3.3, has played the role of "study subject" and it was used in both reuse techniques (conventional and model-based). The quantitative focus was determined

Table 8 Base application details

Constant definition		
Application database name	"airlinedb"	
Database management system name	"derby"	
Database connection driver name	"org.apache.derby.jdbc.EmbeddedDriver"	
Database connection protocol	"jdbc:derby:"	
Joinpoint definition (method execution)		
Joinpoints	**Method execution**	
Connection opening joinpoints	**Class**	**Method**
	Airplane	Landing
	Airport	Opening
	Luggage	Dispatch
	Checkin	Confirm
	Passenger	Onboard
	Flight	Depart
Connection closing joinpoints	**Class**	**Method**
	Airplane	Takeoff
	Airport	Closing
	Luggage	Retrieve
	Checkin	Cancel
	Passenger	Unboard
	Flight	Arrive
Type extensions		
Classes that represent persistent objects	**Class**	
	Airport	
	Luggage	
	Checkin	
	Passenger	
	Flight	

Details of a base application that needs to be coupled to the crosscuting framework.

```
                    ConcreteExtendedConnectionVariabilities0.aj

package persistence.reuse;
import persistence.instantiation.helper.ExtendedConnectionVariabilities;
public aspect ConcreteExtendedConnectionVariabilities0 extends
 ExtendedConnectionVariabilities {
    public String ExtendedConnectionVariabilities.setDatabaseName (){
        return "airlinedb";
    }
    public String ExtendedConnectionVariabilities.setSpecificDatabase (){
        return "derby";
    }
    public String ExtendedConnectionVariabilities.getDriver (){
        return "org.apache.derby.jdbc.EmbeddedDriver";
    }
    public String ExtendedConnectionVariabilities.getJDBC (){
        return "jdbc:derby:";
    }
}
```

Figure 7 Reuse code - first unit. The first generated reuse code fragment contains an aspect that is used to define the "Connection Variabilities" of the framework: these "Connection Variabilities" are provided by overriding methods.

considering the time spent in conducting the reuse process. The qualitative focus was to determine which technique takes less effort during the reuse process. This experiment was conducted from the perspective of application engineers reusing CFs: the study object was the 'effort' to perform a CF reuse.

5.2 Reuse study planning

The first experiment was planned considering the following question: "Which reuse technique takes less effort to reuse a CF?";

```
                    ConcreteExtendedConnectionCompositionRules1.aj

package persistence.reuse;
import persistence.instantiation.helper.ExtendedConnectionCompositionRules;
public aspect ConcreteExtendedConnectionCompositionRules1 extends
    ExtendedConnectionCompositionRules {
    public pointcut openConnection ():
        (
                execution (* baseapp.Airplane.landing(..)) ||
                execution (* baseapp.Airport.opening(..)) ||
                execution (* baseapp.Luggage.dispatch(..)) ||
                execution (* baseapp.Checkin.confirm(..)) ||
                execution (* baseapp.Passenger.board(..)) ||
                execution (* baseapp.Flight.depart(..))
        );
    public pointcut closeConnection ():
        (
                execution (* baseapp.Airplane.takeoff(..)) ||
                execution (* baseapp.Airport.closing(..)) ||
                execution (* baseapp.Luggage.retrieve(..)) ||
                execution (* baseapp.Checkin.cancel(..)) ||
                execution (* baseapp.Passenger.unboard(..)) ||
                execution (* baseapp.Flight.arrive(..))
        );
}
```

Figure 8 Reuse code - second unit. The second generated reuse code fragment contains an aspect that is used to define the "Composition Rules" of the framework. The "CompositionRules" are provided by overriding pointcuts.

```
                                    ParentsDeclaration.aj

        package  persistence.reuse;
        public aspect  ParentsDeclaration  extends  Object {
            declare parents : baseapp.Airplane    implements
                persistence.PersistentRoot;
            declare parents : baseapp.Airport     implements
                persistence.PersistentRoot;
            declare parents : baseapp.Luggage     implements
                persistence.PersistentRoot;
            declare parents : baseapp.Checkin     implements
                persistence.PersistentRoot;
            declare parents : baseapp.Passenger   implements
                persistence.PersistentRoot;
            declare parents : baseapp.Flight      implements
                persistence.PersistentRoot;
        }
```

Figure 9 Reuse code - third unit. The third generated reuse code fragment contains an aspect that is used to define static crosscutting features needed during the framework reuse. By default, all static crosscutting declarations are merged into a single aspect.

5.2.1   Context selection

Both studies have been conducted by students of Computer Science. In this section, they are referred to as "participants". Sixteen participants took part in the experiments, eight of those were undergraduate students and the other eight were post-graduate students. Every participant had a prior AspectJ experience.

5.2.2   Formulation of hypotheses

Table 9 contains our formulated hypotheses for the reuse study, which are used to compare the productivity of our tool with the conventional process.

There are two variables shown on the table: "Tc_r" and "Tm_r". "Tc_r" represents the overall time necessary to reuse the framework using the conventional technique while "Tm_r" represents the overall time necessary to reuse the framework using the model-based technique. There are three hypotheses shown on the table: "$H0_r$", "Hp_r" and "Hn_r". "$H0_r$" represents the null hypothesis, which is true when both techniques are equivalent; then, the time spent using the conventional technique minus the time spent

Table 9 Hypotheses for the reuse study

$H0_r$	There is no difference between using our tool and using an ad-hoc reuse process in terms of productivity (time) to successfully couple a CF with an application.
	Then, the techniques are equivalent.
	$Tc_r - Tm_r \approx 0$
Hp_r	There is a positive difference between using our tool and using an ad-hoc reuse process in terms of productivity (time) to successfully couple a CF with an application.
	Then, the conventional technique takes more time than the model-based tool.
	$Tc_r - Tm_r > 0$
Hn_r	There is a negative difference between using our tool and using an ad-hoc reuse process in terms of productivity (time) to successfully couple a CF with an application.
	Then, the conventional technique takes less time than the model-based tool.
	$Tc_r - Tm_r < 0$

Considering the Reuse Study, there are three hypotheses for the outcome. In the first one, both are equivalent, while in two of them, a technique is faster.

using the model-based tool is approximately zero. "Hp_r" represents the first alternate hypothesis, which is true when the conventional technique takes longer than the model-based tool; then, the time spent to use the conventional technique minus the time of the model-based tool is positive. "Hn_r" represents the second alternate hypothesis, which is true when the conventional technique takes longer than the model-based tool; then, the time taken to use the conventional technique minus the time taken to use the model-based tool is negative. As these hypotheses consider different ranges of a single resulting real value, then, they are mutually exclusive and only one of them is true.

5.2.3 Variable selection

The dependent variable in this work is the "time spent to complete the process". The independent variables are Base Application, Technique and Execution Types, which, are controlled and manipulated.

5.2.4 Participant selection criteria

The participants were selected through a non-probabilistic approach by convenience, i. e., the probability of all population elements belong to the same sample is unknown. We have invited every student from the computing department of Federal University of São Carlos that attended the AOP course, a total of 17 students. Every student had to be able to reuse the framework by editing code during the training. Because of that, one undergraduate student was rejected before the execution.

5.2.5 Design of the study

The participants were divided into two groups. Each group was composed by four graduate students and four undergraduate students. Each group was also balanced considering a characterization form and their results from the pilot study. Table 10 shows the planned phases.

Table 10 Study design

Phase	Group 1	Group 2
General training	Reuse and maintenance training	
	Repair shop	
1ˢᵗ Reuse	Conventional	Models
Pilot phase	Hotel application	
2ⁿᵈ Reuse	Models	Conventional
Pilot phase	Library application	
1ˢᵗ First	Conventional	Models
Reuse phase	Deliveries application	
2ⁿᵈ First	Models	Conventional
Reuse phase	Flights application	
1ˢᵗ Replication	Conventional	Models
Reuse phase	Medical clinic application	
2ⁿᵈ Replication	Models	Conventional
Reuse phase	Restaurant application	
1ˢᵗ First	Conventional	Models

The Study Design contains every phase from both studies. It contains the sequence of operations, technique and the conidered applications.

5.2.6 Instrumentation for the reuse study

Base applications were provided together with two documents. The first document was a manual regarding the current reuse technique, and the second document was a list of details, which described the classes, methods and values regarding the application to be coupled.

The provided applications had the same reuse complexity. The participants had to specify four values, twelve methods and six classes in order to reuse the framework and to couple it to each application. These applications were designed with exactly the same structure of six classes. Each class contained six methods plus a class with a main method which is used to run the test case.

Each phase row of the Table 10 is divided into sub-rows that contain the name of the application and the technique employed to reuse the framework. For instance, during the First Reuse Phase, the participants of the first group coupled the framework to the "Deliveries Application" by using the conventional technique. The participants of the second used the model-based tool to perform the same exercise.

5.3   Operation for reuse study

5.3.1 Preparation

During the maintenance study, the students had to fix a reuse artifact to complete the process. Every participant had to fix every application by using only one of the techniques in equal numbers.

5.3.2 Execution

The participants had to work with two applications; each group started with a different technique. The secondary executions were replications of the primary executions with two other applications They were created to avoid the risk of getting unbalanced results during the primary execution, since some data that we gathered during the pilot study were rendered invalid.

5.3.3 Data validation

The forms filled by the participants were confirmed with the preliminary data gathered during the pilot study. In order to provide a better controllability, the researchers also watched the notifications from the data collector to check if the participants had concluded the maintenance process and had gathered the necessary data.

5.3.4 Data collection

The recorded timings during the reuse processes with both techniques are listed on the Table 11. Each table has five columns. Each column is defined by a letter or a word: "G" stands for the group of the participant during the activity; "A" stands for the application being reused; "T" stands for the reuse technique which is either "C" for conventional or "M" for model-based tool; "P" column lists an identifying code of the participants (students), whereas, the least, eight values are allocated to graduate students and the rest are undergraduate students; "Time" column lists the time the participant spent to complete each phase. The raw data we have gathered during the reuse study is also available as Additional file 1.

Table 11 Reuse process timings

	Primary execution					Secondary execution			
G	A	T	P	Time	G	A	T	P	Time
1	Flights	M	15	04:19.952015	2	Clinic	M	10	02:59.467569
1	Flights	M	13	04:58.604963	1	Restaurant	M	13	03:56.785359
1	Flights	M	8	05:18.346829	1	Restaurant	M	15	04:23.629206
2	Delivery	M	11	05:24.249952	2	Clinic	M	11	04:25.196135
2	Delivery	M	5	05:31.653952	1	Restaurant	M	8	04:33.954349
2	Delivery	M	9	05:45.484577	2	Clinic	M	9	04:41.254920
2	Delivery	M	3	06:16.392424	1	Restaurant	M	12	05:05.524264
2	Delivery	M	10	06:45.968790	2	Clinic	M	3	05:45.333167
2	Delivery	M	14	07:05.858718	2	Clinic	M	14	05:57.009310
2	Delivery	M	6	07:39.300214	2	Clinic	M	5	06:31.365498
2	Delivery	M	2	08:02.570996	2	Clinic	M	2	06:59.967490
1	Flights	M	1	08:38.698360	2	Restaurant	C	2	07:18.927029
2	Flights	C	2	08:42.389884	2	Clinic	M	6	07:45.403075
1	Flights	M	16	10:18.809487	2	Restaurant	C	10	08:56.765163
1	Delivery	C	13	10:25.359836	1	Clinic	C	16	09:20.284593
2	Flights	C	9	10:51.761493	1	Restaurant	M	7	09:23.574403
1	Flights	M	7	10:52.183247	1	Restaurant	M	4	09:25.089084
2	Flights	C	10	10:52.495216	2	Restaurant	C	14	09:27.112225
1	Delivery	C	8	11:39.151434	2	Restaurant	C	3	09:55.736324
1	Delivery	C	15	12:03.519008	1	Clinic	C	15	10:25.475603
1	Flights	M	4	12:17.693128	2	Restaurant	C	5	10:37.460834
2	Flights	C	3	12:26.993837	2	Restaurant	C	9	10:49.014842
2	Flights	C	14	12:49.585392	1	Restaurant	M	16	10:56.743477
2	Flights	C	11	13:04.272941	1	Clinic	C	13	11:04.485390
1	Delivery	C	4	13:16.470523	1	Clinic	C	4	12:06.690347
1	Delivery	C	1	15:47.376327	1	Clinic	C	8	13:38.014602
1	Delivery	C	16	18:02.259692	1	Clinic	C	12	14:37.197260
1	Flights	M	12	20:03.920754	1	Restaurant	M	1	17:09.073104
2	Flights	C	5	21:32.272442	2	Restaurant	C	11	17:11.980052
2	Flights	C	6	23:10.727760	1	Clinic	C	7	19:35.816561
1	Delivery	C	7	23:20.991158	2	Restaurant	C	6	28:02.391335
1	Delivery	C	12	41:29.414342	1	Clinic	C	1	28:18.301114

The timings table contains data captured for each study, in this case, the maintenance study. By analysing this table, it is possible to identify the time of each participant, their group, the technique and the considered application.

We have developed a data collector to gather the experiment data. This system has stored the timings with milliseconds precision considering both the server and clients' system clocks. However, the values presented in this paper only consider the server time. The delays of transmission by the computers are not taken into consideration; preliminary calculations considering the clients' clocks have indicated that these delays are insignificant, i.e., have not changed the hypothesis testing results. The server's clock was considered because we could verify that its clock had not been changed throughtout the execution.

That system was able to gather the timings and the supplied information transparently. The participants only had to execute the start time, which was supervised, and to work on the processes independently. After the test case had provided successful results, which meant that the framework was correctly coupled, the finish time was automatically submitted to the server before notifying the success to the participant.

5.4   Data analysis and interpretation for reuse study

The data of the first study is found on Table 11, which is arranged by the time taken to complete the process. The first noteworthy information found on this table is that the model-based reuse tool, which is identified by the letter 'M', is found in the first twelve results. The conventional process, which is identified by the letter 'C', got the last four results.

The timings data of Table 11 is also represented graphically in a bar graph, which is plotted on Figure 10. The same identifying code for each participant and the elapsed time in seconds are visible on the graph. The bars for the used conventional technique and the used model tool are paired for each participant, allowing easier visualization of the amount of time taken by each of them. In other words, the taller the bar, the more time it took to complete the process with the specified technique.

The second significant information found during the first study was that not a single participant could reuse the framework faster by using the conventional process than by using the reuse tool in the same activity.

Table 12 shows the average timings and their proportions. If we analyze the average time that the participants from both groups have taken to complete the processes, we could conclude that the conventional technique took approximately 97.64% longer than the model-based tool.

5.5   Maintenance study definition

It is necessary to remind here that our objective was to compare the effort in modifying a CF-based application by editing the reuse code (conventional technique) with the effort in modifying the same application by editing the RM. The Persistence CF, shown in the Section 3.3 was again used in the two maintenance exercises. The quantitative focus was measured by means of the time spent in the maintenance tasks and the qualitative focus was to determine which artifact (source code or RM) takes less effort during maintenance. This experiment was conducted from the perspective of application engineers

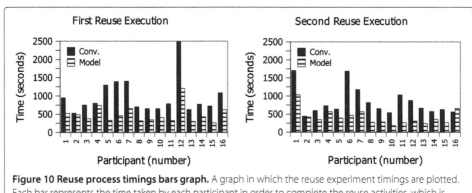

Figure 10 Reuse process timings bars graph. A graph in which the reuse experiment timings are plotted. Each bar represents the time taken by each participant in order to complete the reuse activities, which is identifiable by the participant number.

Table 12 Reuse study average timings

A.	Tech.	Avg.	Sum of Avg.	Percents
First	Conv.	16:13.44008	30:03.79341	66.7766%
Replication		13:50.35333		
First	Model	08:04.980525	14:57.441176	33.2234%
Replication		06:52.460651		
Total			45:01.234586	100.0000%

The Study Average Timings table contains averages for the Reuse Study. It is possible to compare the general time effort needed to complete the activities of both techniques.

who intended to maintain CF-based applications. Therefore, the study object is the 'effort' of maintaining a CF-based application.

5.6 Maintenance study planning

The core question we wanted to answer here was: "Which artifact takes less editing effort during maintenance: the reuse model or the reuse code?" During this experiment we have gathered and analyzed the timings taken to complete the process for each activity.

5.6.1 Context selection

Both studies were conducted by students of the Computer Science Department. In this section, they are referred to as "participants". Sixteen participants took part in the experiments: eight of them were undergraduate students and the other eight were graduate students. Every participant had a prior AspectJ experience.

5.6.2 Formulation of hypotheses

Table 13 contains three variables. "Tc_m" represents the overall time to edit the reuse code during maintenance. "Tm_m" represents the overall time to edit the reuse model during maintenance. "$H0_m$" represents the null hypothesis, which is true when the edition of both artifacts is equivalent. "Hp_m" represents the first alternate hypothesis, which is true when the edition of the reuse code takes longer than editing the RM. "Hn_m" represents the second alternate hypothesis, which is true when the edition of the reuse code takes less time than editing the RM. These hypotheses are also mutually exclusive: only one of them is true.

Table 13 Hypotheses for the maintenance study

$H0_m$	There is no difference between using editing a reuse model and editing the reuse code in terms of productivity (time) when maintaining an application that reuses a CF.
	Then, it is equivalent to edit any of the artifacts. $Tc_m - Tm_m \approx 0$
Hp_m	There is a positive difference between using editing a reuse model and editing the reuse code in terms of productivity (time) when maintaining an application that reuses a CF.
	Then, editing the reuse code takes more time than editing a reuse model during maintenance. $Tc_m - Tm_m > 0$
Hn_m	There is a negative difference between using editing a reuse model and editing the reuse code in terms of productivity (time) when maintaining an application that reuses a CF.
	Then, editing the reuse code takes less time than editing a reuse model during maintenance. $Tc_m - Tm_m < 0$

Considering the Reuse Study, there are three hypotheses for the outcome. In the first one, both are equivalent, while in two of them, a technique is faster.

5.6.3   Variable Selection

The dependent variable analyzed here was the "time spent to complete the process". The independent variables, which were controlled and manipulated, are: "Base Application", "Technique" and "Execution Types".

5.6.4   Participant selection criteria

The participants were selected through a non probabilistic approach by convenience, i. e., the probability of all population elements belong to the same sample is unknown. Both studies share the same participants.

5.6.5   Design of the Maintenance Study

The participants were divided into two groups. Each group was composed of four graduate students and four undergraduate students. Each group was also balanced considering the characterization form of each participant and their results from the first study. The phases for this study are shown in Table 14.

5.6.6   Instrumentation for the maintenance study

The base applications provided for the second study were modified versions of the same applications that had been supplied during the first study. These applicationswere provided with incorrect reuse codes (conventional) and incorrect reuse models (model-based): these incorrect artifacts had to be fixed by the participants. The participants received a document describing possible generic errors that could happen when a reuse code or a model are defined incorrectly. It is important to point out that that document did not have details regarding the base applications; the participants had to find the errors by browsing the source code.

The provided applications had the same reuse complexity: the reuse codes and models had the same amount of errors. In order to fix each CF coupling, the participants had to fix three outdated class names, three outdated method names, and three mistyped characters. It is also important to emphasize that errors specific for the manual edition of reuse codes were not inserted in this study.

Each phase row of the Table 14 is divided into sub-rows that contain the name of the application and the technique employed during the maintenance. For instance, the participants of the first group had to fix the reuse code of the "Deliveries Application" during

Table 14 Maintenance study design

Phase	Group 1	Group 2
General training	Maintenance training	
	Deliveries application	
2nd First	Models	Conventional
Maintenance phase	Flights application	
1st Replication	Conventional	Models
Maintenance phase	Medical clinic application	
2nd Replication	Models	Conventional
Maintenance phase	Restaurant application	

The Study Design contains every phase from both studies. It contains the sequence of operations, technique and the conidered applications.

the First Maintenance Phase, while the participants of the second group had to fix the reuse model to perform the same exercise.

5.7 Operation for maintenance study

5.7.1 Preparation

During the maintenance study, the students had to fix a reuse artifact to complete the process. Every participant had to fix every application. They have fixed each application only once, by using only one of the techniques in equal numbers.

5.7.2 Operation Execution

The participants had to work with two applications; each group started with a different technique. The secondary executions were replications of the primary executions with two other applications They were created to avoid the risk of getting unbalanced results during the primary execution, since some data that we gathered during the pilot study were rendered invalid.

5.7.3 Data validation

The forms filled by the participants were confirmed with the preliminary data gathered during the pilot study. In order to provide a better controllability, the researchers also watched the notifications from the data collector to check if the participants had concluded the maintenance process and had gathered the necessary data.

5.7.4 Data collection

The timings for the maintenance study are presented in Table 15. The column "G" stands for the group of the participant; "A" stands for the application being reused; "T" stands for the reuse technique which is either "C" for conventional or "M" for model-based tool; "Time" column lists the time the participant spent to complete each phase, and finally; and "P" column lists an identifying code of the participants. At least eight values are allocated to graduate students and the rest are undergraduate students; The raw data we have gathered during the maintenance study is also available as Additional file 2.

The data collector that was employed to gather the experiment data stored the timings with milliseconds precision: both the server and clients' system clocks were taken into consideration. However, the values presented in this paper consider only the server time. The delay of data transmission over the network was not taken into consideration. We believe that they are insignificant in this case because preliminary calculations considering the clients' clocks did not change the order of results.

That system was able to gather the timings and the supplied information transparently. The unique task of the participants was to click in a button to initialize the starting time. Once the provided test case had succeed (meaning that the framework was correctly coupled) the finishing time was automatically submitted to the server before notifying the success to the participant.

5.8 Data analysis and interpretation for maintenance study

The data of the second study is found on Table 15. This study has provided results similar to the first study. The first eleven values are related to the model-based tool, while the last

Table 15 Maintenance process timings

	Primary execution					Secondary execution			
G	A	T	P	Time	G	A	T	P	Time
2	Flights	C	10	02:30.944685	2	Clinic	M	5	01:43.801965
2	Flights	C	9	02:54.232578	2	Clinic	M	3	02:17.158954
1	Delivery	C	8	03:02.751342	1	Clinic	C	8	02:34.248260
2	Flights	C	2	03:11.695431	1	Clinic	C	14	02:57.405545
1	Delivery	C	15	03:31.801582	2	Restaurant	C	2	03:01.547524
2	Flights	C	12	03:45.692316	2	Restaurant	C	10	03:09.169865
2	Flights	C	3	05:09.817914	2	Clinic	M	2	03:25.640129
2	Flights	C	5	05:44.462030	2	Restaurant	C	3	03:39.443080
1	Flights	M	8	05:53.407296	1	Clinic	C	7	04:28.998071
2	Flights	C	11	07:08.687074	2	Restaurant	C	6	04:35.517498
2	Flights	C	6	07:38.576312	2	Restaurant	C	12	04:41.052812
1	Flights	M	4	07:53.595699	2	Restaurant	C	11	04:46.028085
1	Flights	M	14	08:14.148937	1	Restaurant	M	8	04:51.290971
2	Delivery	M	3	08:27.092566	2	Clinic	M	6	04:53.800449
1	Delivery	C	1	08:37.138931	1	Restaurant	M	15	04:58.094389
1	Flights	M	13	08:50.185469	1	Clinic	C	15	05:21.846560
1	Flights	M	1	09:15.253791	2	Restaurant	C	5	05:42.389865
2	Delivery	M	5	09:15.934211	2	Clinic	M	10	07:18.533351
1	Delivery	C	14	09:32.031612	1	Restaurant	M	14	07:24.342788
1	Delivery	C	7	10:04.694800	1	Clinic	C	16	07:37.332151
1	Flights	M	15	11:07.617639	1	Restaurant	M	1	07:44.516376
2	Delivery	M	6	11:32.482992	2	Clinic	M	11	08:08.144168
2	Delivery	M	2	11:49.247460	2	Restaurant	C	9	08:13.115942
1	Delivery	C	16	12:12.576158	1	Restaurant	M	13	08:32.056119
1	Flights	M	7	12:27.297563	1	Restaurant	M	16	11:28.592180
1	Delivery	C	13	12:49.443610	1	Restaurant	M	7	11:45.459699
2	Delivery	M	11	13:00.604583	2	Clinic	M	9	12:42.958789
1	Delivery	C	4	13:25.433748	1	Restaurant	M	4	13:57.879299
2	Delivery	M	9	15:51.117061	1	Clinic	C	1	14:46.465482
2	Delivery	M	12	15:56.048486	1	Clinic	C	4	17:55.176353
2	Delivery	M	10	21:23.533192	1	Clinic	C	13	18:02.486509
1	Flights	M	16	32:32.875079	2	Clinic	M	12	25:54.176697

The timings table contains data captured for each study, in this case, the maintenance study. By analysing this table, it is possible to identify the time of each participant, their group, the technique and the considered application.

four are related to the conventional technique. Only the Participant 16 was able to reuse the framework faster by applying the conventional process, which contradicts the results of the same participant in the previous study. This participant said he got confused when he had to correct the reuse model. That was the reason why he had to restart the process from the very beginning, causing this longer time.

The plots for the maintenance study are found on Figure 11. These plots follow the same guidelines that were used when plotting the graphs for the previous study. Considering the timings of the maintenance study, the reuse model edition does not provide any advantage in terms of productivity, since most of participants took longer to edit the model than the reuse code.

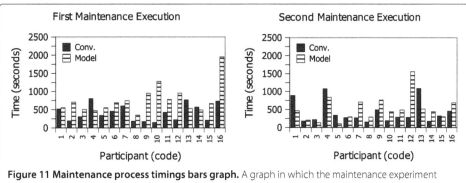

Figure 11 Maintenance process timings bars graph. A graph in which the maintenance experiment timings are plotted. Each bar represents the time taken by each participant in order to complete the maintenance activities, which is identifiable by the participant number.

Table 16 illustrates the average timings and their proportions. Considering only the average time, the participants who applied the conventional technique took less time than their counterparts who used our model-based approach.

6   Results and discussion

6.1   Hypotheses testing for reuse study

In this section, we present statistical calculations to evaluate the data of the reuse study. We applied Paired T-Tests for each execution and another T-Test after removing eight outliers. The time consumed in each execution was processed using the statistic computation environment "R" (Free Software Foundation, Inc 2012). The results of the T-Tests are shown on Table 17, which is actually a pair of tables. The time unit is "seconds".

The first columns of these tables contain the type of T-Test and the second ones indicate the source of the data. The "Means" columns indicate the resultant mean for each T-Test. For a paired T-Test, there is one mean, which is the average of subtracting each set member by its counterpart in the other set. For the non-paired T-Tests, there are two means, which are the averages for each set. In this case, the first set represents the conventional technique; the second set represents the use of the model-based tool. The "d.t." columns stand for the degrees of freedom, which is related to how many different values are found in the sets; "t"and "p" are variables considered in the hypothesis testing.

The Paired T-Test is used to compare the differences between two samples related to each participant. In this case, the time difference of every participant is considered individually; then, the means of the differences are calculated. In the "Two-Sided" T-Tests, which are unpaired, the means are calculated for the entire group, because a participant

Table 16 Maintenance study average timings

A.	Tech.	Avg.	Sum of Avg.	Percents
First	Conv.	06:57.498758	13:55.762733	39.5521%
Replication		06:58.263975		
First	Model	12:43.152626	21:17.305521	60.4479%
Replication		08:34.152895		
Total			35:13.068254	100.0000%

The Study Average Timings table contains averages for the Maintenance Study. It is possible to compare the general time effort needed to complete the activities of both techniques.

Table 17 Reuse study t-test results

T-Test	Data	Means	d.f.	t	p
Paired	First	488.4596	15	5.841634	$3.243855 \cdot 10^{-05}$
Paired	Replication	417.8927	15	5.285366	$9.156136 \cdot 10^{-05}$
Two-sided	Both	$\dfrac{771.4236}{409.4295}$	43.70626	6.977408	$1.276575 \cdot 10^{-08}$

T-Test is a statistical test used to determine the correct hypothesis for both studies. This table lists the results for the reuse study.

may be an outlier in a specific technique, which breaks the pairs. It is referred to as two-sided because the two sets have the same number of elements, since the same number of outliers was removed from each group.

The "Chi-squared test" was applied to both studies in order to detect the outliers, which were then removed when calculating the unpaired T-Test. On the table, the unpaired T-Tests are refered as "Two-sided". The results of the "Chi-squared test" for the reuse study are found on Table 18. The 'M' in the techniques column indicates the use of our tool, while 'C' indicates the conventional technique. The group column indicates the number of the group. The X^2 indicates the result of subtracting each value by the variance of the complete set. The position column indicates their position on the set, i.e., highest or lowest. The outlier column shows the timings in seconds that were considered abnormal.

In order to achieve a better visualization of the outliers, we also provide two plots of the data sets. In Figure 12 there are line graphs which may be used to visualize the dispersion of the timing records. In these plots, the timings for each technique are ordered by their performance; therefore, the participant numbers in these plots are not related to their identification codes.

Considering the reuse study and according to the analysis from Table 17 we can state the following. Since all p-values are less than the margin of error (0.01%), which corresponds to the established significance level of 99.99%, then, statistically, we can reject the "$H0_r$" hypothesis that states the techniques are equivalent. Since every t-value is positive, we can accept the "Hp_r" hypothesis, which implies that the conventional technique takes more time than ours.

6.2 Hypotheses testing for maintenance study

In this section, we present statistical calculations to evaluate the data of the maintenance study. Similarly to the reuse study, we applied Paired T-Tests for each execution

Table 18 Chi-squared test for outlier detection applied on reuse study

Study	T.	G.	X^2	p	Position	Outlier
First	C	1	5.104305	0.02386654	highest	2489.414342
		2	2.930583	0.08691612	highest	1390.72776
	M	1	4.091151	0.04310829	highest	1203.920754
		2	2.228028	0.1355267	highest	482.570996
Replication	C	1	4.552248	0.03287556	highest	1698.301114
		2	5.013908	0.02514448	highest	1682.391335
	M	1	3.917559	0.04778423	highest	1029.073104
		2	2.943313	0.08623369	lowest	179.467569

Chi-squared test is a statistical test used to detect outliers. It was employed to detect eight outliers in the reuse study. These outliers are removed in the last t-test.

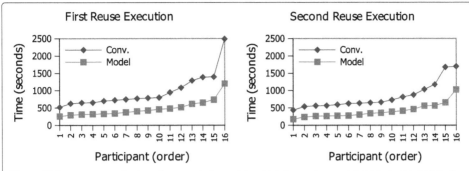

Figure 12 Reuse process timings line graph. A graph in which the reuse experiment timings are plotted. The timings are plotted as points in ascendant order, which are then linked with lines. This graph is useful to visualize the data dispersion.

and another T-Test after removing eight outliers. The seconds that were spent during the process were processed using the statistic computation environment "R" (Free Software Foundation, Inc 2012). The results of the T-Tests are shown on Table 19.

The first column of this table contain the type of T-Test. The second columns indicate the source of the data, which refers to the datasets created for each technique. The "Means" columns indicate the resultant means. The "d.t." columns stand for the degree of freedom; "t" and "p" are variables considered in the hypothesis testing.

The "Chi-squared test" was applied in order to detect the outlier. The results of the "Chi-squared test" for the maintenance study are found on Table 20. These outliers were removed when calculating the unpaired T-Test. On the table, the unpaired T-Test is refered as "Two-sided". The 'M' in the *techniques* column indicates the use of our tool, while 'C' indicates the conventional technique. The *group* column indicates the number of the group. The X^2 indicates the results of an comparison to the variance of the complete set. The position column indicates their position on the set, i.e., highest or lowest. And finally, the outlier column shows the timings in seconds that were considered abnormal.

In order to achieve better visualization of the outliers, we also provide two plots of the data sets. In Figure 13, there are line graphs which may be used to visualize the dispersion of the timing records. In these plots, the timings for each technique are ordered independently. Therefore, the participant numbers in these plots are not related to their identification codes.

If we take into consideration the maintenance study and its analysis illustrated on Table 19, we cannot reject the "$H0_m$" hypothesis that states the techniques are equivalent because all p-values are bigger than the margin of error (0.01%), which corresponds to the established significance level of 99.99%. Therefore, statistically , we can assume that the effort needed to edit a reuse code and a reuse model is approximately equal.

Table 19 Maintenance study t-test results

T-test	Data	Means	d.f.	t	p
Paired	First	-345.6539	15	-3.971923	0.001227479
Paired	Replication	-95.88892	15	-1.191781	0.2518624
Two-sided	Both	431.3323 / 641.0024	24.22097	-2.662684	0.0135614

T-Test is a statistical test used to determine the correct hypothesis for both studies. This table lists the results for the maintenance study.

Table 20 Chi-squared test for outlier detection applied on maintenance study

Study	T.	G.	X^2	p	Position	Outlier
First	C	1	2.350449	0.1252469	lowest	182.751342
		2	2.152789	0.1423112	highest	458.576312
	M	1	5.788559	0.0161308	highest	1952.875079
		2	3.598538	0.05783041	highest	1283.533192
Replication	C	1	1.771974	0.183138	highest	1082.486509
		2	4.338041	0.03726978	highest	493.115942
	M	1	2.422232	0.1196244	highest	837.879299
		2	4.87366	0.02726961	lowest	1554.176697

Chi-squared test is a statistical test used to detect outliers. It was employed to detect eight outliers in the maintenance study. These outliers are removed in the last t-test.

6.3   Threats to validity

6.3.1   Internal validity

- Experience Level of Participants. The different levels of knowledge of the participants could have compromised the data. To mitigate this threat, we divided the participants in two balanced groups considering their experience level and later we rebalanced the groups considering the preliminary results. Although all participants already had a prior experience in how to reuse the CF in the conventional way, during the training phase, they were taught how to make the reuse with the model-based tool and also how to reuse it in the normal way. So, this could have provided the participants even more experience with the conventional technique.
- Productivity under evaluation. The students could have thought that their results in the experiment will influence their grades in the course. In order to mitigate this, we explained to the students that no one was being evaluated and their participation was considered anonymous.
- Facilities used during the study. Different computers and configurations could have affected the recorded timings. However, participants used the same configuration, make, model, and operating system in equal numbers. The participants were not allowed to change their computers during the same activity. This means thatevery participant had to execute every exercise using the same computer.

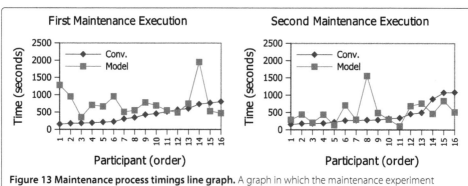

Figure 13 Maintenance process timings line graph. A graph in which the maintenance experiment timings are plotted. The timings are plotted as points in ascendant order, which are then linked with lines. This graph is useful to visualize the data dispersion.

6.3.2 Validity by construction

- Hypothesis expectations: the participants already knew the researchers and knew that the model-based tool was supposed to ease the reuse process, which reflects one of our hypothesis. Both of these issues could affect the collected data and cause the experiment to be less impartial. In order to avoid impartiality, we enforced that the participants had to keep a steady pace during the whole study.

6.3.3 External validity

- Interaction between configuration and treatment. It is possible that the reuse exercises were not accurate for every reuse of a crosscutting framework for real world applications. Only a single crosscutting framework was considered in our study and the base applications were of the same complexity. To mitigate this threat, we designed the exercises with applications that were based on the ones existing in reality.

6.3.4 Conclusion validity

- Measure reliability. It refers to metrics used to measuring the reuse effort. To mitigate this threat, we have used only the time, necessary to complete the process, which was captured by a data collector in order to allow better precision;
- Low statistic power. The ability of a statistic test to reveal the reliable data. We applied three T-Tests to analyze the experiment data statistically to avoid the low statistic power.

7   Related work

The approach proposed by Cechticky et al. (2003) allows the reuse of object-oriented application framework by applying the tool called OBS Instantiation Environment. That tool supports graphical models to define the settings to generate the expected application. The model-to-code transformation generates a new application that reuses the framework.

In another related work, Braga and Masiero (2003) proposed a process to create framework instantiation tools. The process is specific for application frameworks defined by a pattern language. The process application assures that the tool is capable of generating every possible framework variability.

The approach defined by Czarnecki et al. (2006) defines a round-trip process to create domain specific languages for framework documentation. These languages can be employed to represent the information that the framework programming interfaces need during the instantiation and the description of these interfaces. This is a bilateral process, i.e., two transformers are fashioned: a transformer from model to code and a transformer from code to model. Generated codes are transformed back to models. This allow the comparison of the source model with the generated model, which should be perfectly equal. If differences are found, the language or the transformers should be improved in the activity called "conciliation".

Santos et al. proposed a process and a tool to suport framework reuse (Santos et al. 2008). In this approach, the domain engineer must supply a reuse example which must be tagged. These tags mark points of the reuse example that is to be replaced in order to create different applications.

The tags are mapped into a domain specific language that lists information that the application engineer should supply in order to reuse the framework. This domain specific language instances are, then, interpreted by a tool that is capable of listing the points to complete framework instantiation. This is the only related work that uses AspectJ and the aspect-oriented programming.

Our proposal differs from their approach on the following topics: 1) their approach is restricted to frameworks known during the development of the tool; 2) the reuse process is applied to application frameworks, which are used to create new applications.

Another approach was proposed by Oliveira et al. (2011). Their approach can be applied to a greater number of object oriented frameworks. After the framework development, its developer may use the approach to ease the reuse by writing the cookbook in a formal language known as Reuse Definition Language (RDL) which can also be used to generate the source code. This process allows us to select variabilities and resources during the reuse procedure, as long as the framework engineer specifies the RDL code correctly. These approaches were created to support the reuse procedure during the final development stages. Therefore, the approach that is proposed in this paper differs from others by supporting earlier development phases. This allows the application engineer to initiate the reuse process since the analysis phase while developing an application compatible to the reused frameworks.

Although the approach proposed by Cechticky et al. (2003) is specific for only one framework, it can be employed since the design phase. The other related approach can be employed in a greater number of frameworks: however, it is used on a lower abstraction level, and does not support the design phase. Another difference is the generation of aspect-oriented code, which improves code modularization. Finally, the last difference that must be pointed out is the use of experiments to evaluate the approach, while the presented related works only show case studies employing their tools.

8 Conclusions

In this article we presented a model-based approach that raises the abstraction level of reusing Crosscutting Frameworks (CFs) - a type of aspect-oriented framework. The approach is supported by two models, called Reuse Requirements Model (RRM) and Reuse Model (RM). The RRM serves as a graphical view for enhancing cookbooks and the RM supports application engineers in performing the reuse process by filling in this model and generating the source-code. Considering our approach, a new reuse process is delineated allowing engineers to start the reuse in early development phases. Using our approach, application developers do not need to worry about either architectural or source-code details, shortening the time necessary to conduct the process.

We have evaluated our approach by means of two experiments. The first one was focused on comparing the productivity of our model-based approach to the ad-hoc approach. The results showed the improvement of approximately 97% in favor of our approach. We claim that this improvement can be influenced by the framework characteristics but not by the application characteristics. If a CF requires a lot of heterogeneous joinpoints we think this percentage will go down because the application engineer will need to write the joinpoints (method names, for instance) either using both our approach or the ad-hoc one. However, if the CF is heavily based on inter-type declarations and the returning of values, then we claim that the productivity can be even higher, as it is very straightforward to do so while using our approach.

The second experiment was focused on observing the effort in maintaining applications that were developed with our approach (CF-based applications) and with the ad-hoc one. It was not possible to conclude which process takes less effort in this case; however, we believe that they are approximately equivalent. The participants argued that the tool could be improved to avoid opening new forms while entering the model attributes, which, as they claim, had disrupted their work and prevented them from reaching a better performance in this case. It is important that in this experiment we did not provide errors that developers could create while using the conventional approach, since our model approach shields the developers from doing that. We have also provided the raw data gathered during the studies as Additional files 1 and 2.

As the possible limitations of our work, we can mention the following. Once the models have been created on top of the Eclipse Modeling Project, they cannot be used in another development environment. Besides, the code generator only produce codes for AspectJ, therefore, only crosscutting frameworks developed in this language can be currently supported. A simple extension is possible to allow this approach to support the reuse of non-crosscutting frameworks written in Java and AspectJ. Also, we have not yet evaluated how to deal with coupling of multiple CFs to a single base application. Although this functionality is already supported in our approach, some frameworks may select the same joinpoints, which may cause conflicts and lead to unpredictable results.

Long term future works are: (i) providing a support for framework engineers so that they do not have to build the RRM manually. The idea is to develop a tool which can assist them in creating this model in a more automatic way; (ii) performing an experiment to verify whether the abstractions of the model elements are on a suitable level (iii) analyzing the reusability of the metamodel abstract classes.

Additional files

Additional file 1: Contains the raw data gathered during the Reuse study.

Additional file 2: Contains the raw data gathered during the Maintenance study.

Competing interests
The authors declare that they have no competing interests.

Authors' contributions
Every author was important for the completion of this article, however, their previous activities are also important to reach the research results, then, these activities are listed in this section. TG developed the models, model editors and model transformers. He also designed and conducted the studies and the considered applications. This work was also presented as a master's thesis in Federal University of São Carlos, Brazil. RSD was a contributor who developed the related tools in which this work is related to. He developed a repository for crosscutting frameworks that allow their sharing and integrates to the tool described herein in order to provide a full featured crosscutting framework reuse environment. These tools are available as Eclipse plugins. VVdC is a professor at Federal University of São Carlos which is responsible for the crosscutting framework reuse project. He also developed the crosscutting framework used as example and worked on the study executions. OPL is a professor at Polytechnic University of Valencia that provided useful background information regarding model-driven development and code generator tools. He is also part of the crosscutting framework reuse project. All authors read and approved the final manuscript.

Acknowledgements
The authors would like to thank CNPq for funding (Processes 132996/2010-3 and 560241/2010-0) and for the Universal Project (Process Number 483106/2009-7) in which this article was created. Thiago Gottardi would also like to thank FAPESP (Process 2011/04064-8).

Author details
¹Departmento de Computação, Universidade Federal de São Carlos, Caixa Postal 676, 13.565-905, São Carlos, São Paulo, Brazil. ²Instituto de Ciências Matemáticas e Computação, Universidade de São Paulo, Av. Trabalhador São Carlense, 400, São Carlos, São Paulo, Brazil. ³Universidad Politecnica de Valencia, Camino de Vera s/n, Valencia, Spain.

References

Antkiewicz M, Czarnecki K (2006) Framework-specific modeling languages with round-trip engineering. In: ACM/IEEE 9th international conference on model driven engineering languages and systems (MoDELS). Springer-Verlag, Genova, pp 692–706. http://www.springerlink.com/content/y081522127011160/fulltext.pdf

Apache Software Foundation (2012) Apache Derby. http://db.apache.org/derby/

AspectJ Team (2003) The AspectJ(TM) Programming Guide. http://www.eclipse.org/aspectj/doc/released/progguide/

Braga R, Masiero P (2003) Building a wizard for framework instantiation based on a pattern language. In: Konstantas D, Léonard M, Pigneur Y, Patel S (eds) Object-oriented information systems, Volume 2817 of Lecture notes in computer science. Springer, Berlin / Heidelberg, pp 95–106. http://dx.doi.org/10.1007/978-3-540-45242-3_10

Bynens M, Landuyt D, Truyen E, Joosen W (2010) Towards reusable aspects: the mismatch problem. In: Workshop on Aspect, Components and Patterns for Infrastructure Software (ACP4IS'10). Rennes and Saint Malo, France. ACM, New York, NY, USA, pp 17–20

Camargo VV, Masiero PC (2005) Frameworks Orientados A Aspectos. In: Anais Do 19° Simpósio Brasileiro De Engenharia De Software (SBES'2005). Uberlândia-MG, Brasil, Outubro

Camargo VV, Masiero PC (2004) An approach to design crosscutting framework families. In: Proc. of the 2008 AOSD workshop on Aspects, components, and patterns for infrastructure software, ACP4IS '08. Brussels, Belgium. ACM, New York, NY, USA. http://dl.acm.org/citation.cfm?id=1404891.1404894

Cechticky V, Chevalley P, Pasetti A, Schaufelberger W (2003) A generative approach to framework instantiation. In: Proceedings of the 2nd international conference on Generative programming and component engineering, GPCE '03. Springer-Verlag, New York, Inc., New York, pp 267–286. http://portal.acm.org/citation.cfm?id=954186.954203

Clark T, Evans A, Sammut P, Willans J (2004) Transformation Language Design: A Metamodelling Foundation, ICGT, Volume 3256 of Graph Transformations, Lecture Notes in Computer Science. Springer-Verlag, Berlin, Heidelberg, pp 13–21

Clements P, Northrop L (2002) Software product lines: practices and patterns, 3rd edn. The SEI series in software engineering, 563 pages, first edition. Addison-Wesley Professional, Boston, United States of America. http://www.pearsonhighered.com/educator/product/Software-Product-Lines-Practices-and-Patterns/9780201703320.page

Cunha C, Sobral J, Monteiro M (2006) Reusable aspect-oriented implementations of concurrency patterns and mechanisms. In: Aspect-Oriented Software Development Conference (AOSD'06). Bonn, Germany. ACM, New York, NY, USA

Eclipse Consortium (2011) Graphical Modeling Framework, version 1.5.0. Graphical Modeling Project. http://www.eclipse.org/modeling/gmp/

Efftinge S (2006) openArchitectureWare 4.1 Xtend language reference. http://www.openarchitectureware.org/pub/documentation/4.3.1/html/contents/core_reference.html

Fayad M, Schmidt DC (1997) Object-oriented application frameworks. Commun ACM 40: 32–38

Fowler M (2010) Domain specific languages, 1st edition. 640 pages, first edition. Addison-Wesley Professional, Boston, United States of America. http://www.pearsonhighered.com/educator/product/DomainSpecific-Languages/9780321712943.page

France R, Rumpe B (2007) Model-driven development of complex software: a research roadmap. In: 2007 Future of Software Engineering, FOSE 07. IEEE Computer Society, Washington, pp 37–54

Free Software Foundation, Inc (2012) R. http://www.r-project.org/

Huang M, Wang C, Zhang L (2004) Towards a reusable and generic aspect library. In: Workshop of the Aspect Oriented Software Development Conference at AOSDSEC'04, AOSD'04. Lancaster, United Kingdom. ACM, New York, NY, USA

Kiczales G, Lamping J, Mendhekar A, Maeda C, Lopes C, marc Loingtier J, Irwin J (1997) Aspect-oriented programming. In: ECOOP. Springer-Verlag, Heidelberger, Berlin, Germany

Kiczales G, Hilsdale E, Hugunin J, Kersten M, Palm J, Griswold WG (2001) An overview of aspectJ. Springer-Verlag, Heidelberger, Berlin, Germany, pp 327–353

Kulesza U, Alves E, Garcia R, Lucena CJPD, Borba P (2006) Improving Extensibility of object-oriented frameworks with aspect-oriented programming. In: Proc. of the 9th Intl Conf. on software reuse (ICSR'06). Torino, Italy, June 12-15, 2006, Lecture Notes in Computer Science, Programming and Software Engineering, vol 4039. Springer-Verlag, Heidelberger, Berlin, Germany, pp 231–245

Mortensen M, Ghosh S (2006) Creating pluggable and reusable non-functional aspects in AspectC++. In: Proceedings of the fifth AOSD workshop on aspects, components, and patterns for infrastructure Software. Bonn, Germany. ACM, New York, NY, USA

Oliveira TC, Alencar P, Cowan D (2011) ReuseTool-An extensible tool support for object-oriented framework reuse. J Syst Softw 84(12): 2234–2252. http://dx.doi.org/10.1016/j.jss.2011.06.030

Pastor O, Molina JC (2007) Model-driven architecture in practice: a software production environment based on conceptual modeling. Springer-Verlag, New York, Secaucus

Sakenou D, Mehner K, Herrmann S, Sudhof H (2006) Patterns for re-usable aspects in object teams. In: Net Object Days. Erfurt, Germany. Object Teams, Technische Universität Berlin, Berlin, Germany

Santos AL, Koskimies K, Lopes A (2008) Automated domain-specific modeling languages for generating framework-based applications. Softw Product Line Conf Int 0: 149–158

Schmidt DC (2006) Model-driven engineering. IEEE Computer 39(2). http://www.truststc.org/pubs/30.html

Shah V, Hill V (2004) An aspect-oriented security framework: lessons learned. In: Workshop of the Aspect Oriented Software Development Conference at AOSDSEC'04, AOSD'04. Lancaster, United Kingdom. ACM, New York, NY, USA

Soares S, Laureano E, Borba P (2006) Distribution and persistence as aspects. Software: Practice and Experience 36(7): 711–759. John Wiley & Sons, Ltd. Hoboken, NJ, USA. http://onlinelibrary.wiley.com/doi/10.1002/spe.715/abstract

Soudarajan N, Khatchadourian R (2009) Specifying reusable aspects. In: Asian Workshop on Aspect-Oriented and Modular Software Development (AOAsia'09). Auckland, New Zealand. AOAsia, Chinese University of Hong Kong, Hong Kong, People's Republic of China

Wohlin C, Runeson P, Höst M, Ohlsson MC, Regnell B, Wesslén A (2000) Experimentation in software engineering: an introduction. First edition. 204 pages. Kluwer Academic Publishers, Norwell, MA, USA

Zanon I, Camargo VV, Penteado RAD (2010) Reestructuring an application framework with a persistence crosscutting framework. INFOCOMP 1: 9–16

Permissions

List of Contributors

Luis Rivero
Grupo de Usabilidade e Engenharia de Software - USES, Instituto de Computação, Universidade Federal do Amazonas (UFAM), Manaus, AM, Brazil

Tayana Conte
Grupo de Usabilidade e Engenharia de Software - USES, Instituto de Computação, Universidade Federal do Amazonas (UFAM), Manaus, AM, Brazil

Silverio Martínez-Fernández
GESSI Research Group, Universitat Politècnica de Catalunya, Jordi Girona, 1-3, 08034 Barcelona, Spain

Claudia P Ayala
GESSI Research Group, Universitat Politècnica de Catalunya, Jordi Girona, 1-3, 08034 Barcelona, Spain

Xavier Franch
GESSI Research Group, Universitat Politècnica de Catalunya, Jordi Girona, 1-3, 08034 Barcelona, Spain

Helena Martins Marques
Everis, Diagonal, 605, 08028 Barcelona, Spain

David Ameller
GESSI Research Group, Universitat Politècnica de Catalunya, Jordi Girona, 1-3, 08034 Barcelona, Spain

Matheus C Viana
Federal Institute of Sao Paulo, Campus Sao Carlos, Rod. Washington Luis, km 235, Block AT6, 13565-905 Sao Carlos, Brazil
Department of Computing, Federal University of Sao Carlos, Rod. Washington Luis, km 235, 13565-905 Sao Carlos, Brazil

Rosângela AD Penteado
Department of Computing, Federal University of Sao Carlos, Rod. Washington Luis, km 235, 13565-905 Sao Carlos, Brazil

Antônio F do Prado
Department of Computing, Federal University of Sao Carlos, Rod. Washington Luis, km 235, 13565-905 Sao Carlos, Brazil

Rafael S Durelli
Institute of Mathematical and Computer Sciences, University of Sao Paulo, Av. Trabalhador Sao Carlense, 400, 13566-590, Sao Carlos, Brazil

Matias Nicoletti
ISISTAN Research Institute, CONICET-UNICEN, Paraje Arroyo Seco, Campus Universitario, Tandil, Argentina

Jorge Andres Diaz-Pace
ISISTAN Research Institute, CONICET-UNICEN, Paraje Arroyo Seco, Campus Universitario, Tandil, Argentina

Silvia Schiaffino
ISISTAN Research Institute, CONICET-UNICEN, Paraje Arroyo Seco, Campus Universitario, Tandil, Argentina

Antonela Tommase
ISISTAN Research Institute, CONICET-UNICEN, Paraje Arroyo Seco, Campus Universitario, Tandil, Argentina

Daniela Godoy
ISISTAN Research Institute, CONICET-UNICEN, Paraje Arroyo Seco, Campus Universitario, Tandil, Argentina

Sandro S Andrade
Distributed Systems Laboratory (LaSiD), Federal University of Bahia (UFBa), Institute of Mathematics, Department of Computer Science, Av Adhemar de Barros, s/n, Ondina, 40.170-110 Salvador-BA, Brazil
GSORT Distributed Systems Group, Federal Institute of Education, Science, and Technology of Bahia (IFBa), Department of Computer Science, Av. Araujo Pinho, 39, Canela, 40.110-150 Salvador-BA, Brazil

Raimundo J de A Macedo
GSORT Distributed Systems Group, Federal Institute of Education, Science, and Technology of Bahia (IFBa), Department of Computer Science, Av. Araujo Pinho, 39, Canela, 40.110-150 Salvador-BA, Brazil

Amanda S Nascimento
Institute of Exact Sciences and Biology, Federal University of Ouro Preto, Ouro Preto, MG, Brazil

Cecília MF Rubira
Institute of Computing, University of Campinas, Campinas, SP, Brazil

Rachel Burrows
Department of Computer Science, University of Bath, Bath, UK

Fernando Castorand
Informatics Center, Federal University of Pernambuco, Recife, PE, Brazil

Patrick HS Brito
Institute of Computing, University of Campinas, Campinas, SP, Brazil
Institute of Computing, Federal University of Alagoas, Maceió, AL, Brazil

Thiago Gottardi
Departmento de Computação, Universidade Federal de São Carlos, Caixa Postal 676, 13.565-905, São Carlos, São Paulo, Brazil

Rafael Serapilha Durelli
Instituto de Ciências Matemáticas e Computação, Universidade de São Paulo, Av. Trabalhador São Carlense, 400, São Carlos, São Paulo, Brazil

Óscar Pastor López
Universidad Politecnica de Valencia, Camino de Vera s/n, Valencia, Spain

Valter Vieira de Camargo
Departmento de Computação, Universidade Federal de São Carlos, Caixa Postal 676, 13.565-905, São Carlos, São Paulo, Brazil

Printed in the USA
CPSIA information can be obtained
at www.ICGtesting.com
JSHW051441221024
72173JS00006B/1537